ROBIN FURNEAUX

THE AMAZON

THE STORY OF A GREAT RIVER

Foreword by Peter Fleming

READERS UNION
HAMISH HAMILTON
London 1971

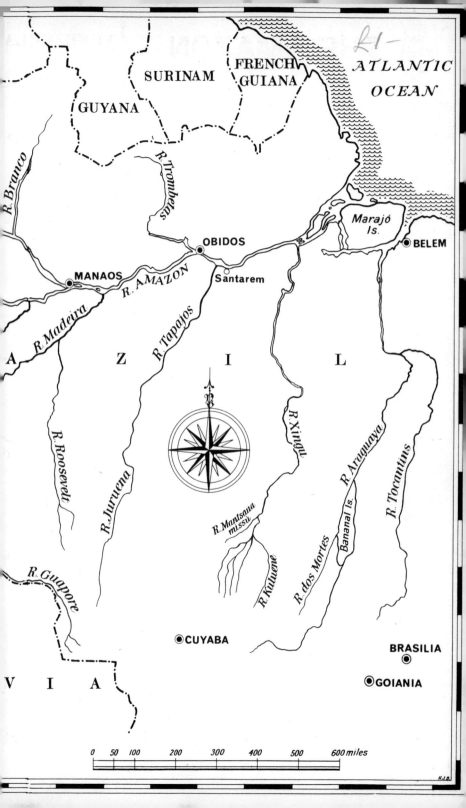

THE AMAZON

A MOUNTAIN STREAM FLOWS THROUGH THE EASTERN SLOPES
OF THE ANDES TO MEET THE AMAZON

CONTENTS

LIST OF ILLUSTRATIONS

A mountain stream flows through the eastern slopes of the
Andes to meet the Amazon   *frontispiece*

Between pages 114 *and* 115

Men and horses crossing a mountain stream

Lake Guatavita, the real El Dorado

A Mojos Indian dancing before the altar

The Jesuit explanation of the Trinity

The reduction of San Jose in Chiquitos

The ruins of a Jesuit seminary near Belém overgrown by
creepers

The murder of de Senièrgues

Caballitos in the Andes

Catching an alligator with lasso

Victoria Regia in a lake by the Amazon

Piranha

The Opera House in Manaos

Putumayo Muchachos with Barbadian overseer

Latex being tapped

Roger Casement

Theodore Roosevelt and Colonel Rondon

Colonel Fawcett

Cuili (central figure on log) who confessed to the murder of
Fawcett's party

Orlando Villas Boas

Kalapolo woman preparing manioc

MAPS

FOREWORD BY PETER FLEMING

GEOGRAPHERS have always recognized the difference between a sea and an ocean. The British, until recently the greatest of the maritime powers, have never been strong on aquatic terminology. We talk, and even the most pedantic historians write, of our 'sea-power', of our 'command of the seas', as essential ingredients in our Imperial expansion and, more recently, in our survival as a nation of free men. But of all the seas on the globe the Mediterranean has so far been the only one in which naval supremacy was of serious importance to us; it is because for a long time we commanded the *oceans* that we retain our liberties, and were able to preserve—or, long ago, to extinguish—the liberties of other peoples.

In freshwater matters we are not merely terminologically at sea. In the United Kingdom nobody really knows how much water we have got, still less how much we need now or may need in the future; floods, though rare and puny by comparison with their counterparts elsewhere in the world, seldom fail to find us unprepared. We think of the Severn (220 miles long) and the Thames (210) as large rivers, difficult at times to control; we know that the Nile and the Amazon are larger, but few realize that they are two hundred times larger, that both are over 4,000 miles long. Seas, if we stop to think, are smaller than oceans; but rivers are rivers the world over and it does not occur to us—why should it?—that on a map of the Irrawaddy Delta the Severn and the Thames would appear, not as rivers, but as *Chaungs*.

Robin Furneaux brings sharply to our attention ('reminds us of' is the standard euphemism) the fact that if the north bank of the

Amazon were in London, the south bank would be in Paris. Sheer bulk is not a promising foundation for legend or romance; but the Amazon, despite the fact that for more than a century it has been navigable as far as Manaos, 800 miles from its mouth, by ocean-going liners, has somehow contrived to retain an aura of mystery, of challenge, of adventure.

Nobody, until now, has tried to piece together the history, in human terms, of this vast river: partly, perhaps, because it flows through the territory of what are now six different republics. The story is not one in which *homo sapiens* can take much pride; in its bizarre pages there are more villains than heroes, more disasters than triumphs. Robin Furneaux, fortified with some experience of travel on the Amazon and its enormous tributaries, has done full justice to his fascinating theme.

PREFACE

I SPENT FOUR months in the Amazon Valley in the winter of 1965. It was an inadequate time to gather any more than sweeping impressions, since the river has over 15,000 tributaries, which together drain an area the size of Western Europe. But we were able to make two expeditions to southern tributaries, the Araguaia at Bananal Island and the Kuluene a few miles away from the village in which Colonel Fawcett was last seen alive. We sailed 2,300 miles up the Amazon itself from Belém at its mouth to Iquitos in Peru and we finished our expedition in the Andes near the river's sources.

The journey from Manaos to Iquitos proved to be the most dramatic part of our travels. We had hired a fishing boat owned by an affable Brazilian who spoke fluent English. It was an unsuitable boat for our purpose, with a maximum speed of six knots, a grossly unreliable engine, little shelter from the sun and none from the rain. Unlike the flat-bottomed steamers more often seen on the river it drew nearly four feet and, since the owner was a poor navigator, we spent much of our time pushing it off sandbanks. For so uncomfortable a vessel it was very heavy.

Our captain, whom we playfully called 'The pirate', persuaded us to buy a large quantity of dried fish in Brazil in order to sell it at a profit in Peru and thus bolster our sagging finances. Unfortunately the beginning of the rainy season soaked the fish as thoroughly as it did us and with more permanent effect, so that we were accompanied up the river by a stench of bad pirarucu. The pirate assured us that this was unimportant; the Peruvians, he said, wanted fish for their soldiers and would not quibble over its condition. Weight was the only criterion, and this would actually have been increased by the rain.

As we neared Iquitos we became increasingly suspicious of the

pirate. He seemed to live in an atmosphere of conspiracy and
to allow mystery to accompany the most trivial of his actions. We
often stopped for no good reason at some floating hut and he would
converse for hours with its owner out of our hearing. His behaviour
became violent and irrational; he would rage and sulk when we
questioned him about the disposal of the fish and once he sat down
by the engines for a day, with a Colt .45 in his belt, brooding over
some imagined slight. On another occasion he attempted, futilely,
to steal a spanner from an American missionary. His knowledge of
the river and his estimate of the time our journey would take were
equally at fault. We often found ourselves sailing up tributaries
and false channels, only to have to turn back when it became clear
that we had missed our course. It took us just over three times as
long to reach Iquitos as he had calculated.

No sooner had we landed at Iquitos than the pirate sold our
fish and left for Lima with the money. The police were unable to
trace him, and when we suggested that his boat should be im-
pounded, they produced the devastating retort that he did not even
own it.

Humiliated and impoverished, we flew up into the Andes for
the last weeks of our journey. It was little consolation when preparing this book to learn that few travellers on the Amazon had
returned without some similar experience.

Fortunately the dangers to one's life are nothing compared to
those menacing one's pocket. If one could believe the authors of
some travel books about the Amazon, to swim in the river would
attract a swarm of piranha, to pass under a tree would tempt the
inevitable anaconda in its branches and to venture into the jungle
would mean almost certain death. We were at first so overawed by
the fearful creatures under water that we refused to bathe in any
river. It was only after seeing Brazilians doing so and after examining them, minutely but in vain, for the absence of any limbs, that
we too took to the water.

We saw many snakes, including the deadly bushmaster, but the
only time we came near to treading on one it proved to be harmless
and as frightened as we were. The Indians we met were almost
embarrassingly friendly and the only loss we sustained at their hands
was the pilfering of a pair of red bathing trunks and volume V of
Gibbon's *Decline and Fall of the Roman Empire*. Mosquitoes were

the only creatures of the Amazon to live up to their evil reputation and the discomfort to which they contributed could at least give one illusions of adventure.

The beauty of some parts of the river stays with me still. Near the Kuluene there is a lagoon where the Kamayura Indians have built their village. The water lies still and clear over the sand and the only movement comes from thousands of phoebis butterflies swarming on the beach like bees. When the sun sets it turns the whole surface of the lake to its own colour, first golden and then, as it sinks below the horizon, a deep red. There are the white beaches on the lower Tapajós with gigantic trees behind them and light blue shallows in front. There are the jagged peaks and ravines of the Urubamba Valley, carpeted with jungle on their steepest slopes.

Historical associations are often strong, perhaps because so little has changed since the discovery of the river. At Machu Picchu it is easy to imagine the last days of the Incas; in Manaos the flamboyance of the architecture, the grandeur imposed on squalor, is a relic and a summary of the Rubber Boom. The ruins of a Jesuit seminary can be seen outside Belém, its stonework penetrated and obscured by vines. Portuguese fortifications more than two centuries old still guard the mouth of the river against foreign invaders. The names of villages and provinces often perpetuate the memory of tribes obliterated long ago.

If the Amazon is full of history it is also singularly short of historians and this is perhaps because it belongs, not to one country, but to six. South American authors have concentrated on the possessions of their own nations and foreigners on their own travels or adventures. The division of the Amazon makes it impractical to follow its political development beyond the point when it was shared by the Spanish and Portuguese Empires. But in most ways this is a happy accident. The Amazon has never been touched by the mainstream of history and its politics have been those of backward provinces in backward countries.

The river can, however, offer shining examples of individual heroism. In Orellana and Colonel Fawcett, in Isabella Godin and Roosevelt and Rondon, in the saintly Jesuit, Father Fritz, and the blaspheming navvies of the Madeira–Mamoré railway, we find men and women pitting themselves against a merciless Nature. Unfortunately, the darker strain in humanity has been as strongly represented in the Amazon Valley. The psychopathic violence of

Lope de Aguirre was followed by the cold, commercial cruelty of
the Portuguese slave trade and finally eclipsed by the horrors of the
Putumayo.

Amazonian literature is as variable as its fauna; this century
has seen such brilliant books of travel as Theodore Roosevelt's
Through the Brazilian Wilderness, H. M. Tomlinson's *The Sea and
the Jungle*, Peter Fleming's *Brazilian Adventure*, Matthew Huxley's
and Cornell Capa's *Farewell to Eden*, and one superlative novel,
Peter Matthieson's *At play in the fields of the Lord*. Most of the
books cited in the bibliography are serious and reliable, but the
submerged nine-tenths, the ramblings of travellers and explorers,
are truly horrific.

An English author who worked in Peru during the Rubber Boom
tells us, 'Where the pigs are raised in the fields, the writer, in the
absence of sanitary arrangements, has been compelled, on more
than one occasion, to protect himself with a stick from the revolting
intentions of the scavenging porkers.'

This modesty is most uncharacteristic; a more normal attitude
is shown by explorers who, when attacked by an anaconda, strangle
the impudent creature in front of their companion's camera, by those
whose days are spent subduing jaguars, alligators and headhunters,
and who rise at dawn as red-blooded as ever, in spite of the attentions
of vampire bats throughout the night. An American explorer can
speak for them:

'I had just been back to Pará and buried one of my followers, who
died of exhaustion'; and again, 'the first explorers of the Mato
Grosso must be men like myself, let the boast be forgiven, who can
bump an old tub over a mud flat without spilling the stores and live
on dried monkeys' tails for a year at a stretch'.

While I cannot myself claim to have bumped an old tub over
anything whatsoever, to have thrust my way into unexplored jungle
or to have escaped from a swarm of cannibal fish, I can truthfully
say that I have hacked a path through some of the most impenetrable
prose in the English language and swallowed clichés that would
have turned the stomach of the most hardened piranha. I only
hope that I have not regurgitated too many of them on to these
pages.

I am deeply indebted to Colonel Eggeling U.S.A.F. for the
results of his investigations into Fawcett's disappearance, to Colonel

Fleming, O.B.E., for his advice on the same chapter, to Father Corbishley S.J. for his assistance on the Jesuit Reductions in Paraguay and for his permission to use the library at Farm Street, to Señora Iriarte of Bogotá for her information on the Indian tribes of the Putumayo; and to Mr. Anthony Huxley for his advice on the wild life of the Amazon; I am also grateful to Mr. William Kellet of the Rubber Growers' Association, Colonel Montgomery of the Anti-Slavery Society, Mr. Nicholas Baring, The Hon. Adrian Berry, Major-General Sir Basil Eugster, C.B., C.B.E., D.S.O., M.C. and Lord Hartwell; and to Miss Christina Pretyman, Lady Emma Tennant and Miss Nike Kent Taylor for their translations. I would finally like to thank all those who helped us in South America, in particular Professor Galvão, Señor Orlando Villas Boas, Señora Perreira, Mr. Patrick Nicholls and Mr. Alec Eaglestone.

PART ONE

THE QUEST FOR EL DORADO

Chapter One

'THE FRESHWATER SEA'

I N THE year 1499, seven years after Columbus's discovery of the New World, a Spanish captain off the coast of Brazil well out of sight of land, was astonished to find that he was sailing through fresh water.

Vicente Yañez Pinzon had made his landfall where the city of Recife now stands, and had taken possession of the country for the Crown of Castile. Then he had followed the coast northward, landing at intervals, but always found himself confronted by fierce and well-armed natives. Pinzon was one of three brothers who had all sailed with Columbus on the great voyage and this subsequent expedition from Seville had been undertaken at his own expense. He found no treasure and it was accounted an unsuccessful venture —but in fact he was the discoverer of the greatest river in the world.

Like all the other Spanish explorers of the New World he imagined that he had reached India. He thought that he must have sailed past the city of Cathay and struck the sub-continent at some point beyond the Ganges. The presence of this great volume of fresh water so many miles from the coast he guessed must be due to 'the vehement course of many rivers, descending from the mountains'.

He turned in towards the shore and eventually anchored in the mouth of a vast river.

Around him as far as the eye could see lay an intricate maze of islands, some of which were large enough to be mistaken for the shore. The water underneath his keel had lost the vivid blue of the tropical Atlantic and had acquired instead an opaque bronze colour, which gleamed like fire only at sunset. Parts of the estuary were

3

broken by shoals and low-lying rocks. The islands were surrounded by carpets of sand, behind which the jungle reared up like a wall. There were no hills or undulations visible on the land. The river merged into sand and the sand into jungle.

The islands seemed fertile and prosperous, but when Pinzon landed he could find no treasure or rich merchandise. He therefore seized thirty-six of the trusting Indians, intending to sell them as slaves on his return to Spain.

When the tide turned it clashed with the force of the river's powerful stream and huge waves rose up beneath the ship, lifting it, the sailors swore, by as much as four fathoms. Pinzon hurriedly beat his way out of the estuary against the trade winds, leaving the river the poorer by thirty-six Indians and one monkey, caught by his sailors, and the richer by a new name—'Santa Maria de la Mar Dulce'.

The 'Santa Maria' was soon forgotten and the newly-discovered river became known as 'La Mar Dulce'—'The Freshwater Sea'.

*

Pinzon had discovered one of the rarest of natural phenomena which, like the Pacific Ocean, the Sahara Desert and the Great Barrier Reef, dwarf everything of their kind. 'The Freshwater Sea' was a more appropriate name than he could have known, for, millions of years before his discovery of the river, all its lower course had formed a vast inland gulf, which received the waters of the Amazon, the Tocantins, the Xingu, the Trombetas and many lesser streams. Over one thousand miles from the mouth, above the cataracts of the Madeira, there was another land-locked sea, 400,000 square miles in area, on the Bolivian plains. And far away in the Andes, at a height of 12,500 feet, there was yet a third great body of water, larger than Lake Superior and a tenth of whose bed is still occupied by Lake Titicaca.

The appearance of the Amazon has changed since the days when it passed through this series of inland oceans, but everything about it remains on the same fantastic scale. At its mouth the river, including the estuary of the Pará, is 208 miles wide and every second its current sweeps seven and a half million cubic feet of water out to sea, with a force that rolls back the Atlantic Ocean and freshens its waters for some 150 miles. The discharge at its mouth is twelve times as great as that of the Mississippi and more than twenty-five times that of the Nile in flood. It exceeds the combined volume of the eight great rivers of Asia, and if all the rivers of the world were united into one vast stream, the Amazon would provide one fifth of its waters. Every day enough sediment is carried out to sea to form a solid cube of earth stretching 500 feet on each side. Marajo, the greatest of the many islands in the Amazon's mouth, is the same size as Switzerland.

The earth is too small for any single river to provide such volume unaided, and the Amazon attracts the waters of every stream in an area only slightly smaller than the Continental United States. Its basin stretches over twenty-five degrees of latitude and from the Atlantic to within a hundred miles of the Pacific. It has over one thousand tributaries, with a combined length of 50,000 miles, which is the same distance as two circuits of the globe at the Equator. It gathers to itself the foaming torrents of the Andes, the meandering brown courses of the Purus and Jurúa, the silted mass of the Madeira, the azure Tapajós and the inky waters of the Rio Negro.

If the size of the Amazon offends European credulity, it is because we are accustomed to thinking in terms of our own cramped little continent. Its gigantic scale may be easier to realize if we super-impose the map of the Amazon system on to more familiar pages of the atlas. Thus if the mouth of the river is placed in Moscow, the Araguaia rises south of Crete, the Madeira deep in the Sahara desert, the Rio Branco in Stockholm, the Putumayo in Liverpool, the Ucayali runs through the Atlas Mountains and the Amazon itself flows through north-west Africa before cutting Spain, France, Germany, Poland and western Russia in half. If we could solve New York's water problem by substituting the Amazon for the Hudson, the valley of the new river would blot out all but the western coastal states and would overlap into Canada, Mexico and Cuba. If the north bank were that of the Thames, the south bank would be in Paris.

The differences in climate and scenery along its course are of course immense, although not so great as they would be if the Amazon lay entirely in a single hemisphere. An inhabitant of the Andes would find conditions in Marajó as strange as a Bedouin the Russian steppes. But the character of the Amazon valley can be described as having a three-fold nature—the tropical rain-forest, the highlands of Brazil and the Guianas, and the rain-swept foothills of the Andes.

From above, the tropical rain-forest resembles an endless green pile-carpet without variations in texture or height; this monotonous landscape is relieved only by occasional rivers, curling their way through the jungle like motionless brown snakes.

On the stream one loses this impression of scale. One may know that the jungle extends for a thousand miles but one can only see a few yards into it. The river sometimes seems deceptively small, for the Amazon, throughout its course, is studded with islands and it often divides into several channels. Parts of the river are confused masses of waterways, where tributaries, bifurcations, the main stream and side-channels all connect with each other and with countless lakes, left stranded at the end of the rainy season.

At low water the banks rear up to a surprising height, like massive, but inadequate dykes. And above them the battle for life is waged with the prodigality of the tropics. Most forests have natural stands of the same kind of timber, but in the Amazon basin every form of plant, shrub and tree jostle each other in their search for light. Palms, laurels, rubber trees, rosewood, mahoganies, 120 different species of cedar, steelwoods, bamboos, chocolate trees, silk cotton trees, figs, acacias, purple hearts, cow trees, Brazil nuts, garlic trees, cashew, balsa and thousands of others sprout side by side. Occasionally the skyline is broken by a vast hardwood rearing its head far above the canopy of the forest.

In this contest for light normal trees become parasites and giant orchids seed themselves in branches sixty feet from the ground. The general effect is of a living wall, impenetrable and ridiculously fertile. Sprays of parakeets explode out of the foliage and flutter noisily across the river. Butterflies of great size and vivid colouring hover around the tree tops, the iridescent blue of the morpho contrasting with the more subdued brown of the brassolidae.

It is a magnificent sight, but also a monotonous one and only in the evening does it become a thing of beauty. Then the sun sinks down until its dying rays shine directly into the forest, lighting up the tree-trunks and revealing the infinite variations of green in the foliage. At the same time the big fish start to feed. Dolphins leap out of the water, show a flash of pink or silver scales, heave a mournful asthmatic sigh and disappear again. The smaller fish jump to avoid their pursuers and, as the duck and macaw make their flights across the river, the evening passes in a liquid symphony of life and death.

The wild life in the river matches the profuse vegetation on its banks. Alligators, though rarer now, were once so common that several explorers complained of the difficulty of steering between them. Countless swarms of turtles cluster on sandbanks during their laying season and an acute observer can still see the monstrous manatee or sea cow nibbling at weeds near the bank, or water snakes writhing their way along the surface.

Lakes, left stranded when the waters fall, boil with life at the end of the dry season, as their fish are concentrated in a smaller area. Wild birds nest around their banks and swoop down to collect the smaller fishes, and alligators and turtles also congregate. Here that vicious little man-eating fish the piranha is at its most dangerous.

Inside the rain-forest there is another world; even if one is no more than a few yards from the river the impression of being deep in the jungle is complete. The sun, which seemed so dazzling outside, now sends thin rays of light, that barely illuminate the ground, through the forest canopy. But even without its rays the heat is stifling. Vast tree-trunks, many of which are supported by elevated roots, like the buttresses of cathedrals, are often overwhelmed by parasites of extraordinary size. The rotting timber of dead trees crackles underfoot and six-foot sprays of orchids shoot out of the living wood far above one's head.

Creepers and vines are everywhere, climbing up to the tops of the highest trees, luxuriating there in the sun, then dropping their tendrils down again to the earth. Sometimes dead trees have no room to fall, but lean instead on their neighbours and wait for their turn to come. The undergrowth is thick enough to make any movement difficult without the use of an axe or machete. Few animals or birds can be seen in the rain-forest; it is too dense and one can only hear the noise of their departure, but the insects are omnipresent. Mosquitoes fly in clouds around one's face and the tree-trunks carry bulbous termite nests. Saüba ants, each with its burden of leaf, march purposefully towards their home.

The astonishing seasonal variation in the water's level allows the river to change its appearance almost as if it were a living thing.*

* The seasonal variation is twelve feet at Belém, thirty-five feet at Obidos, forty-five feet at Tefé and twenty feet at Iquitos. It can be even higher on some of the Amazon's tributaries. The level of the Rio Negro varies by forty to fifty feet and that of the Purus by fifty to sixty feet.

The beginning of the rainy season is accompanied by thunder-storms of incredible violence, with sheet and forked lightning illuminating the river by night as clearly as the sun by day. The wind whips up waves big enough to endanger the small ships that sail on the Amazon and the rain descends like a waterfall. When the stream rises, trees, sediment, masses of grass and sometimes whole sections of the banks are undermined and swept away. A big tree of a 'floating island' may stick on a shoal and be joined by more débris, until, in the next dry season, a new island will appear. The soil is so fertile that, in a few years time, it will be indistinguishable from its neighbours.

Under the force of the flood-stream everything changes, the deep-water channels, islands, shoals and the very course of the stream. The complex filigree of channels is absorbed by the rising water; lakes are swallowed up, banks and islands flooded and tributaries dammed back. For much of its course the Amazon is flanked by low-lying alluvial land and, at high water, this too is flooded to form an inland sea which varies in width from five to several hundred miles. The highlands in the south and the foothills of the Andes are both extensions of the rain-forest. There is no natural interruption between them; they merge into each other.

The Amazon itself is navigable as far as the rapids of the Pongo de Maseriche, which lie about 2,600 miles from the Atlantic, but its great northern and southern tributaries are generally unnavigable for much of their length. The reason for this is that the Amazon Valley, while flat from west to east almost as far as the foothills of the Andes, rises far more sharply to the north and south of the main river. In the south, where the tributaries are longer and their sources farther from the Equator, the rain-forest soon thins out and is eventually left clinging only to the banks of rivers and lakes. The country between the rivers is filled with dry plains and stunted trees. The same conditions can be seen in the headwaters of some northern tributaries.

The Cordillera of the Andes have one of the highest rainfalls of any area in the world. Clouds are swept in from the east by the Trade Winds to be broken on the mountain chain and to shed all their rain on its eastern slopes. This causes dramatic scenery, since the rain-forest survives to an extraordinary height and clings tenaciously to the steepest cliffs. Below, the torrents have cut deep gorges through the mountains for their passage down to the plains of the Amazon and, far above, the tree-line gives way, first to the bare hills, with their granite shining white in the sun, and then to the purer white of eternal snow. The weather is turbulent and quick to turn; each minute alteration of the light gives a subtle difference to the colouring of the jungle, and changes it, through every shade of green, to a deep hazy blue.

It is a violent country. Rain lashes the ground and pounds it into a sodden quagmire. Torrents race down the mountainside, tumbling from level to level, from fall to rapid, with inexhaustible energy. Heavy rainfall upstream has an extraordinary effect on their levels and dry water-courses are suddenly filled with raging floods which pluck up trees and great boulders and carry them down on their crests. A stream can rise over twenty feet in twenty-four hours and be transformed from a brook into a river in the same time.

If one follows the course of the Amazon upstream one notices that to the east of the Andes it sprays out into innumerable streams, like a tree putting down its roots. At first these off-shoots are large rivers—the Napo, the Ucayali, the Pastaza, and the Huallaga. But in the Andes each of these tributaries sprouts hundreds of smaller affluents, which flow down through each mountain valley. It is only after its junction with the Ucayali that the Amazon becomes recognisable as the greatest of rivers. Until then it is only one of many.

By keeping to the greater stream at each division of water one will at last reach a glacier 16,000 feet above sea level; its waters feed a series of lakes before forming a small icy stream, which cascades downhill to Lake Santa Ana and then to Lake Lauricocha. Up here there is no vegetation; the air is thin and bitterly cold; it is a bleak wasteland of rocks, ice and snow. The only sign of life is an occasional giant condor overhead, soaring high or swooping low with motionless wings, the master of the air currents. As the Amazon plunges down the Andes it is joined by other streams and as its size increases its pure glacier water is stained to the brown of the earth by the fury of its descent. For hundreds of miles it races downhill, always unnavigable and often inaccessible, until at last it bursts out of the mountains with irresistible force.

At the time of its discovery, the Amazon supported many tribes of Indians, who, although less advanced than the mountain Indians of Peru and Colombia, had made some progress towards civilization. They were short, thick-set people, of great physical strength. They hunted with blowpipes and bows and fought with bows, darts and war clubs. Many of them were cannibals, but they ate human flesh as a part of their rituals and the act was thought to confer great honour on all those who took part in it.

The finest sites on the river were occupied by Indians of Carib tribes. Their race had originated on the southern seaboard of Brazil and had fought its way up to the Amazon, driving weaker Indian nations into the interior. From the Amazon they travelled north up the Rio Negro, crossed into the Orinoco and settled on its banks. In their frail canoes they sailed out to sea and, by reaching the Caribbean, Mexico and Florida, rivalled the explorations of the Vikings.

The Indians lived in harmony with their surroundings. The river and the forest gave them every necessity of life and they knew all their secrets. They used the branches of a bush to poison fishes in the water, and distilled curare for their darts from the bark of a tree. Their knowledge of herb lore has benefited many travellers Humboldt and Colonel Fawcett were both cured by Indians of troublesome insects that had burrowed under their skin. Woodroffe was cured of worms by a Tucuna woman, and Lidstone was saved from the effect of a scorpion bite. Up de Graff saw leaves being used to cure ulcers on the leg. The Indians themselves produced an effective oral contraceptive from herbs. Hot copaiba oil served them as a primitive anaesthetic and they may have used the bark of the cinchona tree to fight malaria. Some tribes are reported to have practised electrolysis with nature's generator, the electric eel.

They were masters, too, of other crafts, from the manufacture of a true, quarter-inch bore in a ten-foot-long blowpipe, to the shrinking of a human head to the size of an orange. They made delicate pottery and figures in a style reminiscent of the Orient. They were fine archers and if some stories of their skill with the bow are almost impossible to believe, it is well established that they could shoot an arrow straight up into the air and make it pierce the shell of a turtle by their feet. Over a short range their accuracy with the blowpipe was phenomenal.

Although they lacked every product of civilization, they were perfectly prepared for survival in the jungle; but they were not equipped to face the colonization of their country. Their naked bodies would soon be easy targets for steel and lead; their constitutions would be overthrown by new and terrible epidemics and their fragile social fabric would crumble at the impact of a stronger culture.

This then was the stage for a long battle between man and nature, a battle which man has yet to win. The Amazon has always seemed to offer easy and immediate wealth, but has betrayed most of those who sought it. The story of the Amazon is one in which Nature is always dominant, and the affairs of mankind pitifully small in so vast a setting.

Chapter Two

THE RIO ORELLANA

FRANCISCO ORELLANA, a young Spaniard from Estremadura, was, entirely by accident, the first man to lead an expedition down the stream of the Amazon; and for a time his name was given to the river.

The Treaty of Tordesillas, signed in 1494 by Spain and Portugal, had divided the unknown world between their two empires with a longitudinal line drawn 350 miles west of the Cape Verde Islands. The Portuguese were tentative in their attempts to establish colonies on the eastern seaboard of South America, all of which came into their hemisphere, and the early Spanish expeditions to the mouth of the Amazon foundered on the hazards of disease, uncharted waters, hostile Indians, and a country from which it was difficult to wring a living. The survivors of the colonists, who had left expecting to plunder the treasures of the New World, returned home disillusioned and ruined.

In the meantime, the Spanish American Empire was rising in other parts of the continent. In 1513 Balboa crossed the Isthmus of Panama and laid claim to the Pacific Ocean for his ruler. Eight years later Cortes' conquest of Mexico reached its climax with the capture of Mexico City, and in 1532 Francisco Pizarro landed, with fewer than 200 men, at Tumbez on the coast of Peru.

Pizarro's conquest of the Inca Empire was carried out at a bewildering speed. He found himself in November 1532 encamped with his small force in the middle of the Inca's army, his survival apparently dependent on that monarch's whim. The man who thus seemed to hold them at his mercy was the absolute ruler of an empire stretching from Ecuador to Chile and from the desert of the

Pacific coast to the rain-forest of the Amazon. It was not a decadent
empire, but at the peak of its strength, and its ruler and his army
were fresh from victory in a civil war. Nor were there any rival
countries whose troops might be enrolled against the Inca, in the
same way as Cortes had used the Tlascallans against the Aztecs.
Even the Spaniard's most powerful weapon, the horse, was unsuited
to much of the country.

Nevertheless, in the space of one year, Pizarro had accomplished
the impossible: an empire of ten million people, loyal, war-like
and regimented, had been overturned by an army of 200 men.
Atahuallpa, the Inca himself, had been captured, ransomed for a
room full of gold, converted, and then garrotted. His armies and
subjects had been scattered or enslaved; a puppet had been installed
in his place and his executioners had entered Cuzco, the capital
city of the Incas, as conquerors.

Before the Spaniards could consolidate their hold on the country,
however, there was a violent Indian uprising, quelled with the
greatest difficulty, which in its turn was followed by a civil war
between the two Spanish partners in the expedition to conquer
Peru, Francisco Pizarro and Diego de Almagro. This was essentially
a struggle over the plunder of the conquest, for Almagro's men had
arrived too late to share in the ransom of Atahuallpa, nor were they
satisfied by the land allocated to them in the division of the country.
At the battle of Las Salinas the Pizarros were victorious in this, the
first of many Peruvian civil wars.

Thus, by 1538, the conquest was firmly established, the Indians
cowed, and the Spanish rebels crushed. Those who had served the
Pizarros well in the wars were rewarded with vast captaincies, and
among these was Francisco Orellana, who was allotted the country
of la Culata in the province of Quito.

No account of Orellana's early life has survived, but we know that
he was a relation of the Pizarro family, and came from the same
province of Estremadura, where he was born in about 1511. He
apparently went to the Indies in his youth, drawn there like many
Spaniards by the limitless wealth of the New World, and like them,
undeterred by its dangers. He had seen service in Nicaragua before
taking part in the conquest of Peru, during the course of which he
lost an eye, and was a firm supporter of the Pizarros.

The territory given to him was among the most difficult to subdue.
The greater part of the Pacific coast was a desert, arid and empty,

but round the city of Guayaquil, which he founded, the long waste of
sand to the south gave way to dense tropical forest watered by the
Guayaquil river. Orellana's was also an unhealthy region. Its jungles
were infested by mosquitoes, and alligators teemed like worms in
its rivers. The climate was hot and humid and at the time of the
conquest the country was inhabited by intractable Indians who had
already rebelled against Spanish rule and had yet to be subdued.*

For Orellana the country's most serious disadvantage was that it
had too many rivers, swamps and forests to allow him to deploy
his cavalry. Nevertheless, within two years he had reconquered the
Indians and, in accordance with his commission, founded the city of
Santiago de Guayaquil. In 1540 his friend and relative Gonzalo
Pizarro arrived in Quito as governor of the province, and as
Orellana's overlord.

Gonzalo was in many ways typical of his remarkable family. There
can seldom have been a tougher or more courageous group of men
than the conquerors of the Inca Empire, nor one more skilled in the
use of horses and arms, but Gonzalo's bravery was conspicuous
even in this company and he was acknowledged to be the finest
horseman in Peru. He was a natural leader, with a strong per-
sonality, but his nature was tainted by cruelty in the same extreme
form as his good qualities. He lacked the judgment and shrewdness
of his elder brothers, Francisco and Hernando, and his vanity would
not allow him to take advice from those more able than himself.
These limitations were to be fatal later in his career, but in 1540,
when he rode in on a magnificent charger to take possession of the
province of Quito, he must have been an inspiring figure, as full of
promise as either of his brothers.

Gonzalo Pizarro saw this great province, comprising the northern
half of the Inca Empire, as a spring-board for further conquests. As
soon as he had been installed he began to organize an ambitious
expedition to explore and take possession of the unknown country
to the east. Pizarro's expedition had two objectives, first to find on
the inland slopes of the Andes a place where cinnamon trees were
said to grow in great profusion, and secondly to find and conquer
the kingdom of El Dorado, the Golden Man.

The profitable spice trade was in Portuguese hands and stories

* The same spirit of lawlessness was found by La Condamine, who 200 years
later reported warfare in these jungles between Indians and Cimarrones, the
escaped negro slaves.

of great forests of cinnamon were common enough for Pizarro to hope quite reasonably to break their monopoly. The legend of El Dorado recurs throughout the early history of the New World. Sir Walter Raleigh was searching for this country in his last disastrous expedition to the Orinoco and he was merely following the Spaniards of Venezuela. The search was later joined by the Portuguese from Brazil and the Spanish conquerors of New Granada.

Its king, El Dorado himself, was said to wear only a fine coating of gold dust, which was washed off and discarded every evening and a fresh coat applied the next morning over sweet-smelling resin. He was thought to consider the gold dust more beautiful than any garment and less cumbersome and vulgar than gold plates or ornaments, nor as Oviedo, the historian of the Indies, says, 'are the handsome proportions of his body and its natural form concealed or injured'. He adds, sardonically, 'I would rather have the sweepings from the chamber of this monarch than that of the great melting establishments in Peru and in any other part of the world.'

Although the stories of El Dorado came from the legends of the Indians, Gonzalo Pizarro and his followers believed them absolutely. It is easy to understand why, when one looks at the Spanish experiences in the New World and sees how every extravagant forecast had been justified. Indeed nothing in the legend of El Dorado is more fantastic than the true story of the ransom of Atahuallpa, when a room measuring seventeen feet by twenty-two feet was filled with gold to a height of nine feet from its floor. The Indians in the Isthmus of Panama gladly exchanged gold for trinkets, and those in the island of Cubagua would part as freely with their pearls. Soon the great silver mines would open at Potosí and the emeralds of Bogotá would join the pearls of the islands, the gold of Peru and the silver of Bolivia in the galleons bound for Spain. Europe had never seen such wealth as the plunder of the Indies, but the conquistadores thought what they had found so far to be no more than the scratchings from the edge of the continent. We cannot be surprised that they expected more from its heart.*

This was not the first expedition from the Andes down into the

* The legend of El Dorado was not without a factual foundation. Outside Bogotá there is a small but deep lake into which the inhabitants would throw gold ornaments once a year as an offering to their god. A priest would be dressed in gold dust and immersed in the lake's waters. But this ceremony had stopped many years before the conquest.

rain-forest, but all the previous ones had ended in failure and one in disaster. In 1538 Pedro Anzures had led 300 Spanish and 4,000 Indians, including the most beautiful girls in Cuzco, down the eastern slopes of the Andes into the jungle. They learned from the Indians of a rich land far to the east, but were forced to turn back before reaching it because of lack of food. Their sufferings on the return journey were terrible; they ate all their horses, even the offal, which they sometimes lacked the strength to wash. 143 Spaniards died of starvation and the rest were on the point of death when they returned. Most of the Indians died and the living ate the bodies of the dead.

This terrible example did not prevent Gonzalo Pizarro from collecting a formidable army of Spanish volunteers, nor from impressing a suitable number of Indian auxiliaries and bearers. Orellana, one of the first to offer his services, had been sent back to Guayaquil to raise a troop of horse. He returned to Quito too late for Pizarro's departure, which must have been an imposing sight.

The 220 Spaniards were all mounted and provided with an ample supply of arms and ammunition. Pizarro had collected vast flocks of llamas for transport and meat, over 2,000 hogs, and nearly 2,000 hunting dogs—big savage brutes that were set on to wild Indians, a process which the Spaniards called 'dogging them'. These were perhaps the expedition's most versatile animals, available for war, hunting, torture, and in the last resort food.

The army was completed by 4,000 miserable mountain Indians, doomed to die in the thick foetid air of the Amazon, and kept for safety in chains and shackles until the day of their departure. Even without Orellana's reinforcements, Gonzalo Pizarro's army was stronger and infinitely better supplied than that with which his brother had overthrown the Inca.

At the end of February 1541, the herds of animals and the army of Indians attending them and sharing their burdens were accompanied by their proud, confident masters through the gates of Quito. The Spaniards, so lavishly equipped, carried nothing but their arms and each man a small sack for his food. Surrounded by food and labour, their bodies well protected by their armour and their feet firmly in their stirrups, they had nothing to fear.

Orellana's party from Guayaquil rode into Quito soon after their departure, his money exhausted by the purchase of horses and equipment for his twenty-three followers. Disregarding the advice of the citizens not to follow with so few men and so little food, he left at once, survived the attacks of the Indians, and, just when his men were beginning to starve, made contact with Pizarro's party. Although he and his followers had nothing except their arms and horses they were welcomed and Orellana was made Lieutenant-General of the combined forces.

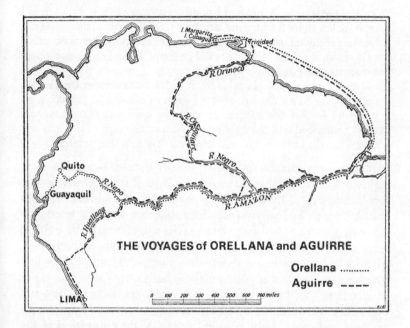

THE VOYAGES of ORELLANA and AGUIRRE

Orellana ....
Aguirre _ _ _ _

The expedition had already suffered the loss of more than one hundred Indians in the cold of the mountains and they now found themselves in a wooded area, unsuitable for the horses, where it rained heavily and incessantly.

They had, in fact, already reached the watershed of the Amazon and few transitions can be more sudden than the change from the bare, icy deserts of the Montana to the steaming jungles on the eastern slopes of the Andes. The rain rotted their equipment and blurred their vision. They had to wade through endless mud and across the innumerable streams in their path. The road down from Quito to the Amazon was afterwards considered to be too difficult even for mules, and the great herds of animals brought by Pizarro became an impossible encumbrance. The horses, their guarantee of

victory, were carefully nursed over every river, suspended by slings
around their stomachs. Richard Spruce, who travelled on roughly
the same route three hundred years later, has left us a vivid account
of its difficulty, and we must remember that his road was already
well worn by other travellers and that it was the easiest way down
from the Montana.

> Road there is none, but only the merest semblance of a track, such as a
> tapir makes to its feeding and drinking places, often carried along the
> face of precipices, where had it not been for projecting roots on which
> to lay hold, the passage would have been impossible. No one ever opens
> a road, no fallen trees have been cleared away, no over-hanging branches
> cut off. From Canelos, the rains set in with greater severity than ever—
> the dripping forest through which I had to push my way, soaking my
> garments so that towards the evening my arms and shoulders were
> quite benumbed and the mud which even on the tops of the hills was
> often over the knees—made our progress very slow and painful.

In conditions equally forbidding Pizarro decided to advance with
eighty Spaniards on foot. After seventy days of fruitless wandering,
in which several of his men starved to death, he found the cinnamon
trees for which he had been searching, but they were scattered over
too wide an area to be of any commercial value. Nearby they found
some debased Indians, living in the lowest depths of barbarism,
whom Pizarro questioned about when they would find valleys and
plains instead of this sodden jungle. The Indians, who had never
seen such things, lacked the wits to invent a satisfactory story, and
when their answers displeased him he had some torn to pieces by
his dogs and others burnt alive. Only one of the chroniclers of the
expedition considered this atrocity worth recording.

On their way back, they found a more advanced tribe with stories
of a rich country further on. Any Indian was likely to tell the
Spaniards something of this sort in reply to their avid questions
about gold,* but in this case it did them no good. Their chief was
seized and those of his followers who resisted were slaughtered.
Pizarro then summoned the main body of the expedition to join him.

A scouting party brought back news of a great river where there
were Indians wearing clothes and in canoes. When the Spaniards
reached this place, on the Coca River, a tributary of the Napo, they

---

* According to Spruce, the Tupi word for 'stone' is the same as the Quecha
word for 'gold'—a fact which would account for many of the wilder stories told
to the Spaniards.

made every effort to be friendly, as they needed the Indians' help to get food. At first all went well, the Indians came and traded in their canoes, but they soon became angry and went away, leaving behind their chiefs and headmen whom Pizarro had had closely watched. The Spaniards seized a few canoes with which they made short journeys to find food, but the river was so full of Indian canoes, paddled with greater skill, that they did not dare go far.

At this stage we learn with a shock that almost all the Indians who had been brought from Quito had already died. It seems extraordinary that none of the chroniclers should have bothered to mention the death of over 3,000 members of the expedition, but the Spanish did not consider the lives of their Indians as being worth recording except when they were badly needed. It may seem equally strange that so many should have died before the real hardships of the expedition began. But the highland Indians usually died of fevers when they were taken down to the jungle and the jungle Indians would die of pneumonia in the mountains.

Pizarro decided to build a brigantine large enough to carry their sick, supplies and munitions, and strong enough to resist attacks from canoes, leaving the horses and some of the men to follow along the banks of the river. At first there were enough settlements to keep them supplied with food, but progress for the men on shore was always difficult. Morasses were common and often there were creeks that had to be swum or bridged. They had no opportunity to explore the country. The settlements along the bank dwindled and eventually disappeared. They had eaten the last of their hogs and their guides told them that they were at the beginning of a great uninhabited area where there was no food to be found, until the river they were travelling on met another great river, where they would find abundant supplies.

The expedition had now been away for about ten months. Almost all its resources had been consumed; several Spaniards and most of the Indians had died and they had achieved nothing except to discredit the myth of La Canela, the land of Cinnamon. Nor had they reasonable expectation of achieving anything further. The stories of rich lands still to come were only pale echoes of the fables told in Quito. The sensible decision would have been to turn back while they still had the means to return; but Spain had not conquered the New World by common sense and caution, and a return to Quito was not contemplated until much later in the expedition.

B

When Orellana offered to take the brig with sixty men to go down-stream in search of food, Pizarro agreed, but told him that he must return within ten or twelve days to the expeditionary force, which would follow down river.

The brig was loaded with their heavier belongings, bedding and a little food. Some of the canoes captured from the Indians were tied alongside. Sixty men, including Orellana, the Friar, Gaspar de Carvajal, who has left us the only account of the voyage, another Friar, the sick, soldiers and sailors, all went on board, and the small, overcrowded boat was taken by the current and disappeared quickly down the river.

From this moment we rely almost entirely on Friar Carvajal's account of their voyage. A native of Trujillo, like Orellana and the Pizarros, he had come to Peru soon after the conquest and established the first Dominican monastery in the country. When Pizarro set out he was still young, vigorous and brave and a natural choice for the expedition. His narrative is conscientious, almost certainly as accurate as could be expected, and annoying to the modern reader only through its omissions. He does not speak of the disagreements among the members of the expedition, of their inevitable hopes and desperation, the threats to Orellana's authority and how he dealt with them. We can imagine the petty discomforts that plagued the travellers and added to the agony of their wounds, hunger and exhaustion, but we must regret the scarcity of any descriptive passages and the dry way in which one of the greatest open boat journeys in history is told.

His vocation gives him some advantages. Dates remain clear in his mind because of the religious calendar, and times of day because of their association with different services. He deals curtly with his own injuries, and his faith never slackens. Sometimes indeed it can be irritating, as when he attributes every stroke of luck to intercession by the Almighty, and describes every defeat of the wretched Indians, who were often only trying to defend their own homes, as the confusion of 'their wicked designs'.

*

On the second day after their departure, the brig hit a sunken log and one of its planks was stove in. If they had not been close to the shore their journey would have ended then and the survivors would have been forced to make a humiliating and difficult return to the main force overland. But the boat was quickly mended and they set off again, gathering speed as the current was swollen by tributaries bearing the melted snow of the Andes.

After three days they had finished all their food, without seeing any signs of human habitation, but they decided to go on. Two more days passed and their hunger became acute, but it was now too late to attempt to row back against the strong current. They were soon reduced to eating leather belts and the soles of their shoes cooked with herbs. Sometimes they would beach the boat and stagger into the woods to search for roots, some supported on staffs and others crawling on all fours. None of them had any knowledge of which roots were edible and inevitably some that they ate were poisonous and those who consumed them became 'like madmen and did not possess sense'.

On New Year's Day, 1542, some of the companions claimed that they could hear drums faintly in the distance. All forgot their starvation and rowed feverishly for the next two days, but without hearing anything further. On the evening of the second day they were sitting in a dispirited group, 'eating certain forest roots', when first Orellana and then the rest heard the drums again, this time plainly. A heavy watch was set in case of a surprise attack, and next morning Orellana made sure that all their arms were ready before they set out.

The Indian village proved to be only seven miles downstream. By the time they reached it the alarm had been given and its inhabitants were ready to defend their homes; but when they saw the Spaniards land their courage failed them and they fled without a blow or a shot having been exchanged, leaving behind a meal they had prepared for themselves.

Later in the day the Indians returned in their canoes and hovered offshore, uncertain what to do; in Carvajal's words 'moving up and down the river like simpletons'. One cannot help feeling that the Friar is being a little harsh, although one can imagine the mood of nervous hilarity of men who have eaten their first meal for a week and may be about to lose their lives for doing so.

Yet looking back over four centuries, we must sympathize with the Indians. Since their earliest tribal memories they have lived in the Amazon jungle, perhaps in the same village on the same bend of the river. The waters rise and fall, game and fish are plentiful or scarce, there are tribal wars, victory or defeat, famines and epidemics and always the struggle for existence in a hard land. These factors form the framework in which the Indian's life always had been lived, and in which he could reasonably suppose it always would be lived. One day, without any warning, a roughly built rowing boat comes slowly round the bend of the river, crammed with haggard, desperate men in strange clothes. Sometimes the Indians fought them, sometimes they greeted them as friends or even as gods, and occasionally they fled into the forest. It did not matter which they did. The Spaniards would soon move on and few of those Indians would see a white man again, but for their tribes life could never be the same. The centuries of disease, exploitation and disintegration were inevitable after that moment.

On this occasion, as on many others, Orellana's amazing gift for languages forestalled any trouble. After speaking to them for a short time in a dialect learned from Indians up the river, he persuaded them to fetch their chief and when he arrived, 'very much decked out', Orellana embraced him and gave him presents. In return the Indians brought them 'meat, partridges, turkeys and many kinds of fish'. The next day he formally took possession of the chiefs and of their lands, a practice he followed whenever the circumstances allowed it. Carvajal unfortunately tells us nothing of the Indians' reactions, except that their friendly attitude and gifts of food continued.

On the same day Orellana called a meeting and told his companions that he had decided to return up-river to Pizarro. The voyage downstream had been difficult enough, but the journey they had completed in nine days would take over a month in reverse, and it might even be impossible to move the brig against the swollen current. His followers presented a petition to this effect through the newly-appointed scrivener (as indispensable an adjunct to any Spanish conquest as a priest), begging him not to push them into treason by insisting on this plan. Orellana at last decided that they were right and agreed to lead them on downstream, on condition that they waited where they were for Pizarro for three to four months or as long as their food held out. They were to spend their time building a larger boat, for the rest of the party if it arrived, or for themselves if it did not.

Building a boat with their resources was not easy. Bellows were constructed out of their leather buskins, leaving some barefooted; other tools were improvised and every surplus scrap of iron was commandeered for nails, two thousand of which were made. Charcoal was prepared and timber cut; but before the boat was completed the Indians became less friendly and the expedition lost its supply of food. Seven Spaniards died, perhaps from disease rather than hunger. It was clear that they would have to leave.

In a last effort to get in touch with Pizarro, who had still not appeared, Orellana offered the services of guides and the sum of one thousand golden castellanos to any six men who would return with a message. Only three anonymous heroes volunteered and so on the day of Our Lady of Candlemas, February 2, 1542, the other Spaniards loaded the unfinished boat on board and set off again downstream.

The circumstances in which Orellana abandoned Pizarro blackened his name among historians for a long period. Pizarro himself, in his report to the Spanish king, complained that Orellana deserted against orders and that he carried off all the arquebuses, crossbows, munitions and iron belonging to the force. A wilder story, in fact a pure invention, is given by the Inca Garcilasso da Vega, and was followed, uncharacteristically, by Prescott in his *Conquest of Peru*. According to this version it was Orellana who suggested that they should sail downstream and only one cavalier and Friar Carvajal objected to abandoning their comrades. Orellana then mistreated Carvajal and marooned the cavalier in the woods to die an agonizing death where he was later found running, naked and bearded, by Pizarro's men. This and less colourful accusations are carefully refuted by Professor Medina in his book, *The Discovery of the Amazon*.

The arguments that Orellana had no other course of action open to him are convincing. It would be a considerable achievement to row his brigantine against the swollen waters of the Coca river, let alone to avoid the starvation which he had only just escaped when he had the full force of its current behind him. A canoe-load of men might reach Pizarro, but Orellana had neither enough volunteers to man the canoe, nor the supplies to await his leader's arrival. But one cannot help feeling that Orellana knew all this throughout, and that both his announcement that they must return upstream and his call for volunteers were disingenuous manoeuvres, calculated to convince any official enquiry that his hand was forced.

*

On their way downstream the expedition had intended to visit the village of a friendly Indian chief named Irrimorrany, who had already brought them food at their last resting place. But he lived a short distance up one of the more turbulent tributaries of the Napo river and the meeting of the two swollen waters caused whirlpools to form and large pieces of driftwood to be sucked from one side to the other. The brigantine was tossed from bank to bank, quite out of control, and as they were spat out of the maelstrom, the Spaniards, realizing how lucky they were to be alive, steeled themselves to endure another two hundred leagues of barren country.

They rowed on, day after day, through a wilderness which seemed to last forever. Each bend in the river brought them the same claustrophobic view of the great flat surface of the stream hemmed in by the dark greens of the jungle. There were no animals to kill, no human beings to rob. Their ordeal lasted from February 2, when they left one Indian village, to February 8, when they reached the next; it was a week of hard work at the oars without food.

On Orellana's orders they approached these new Indians with friendship, offering them presents and asking for food. They were brought many turtles and parrots to eat and told to rest in an uninhabited village on the far bank; but in the middle of the night, they were attacked by an enemy as bad as hunger—mosquitoes in swarms great enough to cause even a conquistador to surrender and move on.

The next day they found their friendliness again rewarded. Indians appeared with canoes loaded with more food, and wondering at the way that Orellana spoke their language. Pizarro in these circumstances would have stormed the Indian village, seized the food, guides, and slaves he needed, and butchered any natives who resisted. Such an action would have cost them their lives, for they were in the country of the Overlord, Aparia the Great, who was soon to show Orellana and his men such kindness. Without his friendship they could never have assembled their second brigantine and without its protection they would have been killed by the warlike tribes of the lower river.

They continued downstream well supplied with food until the point where the Napo river is swallowed up by the Amazon. Here they were given partridges and turtles 'as large as leather shields' and told that all this food had been sent to them by the command of Aparia himself. The Spaniards were then guided to his settlement,

but as they approached, many warriors armed for war ran down to
the bank. Orellana talked to them in their own language, calmed
them and landed. Carvajal comments: 'His understanding of the
language, was, next to God, the deciding factor by virtue of which
we did not perish,' a standard form of expression for the conquistadores, similar to the often used 'next to God we owed our
victory to the horses'. Even in Carvajal's short account, Orellana's
linguistic skill is soon replaced by the crossbows and then by the
brigantines. Belief in God's support and a sturdy reliance on their
own resources were mixed as thoroughly in the minds of the
Catholic conquistadores as in those of Cromwell's Puritan army.

Aparia made his guests welcome and had food brought, turtles,
manatees, fish, partridges, cats and monkeys. A most peculiar
conversation followed, Orellana explaining, in the words of Carvajal,
'that we were Christians and worshipped a single God, who was the
Creator of all created things, and that we were not like them that
walked in the paths of error, worshipping stones and images . . . ;
and how we were servants and vassals of the Emperor of the
Christians, the great King of Spain . . . to whom belonged the
territory of all the Indies and many other dominions and kingdoms
throughout the world, and that it was by his command that we were
coming to that land, and that we were going to make a report to
him on what we had seen in it.'

The Indians were suitably attentive, and replied with a piece of
advice which, although irrelevant, was certainly useful, that they
should avoid the land of the Amurians or Grand Mistresses, for
the Spaniards were few and would be killed.

Aparia then asked Orellana who they were, showing an under-
standable confusion at his first speech. The Spanish captain patiently
repeated it and at the end, abandoning his proselytizing, added
that they were the children of the sun. This announcement delighted
the Indians who worshipped the sun, and throughout their lengthy
stay in Aparia's country they lacked for nothing.

The next day Orellana summoned all the overlords, took possession of them in the King's name, and caused a tall cross to be raised
'in which the Indians took delight'. He wisely decided to use this
friendly village as a base to build the second brigantine, essential
for their survival, for if they were attacked while in canoes, the
Spaniards would be overwhelmed by the Indians' greater numbers
and skill.

They were faced with a formidable task, for although the expedition included one woodworker and a few sailors, none of them had any experience of boat-building or any mechanical skill. Their confidence cannot have been improved by the condition of the brigantine which they had constructed earlier with the assistance of Pizarro's men. This boat was rotting, unseaworthy and in need of almost as much work as the new one.

It was more than a matter of building a brigantine strong enough to protect them from Indians throughout their passage of the river; these boats must later carry them from the mouth of the river to the nearest Spanish settlement and they might never again have time to repair them in safety. Throughout their task they were plagued by mosquitoes, so troublesome that while one man was working, another, and sometimes even two, had to fan him to keep them at bay. The Indians helped by giving them fans for the insects, resin for tar, and cotton for oakum, and, most important of all, continued to supply the Spaniards with food.

They left Aparia's village on the eve of the Evangelist St. Mark's day, April 24, 1542, but for a full eighty leagues they were within his country and Aparia himself visited them twice, bringing food on each occasion. As the chief to whom they owed so much left them for the last time, Carvajal does his best to ruin the record of civilized behaviour, rare enough among Spaniards in the New World, by justifying it almost defensively. No ill-treatment was meted out to Aparia in order, according to the Friar, that he should retain affectionate memories of the Spaniards and be the more easily reduced to obedience when the country was colonized. He admits that good relations with the Indians also brought them supplies of food, thus making their passage easier, but fails to raise their relationship to the level where friendship would be the natural result of gratitude.

*

Soon after their departure from Aparia's country their supplies of food again ran out and they were reduced to what Carvajal calls 'our customary fare, which consisted of herbs and every now and then a bit of roasted maize'. Their misery must have been relieved by an incident so laughably unlikely that it might even have been true. Diego Mexia, the woodworker, aimed a bolt from his crossbow at a bird; as he fired the irreplaceable nut fell off his bow into the water and was lost, but a few seconds later one of his companions pulled a great fish out of the river on his line and, when it was opened, they found the nut in its belly. This extraordinary incident was witnessed, Carvajal says, by all the crew.

Six days later they arrived in the province of the great chief Machiparo. Although the banks of the Amazon were more densely populated in those days than at any time since,* Carvajal undoubtedly exaggerates the power of the Indian monarchs along their route and the number of their subjects. Thus Machiparo is described as having 50,000 warriors at his command, all aged between thirty and seventy, and allied with Omagua, an equally powerful chieftain, he is said to have fought defensive wars against even greater tribes in the interior.

These descriptions and particularly the figures could only have come from the Indians, who are seldom reliable sources and notoriously unable to count. Linguistic difficulties may have helped and the Friar was credulous enough, as his later story of the Amazons shows. His estimates of the numbers of Indians who attacked them are as unlikely as his descriptions of the broad highways leading into the interior and the magnificence of the great Indian houses. The Spanish wanted the area to be thought as advanced as possible, so that its colonization would be authorized, and the more powerful their enemies, the more credit they would gain by surviving their attacks. There was, however, no need to exaggerate Machiparo's hostility and his power was nearly enough to finish the expedition.

They were suffering from hunger and exhaustion when they saw the first of Machiparo's villages, but they were forced immediately into a relentless battle by river and land, which was to last for as long as they remained in his kingdom. A swarm of canoes intercepted them, full of armed warriors shouting and playing their trumpets and drums and threatening to devour them. The Spanish made ready their weapons, a pitiful three arquebuses and four or five crossbows, and found to their dismay that their powder was damp and that only the crossbows could be used; but they were plied so skilfully that the Indians were forced back.

The running fight continued down to the village, the two brigantines locked together and circled by canoes. On the banks of the river by the village more Indians were drawn up, ready to defend

* See also accounts of the expedition of Pedro de Ursua and Lope de Aguirre and that of Pedro Texeira.

their homes, but the Spaniards beached the brigantines and put them to flight. Orellana intended to rest in the village once he had won it, but discouraged by its size and by the constant assaults of the Indians on the water, he ordered a party of a dozen men to seize what food they could find. Both parties were attacked from the shore by great numbers of natives and although they beat off each foray the Indians allowed them no rest but returned again and again. Eighteen of the companions having been wounded, one mortally, Orellana reluctantly ordered a retreat, but their troubles continued on the water.

The Indian canoes harassed them throughout the night, allowing them no rest; Indian reinforcements arrived hourly, while the Spanish rowed and fought on, hungry and exhausted. The condition of their wounded must have been terrible, without medicine, food or sleep and trampled on by their defenders. At one time a small uninhabited island seemed to give them a chance to eat and to rest a little, but the Indians followed them on to it and forced them to re-embark under the threat of a concerted attack from land and river.

As the agonizing pursuit dragged on and the Spaniards weakened, sorcerers appeared in the canoes surrounding them, their bodies grotesquely smeared with paint, blowing ashes into the air and whipping up the frenzy of the attack. At length the Spaniards were trapped in some narrows by an ambush on land and a greatly superior force on the water. The chief of the war party stood up as the Indians closed in for the kill and a lucky shot from an arquebus struck him full in the chest. The Indians were so disheartened by the death of their leader that they allowed the Spaniards to escape to a wider part of the river.

The chase continued for two days and nights until they had left the land of Machiparo. During all this time they had been unable to eat at all, although they had a little food on board.

*

The survival of Orellana's men in battles against great odds was due to their superior arms and sturdier boats. The Indians would fight with bows and war-clubs, neither of them very serious threats to men protected by armour. The Spaniards would reply at long range with their arquebuses and crossbows and at close quarters with their swords, all lethal against naked men. Even so, if the

Spaniards had been in canoes, they would have been utterly destroyed in the first determined attack, as a canoe manned by Indians could always upset one less skilfully handled. But the canoes of the Indians were helpless against solid rowing boats like the brigantines, which could not be sunk, and which, with their higher sides and formidable defenders, were almost impossible to board. Thus the Indians could only rely on their numbers to wear down the invaders' strength.

Once Machiparo's followers had abandoned their pursuit the Spaniards ate what food they had, and found more in a small village which they captured without difficulty. After a few days' welcome rest, they set out again, passing the mouth of the Jurúa river and entering a thickly populated area.

Machiparo's attacks forced Orellana to adopt new tactics in his dealings with the Indians. He now forbade his men to land and if one bank had many villages the brigantines would row down the far side of the river. When they needed food they would raid a small village, but they would never sleep near any Indian village except as a last resort. For a time this policy worked well; they met with varying treatment from the Indians, some giving them food, others attacking them with fleets of war canoes. Often the natives would paddle alongside the Spaniards and try to talk to them, but in languages which even Orellana failed to understand.

On June 3 they reached the mouth of the Rio Negro and Carvajal recorded the phenomenon of the meeting of the waters with awe. It was and it remains a staggering sight. The Rio Negro is over ten miles wide near its mouth; its tributaries splay deep into the north of the continent, achieving through the Casiquiare a navigable link with the Orinoco system. Its tentacles reach out into Guyana, Venezuela, and far into Colombia. In any other continent it would be a great river in its own right, but it is not even the greatest of the Amazon's tributaries.*

At the point where it flows into the main river its inky-black waters, like a limitless tide of Guinness, meet the deep yellow of the Amazon and are turned sharply aside by the stronger stream. From an aeroplane it seems as if a drunkard has drawn a line across its mouth, and even on the water the change from black to yellow is

* It is third to the Madeira and Ucayali. The extraordinary colour of its water is due to decomposed vegetable matter. There are many smaller 'black waters' in the Amazon system.

immediate. For some distance the two waters run side by side
without mingling, until at last the Rio Negro is absorbed without
even darkening the yellow of the Amazon. Nothing gives a more
impressive illustration of the Amazon's size, and this is before it
gathers the waters of the Madeira, the Tapajós, the Xingu, the
Tocantins and many lesser tributaries.

Few of the names given by Orellana's expedition have endured,
indeed the Spaniards often failed to name even the largest rivers.
The Napo they called la Canela, the Jurúa the Trinidad, the Madeira
the Rio Grande, but the Rio Negro was so obviously the right
name, both in Spanish and in Portuguese, that it has lasted until the
present day. Apart from the story of the Amazons, which eventually
gave the main river its name, it is the only lasting memorial to the
men who discovered it.*

*

The expedition continued downriver, still avoiding unnecessary
battles and taking food from the smaller villages. The Indians on
the banks were openly hostile, challenging them to fight and
taunting them for fleeing, but there were no serious attacks until
June 7, the day before Corpus Christi. Then they seized a small
settlement inhabited only by women without any resistance, and
found there a large quantity of fish. Orellana wished to take as much
food as they could carry and continue their journey before the
Indian men returned, but he relented when his followers implored
him to allow them to celebrate the festival on land and in comfort.

At sunset the Indian men returned from their fields, astonished
and furious that the Spaniards should have taken possession of their
homes. At first they stood and shouted at them to leave, then when
this failed they attacked, but in a muddled indecisive way which
was easily repelled. Orellana ordered his men to sleep in their
armour and a more determined attack came at midnight from three
sides of the village. The sentries were wounded and the Indians
were in among the sleepy, gorged Spaniards before any resistance
could be made. Then Orellana came out shouting, 'Shame, shame,
gentlemen, they are nobody; at them!' and the Indians were routed.

Orellana released one captured Indian with his back ripped wide
open by the slash of a dagger, to show those who had escaped the

* There is a village called Orellana on the Ucayali river in Peru which he
never saw.

danger of attacking the Spaniards. His other prisoners he hanged in the morning for the same reason, and every house in Corpus Christi village was burned to the ground.

This is the first occasion on which Orellana behaved with the wanton cruelty typical of the conquistador, and even at his worst he was comparatively restrained (Pizarro would have burned the Indians as well as the houses). It is likely that he was both provoked by his own weakness in giving way to his men's demands and driven to desperation by the Indians' constant hostility. They never again camped in an Indian village.

After further skirmishes they entered what they took to be the realm of the Amazons of which Aparia had warned them. Rounding a bend in the river they saw 'many villages and very large ones, which shone white'. Indians came out to meet them. Orellana talked to them in a peaceful manner, but they jeered and said that others were waiting for them downstream who would bind them and take them to the Amazons. As the Spaniards were again short of food, it seemed sensible to collect some at once, if they were to be faced with a long running fight on the river. But this raid nearly ended in disaster.

The village was defended by a horde of warriors, who resisted with ferocity, and Carvajal was struck 'in one side with an arrow, which went in as far as the hollow region'. On shore the bitter fight continued for an hour. The Spaniards noticed women fighting among the Indian ranks and using their war-clubs to strike down any warrior who fled. Carvajal describes them as 'very white and tall and having hair long and braided and wound about the head, and they are very robust and go about naked, but with their privy parts covered'.

The Indians were slowly driven back, disputing every inch of the ground, but the Spaniards had won a respite rather than a victory for more Indians were pouring in by land, and a fleet of canoes had assembled on the river. They were thankful to be able to regain their boats and get safely back into midstream, empty-handed and so tired that they could not row but sat exhausted and allowed the current to take them downriver.

A second attempt to find food, later in the day, at a village which appeared to be deserted, ended in another fight and the poor Friar, already in agony from the wound in his side, was struck in the eye by an arrow.

It was a bad day for the companions, although it had started harmlessly enough, with an unwounded Carvajal preaching in praise of St. John the Baptist, to whose intercession he now ascribed his survival. The province was named San Juan in honour of the saint and because it was discovered on his day.

Throughout this province they were harried by the Indians and given no chance to find food and little to rest. When they had left San Juan behind them Orellana at last found time to question an Indian trumpeter whom they had captured in the first village, and from him they learned the strange story of the Amazons.

He told them that the women who had fought against them lived in the interior of the country and that many provinces were subject to them. Their villages were built of stone and inhabited only by women. When they wished they would make war on a neighbouring overlord and capture husbands for themselves. If their children were female they would raise them and train them in the arts of war, but if they were male, they would be killed or returned to their fathers.* They had much gold and silver, both as idols in their temples and as plates in their homes. Their appearance was as exotic as their possessions, magnificent blankets draped around them, or sometimes flung over a shoulder, golden crowns on their heads, and hair so long that it reached the ground. Animals, which the Spaniards guessed to be camels, carried them from place to place, and there were other unidentifiable beasts 'as big as horses, and which had hair as long as the spread of the thumb and fore-finger . . . and cloven hoofs and people kept them tied up'.

Apart from Carvajal's account of the Indian women leading their men into battle and Aparia's warning to the companions, this man's tale is the main authority for the legend of the Amazons. For centuries afterwards many people believed it implicitly while others derided Orellana for giving credence to such a fantastic story.

At first sight the legend is founded entirely on the hearsay evidence of one frightened Indian, for it was not unusual, in the Indies, to find women fighting alongside their men. But the same story—of 'the women who live alone' meeting men solely in order to breed and keeping only their female children—is a part of Indian folklore throughout the Amazon and Orinoco basins and in the

* When the Amazons parted from their men they would give them gifts of green jade-like stones. These 'Amazon Stones', once common, are now very precious and scarce.

northern headwaters of the Paraguay. The stories told to Raleigh and Orellana were repeated with few changes to La Condamine two hundred, and Spruce three hundred years afterwards, and Mission Indians, in their confessions, claimed to have visited the Amazons and to have been rewarded by gifts of gold and green stones.

The consistency of the evidence over such extents of distance and time was enough to convince La Condamine, Spruce, Acuña and Southey of the Amazons' existence and even Humboldt preserves a guarded neutrality. Spruce theorizes that they may have been the descendants of a fugitive vestal community from the empire of the Incas.*

If one discounts the marvellous stories of strange animals, exotic clothing, and inexhaustible wealth, there is nothing incredible about the legend. Compared to many widely-believed stories of weird tribes inhabiting the Amazon Valley that of the Amazons themselves is almost pedestrian.

*

After San Juan the Spaniards had a moment of peace, for the natives, although still hostile and, according to the trumpeter, cannibals, lacked the determination of the subjects of the Amazons. At the next village one of the companions was killed by a poisoned arrow, the first they had seen. On Orellana's orders they built railings along the sides of their brigantines to protect themselves, an imaginative and successful defence against these weapons. Afterwards they were shepherded down the river by an armada of pirogues and canoes but without being forced to fight, until at last they saw, with rapture and an ecstatic sense of deliverance, the first signs of the tide. It was mercifully hidden from them that they were still six hundred miles from the sea.

The next day they were assaulted by a different tribe, who fell upon them 'like ravenous dogs'. The canine analogies favoured by Carvajal are surprisingly apt. The running fights on the river were more like bull-baiting than war, the Indians, or the dogs, lacking

* He also advances the attractive theory that the legend of El Dorado may have originated in stories of the wealth of Peru brought across the continent and back again in such a distorted form that the Spaniards failed to recognise them. If he was right, those who perished in the fruitless expeditions to the Amazon were searching for a kingdom which they had already conquered and which they were indeed inhabiting at the time.

the armaments to hurt the bull and relying on their numbers to
wear him down and on their speed to escape injury. On this, as on
most occasions, the bull was victorious. A lucky shot from an
arquebus killed two Indians and many others were so astounded by
this that they fell into the water, where they were easily despatched.
Another of the companions was killed by a poisoned arrow and
Carvajal described his death:

> At the moment that it struck him he felt a great pain, and it was
> immediately evident that he was mortally wounded, and he confessed
> his sins and set his soul aright. It was a thing that inspired great pity
> on us to see him; for the foot in which he had been wounded turned
> very black and the poison gradually made its way up through the leg,
> like a living thing, without its being possible to head it off, although
> they applied many cauteries to it with fire; and when it had mounted
> to his heart, he died, being in great pain until the third day, when he
> gave his soul to God, who had created it.

From this moment they avoided inhabited areas whenever
possible and pressed on towards the sea. The railings round their
boats were probably built near the point at which the Tapajós enters
the Amazon, where the little town of Santarem now stands. Soon
they entered the maze of islands which filled the mouth of the river
and here they were again forced to attack a village to find food.

This, their last fight, came nearer to disaster than any. As they
came in to beach the boats the smaller brigantine struck a submerged log, which stove in a plank, and swamped. They hauled the
damaged boat on land where they were at once ambushed by many
Indians and forced back to the brigantines, only to find that the
tide had betrayed them and that the larger boat was high and dry.

In this desperate situation, cut off from any means of escape,
Orellana again showed his qualities as a leader, dividing his force,
half to hold off the Indians and half to refloat the boats and carry
out rough repairs on the smaller brigantine.

After three hours' work the second party had finished their task,
but the fighting was still raging on the beach and it was evidently
not possible to re-embark until the Indians had been put to flight.
At length they were driven off, discouraged at seeing the boats
afloat again. After their victory the Spaniards were even able to find
a little food.

The next day they stopped in a secluded part of the river to
repair the small brig, a task which took them eighteen days. The

food they had seized at the last village was soon consumed, and they were again on the brink of starvation, eating only maize counted out by the grain, but their luck held; a dead tapir came floating down the stream still warm—nearly a week's food for the whole expedition. They still had to make the boats seaworthy, but their present haven was not suitable for beaching. Sailing through the islands they found a good beach, however, and continued the inspired improvisation which had started with the building of the smaller brigantine far away on the upper reaches of the Coca river.

Rigging and cordage were made out of vines, and sails out of blankets; masts were fashioned out of forest trees, and stones used for anchors. Both boats were thoroughly repaired, decks and upper constructions added, and crude pumps and rudders made.

They spent fourteen days on this work, living off the flotsam of the foreshore, for their food would be needed only too certainly at sea. When they set out they found great difficulty in leaving the river-mouth under sail. The progress they made, tacking with their blankets close-hauled against the Trade Winds, would often be lost when the tide turned and they dragged their inadequate anchors back into the river. The water was sometimes so deep that they could not use their anchors at all, and sometimes so shallow that they grounded and everyone leaped out to push the boats off before they were broken by the waves.

At length the two wretched boats came out of the river's mouth and turned north, with little food, no pilots, no compass or charts and no idea of what course to set even if they had had the means to follow it. They headed up the coast until, on the day of the beheading of St. John (August 29, 1542), the two boats that had survived so many dangers together were separated by night. St. John the Baptist was not the expedition's lucky saint, in spite of his intercession over Carvajal's wound. On his saint's day they had been attacked by the Amazons and on the day of his death they were separated.

Both Carvajal and Orellana were on the *Victoria*, as they had called the larger brigantine. They continued their journey, dejected and alone, until they passed by the north shore of Trinidad which they must have mistaken for the mainland, and following its line were trapped in the Gulf of Paria. It took them seven days without rest at the oars to force their way out against the sea and wind, living only on a plum-like fruit which they called 'hogos'. They named the Gulf 'The Mouth of the Dragon', for as Carvajal wrote, 'we came very close to staying inside there for ever.'

Two days later, having no idea where they were, they reached the rich pearl fisheries of Cubagua and there they found the smaller brigantine which had arrived before them, on the day that they had escaped from the Gulf.

Any relief from deprivation, however mild, gives a disproportionate feeling of luxury. Orellana's men had been suffering from malnutrition, wounds, sickness and exhaustion with very little relief for over eighteen months, and during all this time death had never been far away. Their joy at finding their companions alive and their dangers at an end must have been indescribable.

On his voyage down the Amazon Orellana had displayed magnificent qualities of leadership. He was decisive, inspiring, courageous, cool and far sighted, and apart from a tendency to defer to his men's wishes it is difficult to find fault in him. The building of the second brigantine, the construction of shields against poisoned arrows, the comparatively pacific attitude towards the Indians, all were right. His coolness in battle was exemplary and his self-control, when racked by hunger, was greater than that of any man under his command. He had sufficient ruthlessness to make himself feared and obeyed, but he avoided fighting whenever possible. Above all he was lucky, not only in his narrow escapes from the Indians, which can be credited largely to the Spaniards' skill and courage, but in avoiding disease and starvation. Many later expeditions, far better equipped, were decimated by malaria and yellow fever, but Orellana lost only seven men out of sixty from natural causes, and Carvajal says that they died of starvation.

As a result of Orellana's discoveries the great river was no longer known as 'the Freshwater Sea', or by its other, less imaginative name, 'the Rio Grande'. Now it was spoken of as 'the River of the Amazons' or 'the Rio Orellano'.*

*

The sufferings of Pizarro's men, whom Orellana had left on the Coca river, had been appalling. Having lost Orellana and being

---

* It had also sometimes been called 'the Marañon'. This inconsistency persists to the present day. Different stretches of the same river are known as 'the Amazon', 'the Marañon', and 'the Solimoes'. But 'the Rio Orellana' has gone the same way as 'the Rio Grande' and 'the Freshwater Sea'.

unable to find food where they were, they were reduced to such expedients as bleeding their horses once a week and cooking the blood with herbs in their helmets. These attempts to eke out their supplies soon ended and they turned to lizards, frogs and roots to keep themselves alive.

It was only in these straits that Pizarro gave the order to return to Quito, a journey so terrible that only eighty Spaniards survived the march, many of them broken in health forever. They limped into Quito haggard, ragged and on foot, in June 1542, nearly a year and a half after their splendid departure through the same gates.

Most of Orellana's men returned to Peru after the expedition, where they were inevitably involved in the civil wars that followed the conquest. All of them sided against their old commander, Gonzalo Pizarro, and many took part in the battle of Xaquixaguana which ended the rule of the Pizarro family.

The Friar, Carvajal, also returned to Peru, where he rose high in his order and lived on, his constitution unshaken by all his hardships and sufferings, until 1584 when he was about eighty years of age. His funeral was attended by every person in Lima of any distinction. Apart from their leader, neither he nor any other member of the expedition ever returned to the Amazon. One can understand why.

Orellana's remaining days were to be fewer than Carvajal's and less distinguished. His ambition had come through the ordeal unquenched, and his first action after returning to Spain was to petition the king to make him governor of the area he had explored, now called New Andalusia. Orellana received his authority but no grant of money, and the costs of the new expedition were too high for his thin purse; he borrowed what he could, but when he could raise no more, and his men were already becoming restless, his fleet of four ships was announced to be unfit for its purpose by the royal inspectors. Faced with the alternatives of a life of poverty in Spain and a last desperate gamble, which could only be justified by outstanding success, Orellana took the conquistador's decision and on May 11, 1545, he sailed, unauthorized, over the bar.

From the start the expedition was disastrous. Sickness ravaged his fleet when they stopped at Tenerife to re-equip. He lost ninety-eight men and sailed on with only three ships; another was lost before they reached the mouth of the Amazon. The two remaining ships made their way a hundred leagues up the river where Orellana stopped to build a brigantine. More men were lost from starvation and disease; there were too few survivors to hope to found a colony and they had eaten all their horses and dogs.

Orellana himself was ill, but leaving some men behind, he headed upstream, hoping to reach the land of San Juan and to barter for silver and gold which he could take home to propitiate the king. He failed, in the maze of islands and tributaries, even to find the main arm of the river which would have led him to this country.

Forced at last to turn back, he tried to collect food for the sea-journey home and seventeen men were shot by Indians. For the first time in all his ordeals he must have given up hope.

Ill and dispirited, Orellana died and was buried on the banks of the Amazon, its conqueror and its victim.

Chapter Three

THE EARLY EXPLORERS AND
COLONISTS 1530–1668

NEITHER THE failure of Orellana's and Pizarro's search for El Dorado, nor their terrible sufferings prevented other explorers from following them. The second half of the sixteenth century saw many well-found expeditions plunging down from the safety of the Andes into the unknown world beyond.

These early explorers of the Amazon showed incredible courage and endurance; often hungry, sometimes lost, and always disappointed, they struggled and cut their way across the continent, prepared to live a miserable life almost indefinitely in the hopes of a limitless reward. They did not always take the easy way of following the rivers wherever they led, but would abandon their boats, hack their way through the jungle, and accept their chances of death through thirst or starvation. Dragging their horses behind them, their sweat flowing down inside their armour, they would struggle on—often for several years.

Some of the earliest and most daring of the explorers were, surprisingly, Germans, from a colony at Coro on the coast of Venezuela given to the Velser merchants of Augsburg by the Emperor Charles V. In 1528 they established a settlement there under Ambrosio de Alfinger, who two years later led 200 Spaniards and Germans up the Magdalena in search of richer lands. During his expedition Alfinger showed a callousness and cruelty towards the Indians worthy of the worst of the conquistadores. He had iron bands rivetted around the necks of his bearers and connected with a long chain, so that it was impossible to release any of them, except those at each end, without undoing others. But Alfinger was an

impatient man and when one of his Indians became too exhausted or
too sick to continue, he would order the man's head to be removed,
to avoid the inconvenience of loosing his fellows. After a year spent
in plundering the Indians, Alfinger was killed by them and his
followers returned to the coast in 1532 laden with gold.

In 1536 George of Spires, Alfinger's successor, led another
expedition down through the headwaters of the Uaupés to the
upper reaches of the Caqueta—a distance, as the crow flies, of 800
miles over some of the most difficult country in the world. This
expedition, while unsuccessful commercially, was not disfigured by
such atrocities as those of Alfinger. George of Spires' lieutenant,
who was under orders to join him, struck out instead on his own
and arrived on the plains of Bogotá shortly after its conquest.

Philip von Huten, another German colonist, travelled down to
the headwaters of the Caquetá in 1541; there he wandered for a full
year, hungry and lost, but encouraged by stories of the fabulous
wealth of the Omagua Indians which made him identify their
kingdom with that of El Dorado. Von Huten found the Omaguas,
but was wounded by them and driven back into the country of the
friendly Uaupés Indians—a tribe which is said to have cured him
in a most remarkable way. Seeing that their visitor could find no
relief from the pain of his wound, they dressed an old and useless
slave in his armour, mounted him on von Huten's horse and then
thrust a lance into the same part of his body as that in which the
German had been wounded. The old man was then dissected, the
angle of the lance thrust discovered and von Huten cured.

But this sacrifice was in vain, for when the German returned to
Coro, he found the government of the colony usurped by a soldier
named Carbajal, by whose command he was seized and decapitated
with a blunt machete. Carbajal, in his turn, was deposed and
executed by the Spanish authorities, who, because of the general
chaos, took this opportunity of removing the colony's government
from the Germans.

*

The courage of the German explorers had met with little reward
and it is ironic that, slightly more than a hundred miles from their
settlement at Coro, unimaginable wealth lay hidden under the salty
waters of lake Maracaibo—wealth which, although greater than all
the treasures of Peru, was not in a form that could have been

exploited or even recognized at that time, but which had to wait for centuries before being found by a new breed of pioneers from the Standard Oil Company of New Jersey.

In the meantime there were many Spaniards ready to continue the search for El Dorado. There was Juan Alvarez Maldonado, the most corpulent and fortunate knight in Peru. In 1566 he crossed the Andes and descended its jungle slopes, where he met another Spanish expedition bent on exploring the same area. Instead of combining forces or going their separate ways—and there was an unknown continent in front of them—the two parties fought each other with insane ferocity until only a handful survived, all of whom were easily captured by Indians. Maldonado, preserved by his good luck, escaped three years later and returned to Peru—the only member of either expedition to do so.

There was Martin de Proveda, who led his soldiers in a bold sweep out from the land of Cinnamon, across the Putumayo and Caqueta, and who ended, exhausted and without profit, in Santa Fé de Bogotá, having crossed the paths used by Philip von Huten in his travels from Venezuela. But the most remarkable of the early explorations was that undertaken in 1560 by Pedro de Ursua, Fernando de Guzman and their assassin, the terrible Lope de Aguirre.

Ursua's travels were brought about by an impressive journey— more a migration than an expedition—by a group of Brazilian Indians* seeking refuge from Portuguese oppression. These Indians left their homes on the Atlantic coast of Brazil, ascended the Amazon and, after ten years of wandering, found their way to the Spanish Province of Quito.

Ever since Philip von Huten's defeat at their hands, the Omagua Indians had been identified with the legend of El Dorado and the Brazilians' account of their dealings with this tribe confirmed his stories of their wealth. The Omaguas had eagerly given gold ornaments in exchange for the Brazilians' iron and had asked them to tell the Spaniards that they would be welcome to trade on the same terms.

An expedition, guided by some of the Brazilians and commanded by Ursua, an experienced officer, was sent out to find this accommodating tribe. Ursua established a small village on the Upper Huallaga, built his boats there and sent advance parties downstream to collect food supplies. By this careful preparation he hoped to avoid the disasters suffered by other explorers of the Amazon in

* Probably members of the Tupinamba tribe.

the first stages of their journeys, but from the start his expedition was plagued by mutiny. Sometimes he himself was to blame, as when he brought with him his mistress Dona Inez de Atienza—a decision that could only cause jealousy and resentment. He was warned by friends in Peru to leave her behind and to dismiss a number of known dissidents, who were plotting against him before his voyage had begun, but in both cases he ignored their good advice. Sometimes the men's discontent was due to bad luck; the woods around his village yielded an unsuitable timber for building brigantines, and, unable to load horses on board the brittle craft, Ursua ordered them to be let loose, thus depriving his followers of their most valued possessions.

But the main cause of mutiny was the calibre of his men. In 1559 the last of the early Peruvian rebellions had been stamped out and a period of administration succeeded an era of conquest. Yet there were many men in Peru unsuited to any work save battle and conquest, and some of them were already wanted by the authorities for fighting against the government. Ursua had, in the past, proved himself to be an able captain and a successful Indian-fighter, but on his last journey he never had control over his men. Pizarro, Orellana and von Huten had led adventurers and conquistadores, but Ursua was in command of pirates, needing the iron hand of a Morgan, Blackbeard or Aguirre to keep them in check.

The expeditions which Ursua sent out to collect food disobeyed their orders and devoted their time instead to the massacre of Indians. As a result the main body sailed down the river hungry and festering with revolt. Ursua punished mutineers and deserters by forcing them to row alongside their Indian slaves, while their companions mocked them, some for their own amusement, others to foment trouble against their leader. The mutineers also exploited the men's natural jealousy of Inez de Atienza, claiming that she was the real leader of the expedition and that any of them could be made galley-slaves at the whim of a whore. They described in lascivious detail the deplorable amount of time that their leader spent in dalliance with her, when he could and should have been sharing the honest discomfort of their quarters.

In a short time these petty grievances had grown into a general agreement on revolt. The rebels lacked only a leader but, as members of such a class-conscious society, they demanded of their captain at least some pretensions to noble blood.

Fernando de Guzman, the only man in the expedition with this qualification, was, for a time, well-disposed towards Ursua. But when the latter arrested his mulatto servant for stealing from friendly Indians, his vanity was outraged. Guzman agreed to take command and to maroon Ursua and those loyal to him on the river bank. This plan was too humane for the dark mind of Lope de Aguirre, the real leader of the mutiny and one of those rare characters of unrelieved evil.

Aguirre saw the expedition from the first, not as a search for El Dorado, but as a promising body of men with whom to seize power in Peru. Some slight in the past left this mysterious man with a festering grievance against society, which overrode any ambition or greed, and which was to manifest itself in alternate bouts of savagery and petulance. For the moment he was cunning and withdrawn, and by playing skilfully on Guzman's punctured vanity he had already persuaded him to usurp Ursua's position. This, the crucial decision, transformed Guzman from an honourable officer into a mutineer. It was the first pipe of opium for the addict, the first glass of cider of the temperance ballads. Aguirre was a realist, who recognized the futility of half-measures in rebellion. Having made Guzman a mutineer it was not hard to persuade him to become a murderer as well.

Aguirre waited for a favourable moment. Then, when Ursua was resting alone on his hammock by the mouth of the Putumayo, his killers approached. Ursua asked them what they wanted; they made no reply but came at him with their arms and stabbed him to death before he could reach any weapon. Even after the murder of their leader the deep-rooted conservatism of their natures made the mutineers draw up a long petition to the king, in which they protested their loyalty and listed their wretched grievances against Ursua. But when the document came to Aguirre, he shocked them by signing it: 'Lope de Aguirre, the traitor', to show that, however successful their search for El Dorado might be, they could now expect no mercy from their monarch. In a final rejection of all Spanish authority Guzman was appointed 'Prince of Peru' and every member of the expedition was allocated lands in that country in anticipation of its conquest.

Guzman, in spite of his elevation, was incapable of restraining Aguirre, who, as a result, was free to display his true character for the first time. Every man even suspected of affection towards Ursua was murdered first, followed by those who had in any way offended Aguirre. Inez de Atienza was one of the first to die—her neck cut by the assassin's knife because it was thought inconvenient to carry all her belongings on the boats. Aguirre needed no stronger excuse than this, and throughout his passage of the river, the sword, the knife and the garrotte were seldom idle. Guzman's reign, short and futile, ended in an appalling massacre at a place which even Aguirre's followers called 'The town of the butchery'.

The chronicle of Aguirre's crimes is sickening and monotonous, but a far more interesting subject is the course taken by his boats. The murder of Ursua took place just below the mouth of the Putumayo and Guzman died near the mouth of the Japura. Since Aguirre finished his voyage at the island of Margarita, a few miles away from Orellana's landfall at Cubagua, it would seem natural for him to have followed the same course—down the Amazon and north-west along the coast, then either through the Gulf of Paria or by the safer route north of Trinidad. But several authorities, including Padre Simon, who, in 1623, wrote the best history of Aguirre's voyage,* Acuña, Acosta and Sir Clements Markham, were all convinced that he sailed up the Rio Negro, crossed into the Orinoco system by the Casiquiare and finally entered the ocean not through the mouth of the Amazon, but by that of the Orinoco. The first established passage of the Casiquiare was by Portuguese slave traders in 1743 and for Aguirre to precede them by nearly two hundred years would have been an astonishing achievement.

Aguirre was obsessed with a passion for revenge against the authorities in Peru, strong enough to overcome his lust for gold. But he knew that his followers were not so afflicted, and that they would never return to a hopeless rebellion once he allowed them to become the masters of so rich a country as the Omaguas'. As soon as he had taken over command, the expedition, which had been formed to find the Omaguas, now took every precaution to avoid them. According to Padre Simon, Aguirre turned out of the main channel of the river 'and navigated three days and a night in a westerly direction'. This indicates that he ascended either the Rio Negro itself or an arm of the Japura connecting with it.

One of the great difficulties in following Aguirre's course is that

---

* Simon drew much of his information, without acknowledgement, from a manuscript written by Francisco Vasquez who actually accompanied Aguirre.

he himself had no idea of where he had been. Nor did he leave behind a competent chronicler, the Friar who might have given some clues to their whereabouts having died under Aguirre's own sword. His men called every water on which they sailed the Marañon and gave themselves the name of Marañones. There was for some time afterwards a confusion between the Amazon and the Orinoco, which supports the view that Aguirre sailed down the latter, and the survivors of his voyage maintained that the Amazon's mouth was opposite Trinidad.

Padre Simon's text is unable to settle the question, although all that we require from him is some indication of whether they travelled upstream north-west on a black river interrupted by rapids, or descended a navigable yellow river in an easterly direction. There are some statements which have been seized upon to prove that they travelled by the Casiquiare. Simon describes their resting at a village of an Indian tribe, the Arnaquina, similar in name and in cannibalism to the Arekainas seen by Wallace on the Upper Rio Negro. It has been argued that Aguirre could not have met these Indians elsewhere, but on closer examination this argument rebounds. According to Simon the river near their village had a tidal effect, which the Rio Negro does not have, and the explorers expected to enter the sea soon after—a hope beyond the most sanguine of travellers who has been sailing upstream for some thousand miles. In fact the whole of this passage suggests that they were descending the Amazon at the time.

The Amazon route is supported by Simon's description of the mouth of the river, which resembles that of the Amazon more closely than that of the Orinoco, and as far as negative evidence is concerned, by the absence of any comment on rapids and portages, which are common on the Rio Negro and the Orinoco, but which do not exist on the lower Amazon.

The dates at which Aguirre was in particular places are very precisely stated by Simon. It took him ninety-four days from a point where he mended the brigantines to reach the sea, and another seventeen days at sea before he arrived in Margarita. Both these figures suggest that he never left the Amazon for long. The stop for repairing and replacing their boats was soon after Ursua's murder at the mouth of the Putumayo and ninety-four days would seem far too short for such a difficult passage as that of the Casiquiare. The Amazon again is over twice as far from Margarita as the Orinoco.

Aguirre had a fair wind and a steady sea, but Orellana did the journey from the mouth of the Amazon in eighteen days, seven of which he spent trapped in the Gulf of Paria. In favourable conditions one cannot see Aguirre taking the same time as Orellana in the same type of boat for a journey of under half the distance.

The final argument against the Casiquiare is the overwhelming unlikelihood of Aguirre knowing that it existed. And unless he did know, it is a strain on our credulity that he should be said to have picked by chance the only one of the Amazon's thousand tributaries to connect with another river system, and that he should have chosen the right course in the main divisions of the Rio Negro to reach it. The contemporary confusion over the two rivers can only be answered by the fact that Aguirre himself had no idea at all of where he had been* and it would be remarkable if he could then tell where he had emerged.

At the mouth of the river, which must almost certainly have been the Amazon, Aguirre abandoned the hundred Christian Indians with him to the mercies of the cannibals who lived there. He had laid in so little water for the voyage that his men had to be rationed to one quarter of a gallon a day while toiling at the oars under an equatorial sun. Their leader felt himself to be above such petty restrictions and took copious draughts whenever he felt so inclined, and, terrified of desertion by the second brigantine, he removed their compass and made them follow him day and night.

He landed secretly on the coast of Margarita, at a bay still known as 'The Tyrant's Port', and swiftly seized the island. In a few months of wayward viciousness he destroyed some sixty years of sober government. No one was safe, and denunciation even of his most trusted accomplices led at once to their death. Like a Zulu despot he kept a group of killers around him, ready to destroy anyone at a word or a gesture. He became accomplished at giving an imperceptible nod or wink while apparently forgiving an enemy, that would send his men running after the happy fool to drag him away. Only one man survived his sentence of death, and he, an equally depraved creature named Llamoso, least deserved to do so.

Aguirre had murdered Martin Perez, his own lieutenant, on being

---

* Aguirre wrote in his querulous letter of defiance to the King of Spain, which so shocked Padre Simon's orthodox soul that he could not bring himself to reproduce it in print: 'God knows how we came through that great mass of waters.'

informed that he was plotting against him. Llamoso had also been denounced, but when his killers came for him, he rushed to Perez's body, which was lying, hacked into pieces, on the ground, and, in Simon's words, 'threw himself upon it, shouting "Curse this traitor, who wished to commit so great a crime! I will drink his blood!" and, putting his mouth over the wounds in the head, with more than demoniac rage, he began to suck the blood and brains that issued from the wounds, and swallowed what he sucked, as if he were a famished dog'. Aguirre, mollified by so convincing a demonstration of loyalty, restored him to his positions.

When his own lust for blood was at last satiated and the whole of Margarita grovelled in terror before him, Aguirre crossed to the mainland and captured the small town of Barburata. He advanced inland with a force already depleted by his own barbarities. He planned to march to Peru and capture the country, as he announced in a letter which he now wrote to the King of Spain, in whose pages megalomania warred with self-pity. But soon after leaving the coast he met a royalist force and his miserable army melted away, leaving him and his daughter in his tent. As the Spanish soldiers approached, he stabbed her to death, saying that he could not allow her to live to be mocked as the child of a traitor. His captors, after some argument, decided to kill him at once. One of them lifted his arquebus and fired, striking him obliquely.

'That was not well aimed,' said Aguirre.

The next bullet took him in the chest.

'That has settled the matter,' he said, and died.

Very little is known of Aguirre's life except for its violent climax. He was notable throughout the expedition for a sullen hypersensitivity and an inability ever to forgive a wrong. He had a child's mind and the cunning of a wild animal. Markham repeats an interesting passage from Garcilasso Inca de la Vega, a contemporary historian, which seems almost certain to concern the tyrant and which fully explains the origins of his hatred for Peru.

In 1548 a party of 200 soldiers had left the mines of Potosí, with Indians laden down with their baggage, although it was against the law to use native labour for such a purpose. The authorities allowed all of them to pass, with the exception of a soldier called Aguirre, who was seized and, since he could not pay the fine, sentenced to 200 lashes. In spite of his own pleas for death instead of so debasing a punishment and the entreaties of the townsmen that he should be pardoned, Aguirre was stripped, tied on a horse, taken to the post and flogged.

Aguirre waited until the end of the judge's term of office and then followed him everywhere, waiting for an opportunity to avenge his tarnished honour. In the meantime he would not mount a horse or wear a pair of shoes, for he said that such luxuries were not for flogged men. The chase continued from city to city for over three years, until the judge at last thought himself safe in Cuzco. But Aguirre found him there, broke into his house and stabbed him to death in his own library. He was sheltered by friends and smuggled out of the city disguised as a negro slave.

One can see, in this Aguirre's character, the same implacability and pride as were evident in the tyrant's, and for such a person it is unlikely that the death of one man could erase the shame of a flogging. Garcilasso's passage ends: 'Thus Aguirre escaped, and this was one of the most wonderful things that happened in Peru in those times. The insolent soldiers said that if there were more Aguirres in the world, judges would not be so free and tyrannical.'

*

After the death of Orellana, the Amazon was ignored by colonists. Spanish and German adventurers might traverse the wildest reaches of its headwaters, but the mouth of the river was left to the bones of the followers of Orellana and Diego de Ordaz. Portugal and Spain both had their slender resources fully extended in the development of their existing colonies in the New World. It seemed as if their empires might eventually meet around the mouth of the Amazon, Spain by advancing south-east along the Venezuelan coast, Portugal by expanding to the north along that of Brazil. But, as the two countries were united from 1580 to 1640, there was little competition between them.

At the end of the sixteenth century, this comfortable arrangement was shattered by the appearance first of Dutch and then of English colonies on the Amazon. The events that followed form a violent and almost unknown chapter in colonial history, but they are, unfortunately, poorly documented and the scanty sources in the three countries involved seldom agree. The Portuguese, for instance, were apparently incapable of distinguishing between the English, Irish, French and Dutch, all of whom had colonies on the Amazon at one time or another, while the colonists were more concerned with making profits than with keeping records. We are fortunate in having the scholarship of Mr. James A. Williamson and the Rev. Dr. George Edmundson* to give continuity to this extraordinary story.

Both England and the United Provinces had been attracted to the fabulous riches of the New World since Raleigh's first voyage to the Orinoco in 1595, and even before this date a lucrative, if illegal trade had sprung up between their ships and the Spanish settlers of Venezuela. They brought in cloth, slaves and manufactured goods and took out pearls and tobacco. Their intrusions provoked vigorous retaliation from the Spanish authorities, who forbade the cultivation of tobacco in Caracas and Venezuela and ordered the eviction of every inhabitant of the smuggling town of Cumanagoto. But it soon occurred to the foreigners that it would be more profitable to grow their own crops than to buy them from others. In 1599 the Dutch sent out an expedition, which sailed safely in through the unguarded mouth of the Amazon and established two settlements at the mouth of the Xingu river. Here they built two forts, loyally named Orange and Nassau, and planted sugar cane and tobacco under their walls.

Five years later, in 1604, an English colony was established on the Wiapoco river, now known as the Oiapoque, some 400 miles north of the Amazon. In 1610 Sir Thomas Roe sailed 200 miles up the Amazon in his ships and another hundred in his boats, and as a result of this voyage, an English colony was founded by the mouth of the river some time between 1611 and 1613. The early colonists suffered terribly from disease, but their relationships with the Indians and with each other were excellent and demand for their crops insatiable. Encouraged by their success, the French and Irish also sent out colonists, and more English and Dutch arrived. Anglo-Dutch and even Anglo-Dutch-French colonies were formed, these combinations being possible because of the large numbers from the three nations to be found in the United Provinces at the time.

An extract from the contemporary historian of the settlements, Major John Scott, gives some picture of the lives led by the early colonists:

In the yeare 1616, one Peeter Adrianson, in the Golden Cock of Vlushings, sayled for the Amazones, and having been as high as the entrance of the Strait, they feared they might be in a wrong chanel, returned Back again, and between the River Coropatube and the River

* See Bibliography.

Ginipape on a peninsula by a little river on one side and an Arme of the Amazones on the other side, they built a fort, many of these people were English that then Inhabited in Vlushing and at Ramakins, towns then in the hands of the English. They were one hundred and thirty men and fourteen of them carryed their famelies to plant with them, they had Bread, Pease, Beefe, Porke, Bakon, Otmeal, Vinegar, and twentie Hogsheads of Brandey, a store for one whole yeare, besides their ship provisions they had a fair corispondence with a nation of Indians their Nieghbours, called Supanes. The ship haveing stayed their four months till their ffort was finished, and some Huts built, without as well as within the ffort, the Indians assisted them in planting Tobacco, Annotta, a red dye, a Bastart Scarlet. Things in this condition, the ship leaves them sayling for Zeeland, but returns the yeare ffollowing, with recruites of all things necessary. But Bread and Meat was not at all now wanting, they loaded the ship with Tobacco, Anotta, and Specklewood, the Loding was sould for Sixtie Thousand pounds sterling money.

*

By 1620 the lower reaches of the Amazon supported a number of thriving colonies. There was an Anglo-Irish settlement at Sapanapoco on the Ilha dos Porcos and an Irish fort on the northern bank at Taurege. The English were on the Rio Jari and the Rio Paru, the Ilha Grande de Gurupá and the Tapajós, the Dutch in Gurupá, on the Xingu and on the main river. The French established themselves on the island of Maranhão.

The Portuguese could not be expected to stand by while foreigners colonized an area within their sphere of influence. In 1615 an expedition under Francisco Caldeira expelled the French from Maranhão and sailed on to the estuary of the Pará where they founded the settlement of Nossa Senhora de Belém. Dissensions among the Portuguese, and revolts by their Indian neighbours, prevented them from taking any immediate action against the English and Dutch. But the war when it came was swift and brutal. In spite of the size of the area at stake the strategic issues were childishly simple. The Portuguese had built Belém in the estuary of the Pará, rather than that of the Amazon, and they were now compelled not only to drive their opponents from the forts which they were occupying, but to establish a well-placed fort of their own which would prevent them from returning.

In 1623 the governor of Belém achieved all these objects, by

defeating a combined Anglo-Dutch-French force, destroying the
Xingu forts of Orange and Nassau, and building a fort at Mariocay
on the site of the present village of Gurupá. The Dutch captured
Mariocay in the same year, but in 1625 it was recaptured, the
Portuguese commander, Pedro Texeira, forcing the garrison's survivors to seek refuge in the remaining English settlement. He captured
this too and slaughtered its defenders, before turning his attention
to the short-lived Irish Empire; the Irish, being only seventy in
strength, surrendered and relied on their common religion for good
treatment, but, in spite of this bond, fifty-four of them were mass-
acred and the rest imprisoned. The Portuguese, in ten years, had
made themselves undisputed masters of the lower Amazon.

There were various attempts by both English and Dutch to re-
establish themselves. But, for England, the attractions of the
Amazon had disappeared with the success of the Virginian tobacco
plantations, and the few merchant adventurers who sailed for the
southern hemisphere did so without adequate resources. The United
Provinces were fully occupied with their attempt to conquer Brazil.*

Both England and the United Provinces established more
successful colonies in Guiana, between the Spanish and Portuguese
empires. From their settlements by the mouth of the Essequibo the
Dutch sent expeditions up that river, across the portage to the Rio
Branco, down the Rio Negro and out into the Amazon and Madeira.
They would bring down iron goods and take back slaves. The
Portuguese, to stop this lucrative traffic, built a fort by the mouth
of the Rio Negro, on the site of Manaos, but the Dutch, although
cut off from the Amazon, continued to trade with the Indians of
the Rio Negro until 1720, when a mission was built at the mouth
of the Rio Branco.

The English never returned in force to the Amazon. Lord
Willoughby's well-found colony of Surinam might have expanded
southwards, but it was given to the Dutch in the peace treaty of
1668.† And it was not until the time of the Napoleonic wars that
Britain acquired another colony in South America.

In retrospect, the most surprising aspect of this story of European
attempts at colonization is the ease with which the Portuguese

---

* Brazil was, until independence, a separate country from Pará and Maranhão.
† The short life of Surinam as an English colony was enlivened by the
discovery of the electric eel and the publication of the first novel by any woman
in the English language—Mrs. Behn's *Oroonoko : or, the Royal Slave.*

C

expelled the intruders. Two sharp, merciless campaigns in 1623 and 1625 were enough, and they took place at a time when the Dutch were conquering large parts of Brazil.

The short answer, so far as the English were concerned, is that until 1649 all colonial expeditions were commercial ventures, unsupported by the government. Capital to finance the Amazon plantations was raised from speculators and the whole operation was seen in terms of profit, never of conquest. There was no great corporation behind each plantation, no western equivalent of the East India Company. In peace and in war every settlement was dependent on its own resources and in peacetime this sytem worked well. The colonists were both strong enough to resist attacks by savages and less likely to be attacked than Portuguese forts, because all that they asked of the Indians was freedom to trade and grow their crops. The Anglo-Dutch settlement on the Tapajós was destroyed by Indians, but otherwise the planters seem to have enjoyed a far better relationship with them than did the Portuguese. The Dutch were somewhat better organized; while entirely commercial in their approach, their colonies were backed by a West India Company, but both they and the English were helpless when opposed to a nation ready for war.

The second reason for the weakness of the early colonists was that both nations had more attractive lands to settle. The colonies in Virginia had no natural advantages over those in South America, but they were free from attack by other European powers. Thus the richer and better supported expeditions sailed to North America, where they might have to fight Nature but where man would leave them alone.

One particularly momentous decision was made on these grounds. In 1620 the Pilgrim Fathers had decided to cross the Atlantic, found their own settlement and live in freedom from religious persecution. A strong body among them held that they should go to South America, either to Guiana or to the Amazon; but this suggestion was rejected, presumably for fear of interference from the Spaniards and Portuguese. The Pilgrim Fathers' decision influenced great numbers of Puritans to follow them to New England.

With so many rivals in the New World the few expeditions to the Amazon found it impossible to raise an adequate amount of capital. Opposed as they were to the forces of a determined nation, they were doomed to defeat. But it is fascinating to speculate on what would have happened had the Pilgrim Fathers' decision gone the other way. Would the Amazon Valley now be a thriving industrial state, or would they, like other northern colonists, have succumbed to the torpor of the tropics?

The name of Pedro Texeira, the victor of the war, will be associated with the Amazon for as long as that of Orellana, for if one of these men was the first to descend the river, the other was the first to make the same journey in reverse. In his epic expedition from Belém to Quito and back, Texeira was guided by Spanish Franciscans who had already made the passage downstream and piloted by Matthias Matteson, a survivor of the Anglo-Dutch settlements. His party of 2,000 was far too strong for any Indians to attack, and too well supplied with hunters and fishermen to go hungry. Each day their catch in the river reminded the fathers of the miraculous draft of fishes. Through his strength and skill Texeira avoided all the difficulties that had made Orellana's voyage so miserable, and he reached Quito without having suffered any serious setback.

Two Jesuits, Acuña and Artieda, accompanied him on his return down the river, and we are indebted to them for the first full description of the tribes on its banks. Theirs is a colourful account. They were accurate enough about the Indians they saw, but entirely credulous about those living inland. Thus their narrative contains startling passages about nations of giants and dwarfs and one peculiar race whose feet grew backwards. Perhaps their most valuable contribution was to confirm Carvajal's account of the density of the Indian population of the Amazon. Acuña estimated that there were 150 tribes on the river, living often so close together that the sound of an axe could be heard in a neighbouring village.

It was now nearly a hundred years since Orellana's descent of the Amazon, and, except for those living in the area around its mouth, its inhabitants had suffered little interference. But their century of grace was over, and already Acuña saw Portuguese slaving expeditions as far west as the Tapajós. Soon the whole main river would be unsafe ground for any Indian.

Chapter Four

THE JESUITS 1549-1767

THE SEARCHERS for El Dorado had traversed the Amazon from north to south and from west to east, but their journeys had been without effect. They would leave an Indian village the richer by a few beads or the poorer by a few lives and continue their hopeless quest. The English and Dutch planters had scratched the surface of the land for the few years of peace they were allowed, but the next phase in the river's history was to change the lives of all whom it touched and it had already started long before Aguirre's terrible voyage.

The first Jesuits landed in Brazil in 1549, to find the Portuguese settlers holding an uneasy grasp on the coastal strip. Other religious orders were then content to minister to the colonists and raised no objections when their flock enslaved the neighbouring Indians. But the Jesuits, under their leader Nobrega, had come to South America to convert the heathen.

The Indians they met were Caribs by race, most of whom belonged to the Tupinamba tribe, which was later to guide Ursua and Aguirre down the river. They were a powerful and numerous tribe of warriors, distinguished by their skill as archers and their distressing addiction to cannibalism. This deeply embedded habit proved to be the greatest single barrier to their conversion. The Jesuits would attend their cannibal feasts, wincing with distaste and with holy water secreted in their sleeves, with which they would surreptitiously baptise the victims. They only conquered the cannibalism of the Indian adults by concentrating on their children who, once converted, could be trusted to work on their parents and to report any relapse into their old ways.

54

Religion was made as attractive as possible by laying emphasis on processions and music. Nobrega would take four or five choristers with him on his preaching expeditions and enter each village singing the litany. One of his followers made an equally successful appeal to another side of the Indian character by appearing vigorously flogging himself for their sins, until his body ran with blood.

During epidemics, tribal wars and cannibal feasts, the Jesuits baptised all those in danger. One tribe, which noticed that most of those who received baptism died soon afterwards, drew the conclusion that the baptismal waters must contain a subtle poison. But the Jesuits' devotion triumphed over all misunderstandings and obstacles until, ten years after their arrival in Brazil, they had won thousands of converts. Then their success was threatened from an unexpected quarter.

The Portuguese settlers had every reason for gratitude to the Jesuits, since, through their efforts, formidable enemies had been transformed into formidable protectors. When the wild Indians attacked, the converts would now join the Portuguese in the defence of their settlements, but their standing as allies and Christians did not, in Portuguese eyes, preclude their use as slaves. As the number of converts swelled, the supply of wild Indians for slave labour dwindled. To prevent the converts being enslaved, the Jesuits persuaded them to live together in large settlements, known as Reductions. By 1600, half a century after the Society began its work, all the Indians of the coast had been gathered together into these Reductions, where they lived under the pure but austere superintendence of the Jesuits.

This achievement had been accelerated by the slave hunters, who always fomented tribal warfare to ensure that there should be an adequate supply of captives. War, slavery and the Reductions between them consumed the Indian population of the coast and drove away the survivors to dispute the territory inland with their traditional enemies, the Tapuya. By 1600 both slaver and missionary had to travel deep into the continent to find new bodies and new souls.

On one of these expeditions the Jesuits found themselves anticipated by an Indian, who had converted a tribe and christened all its males 'Jesus' and all its females 'Mary'. His eccentric liturgy included an appeal to 'Mary the wife of God' and the only image displayed was that of a waxen fox. In South America there was always competition between two antagonistic groups. The slaver wished to debase the Indian for his own commercial advantage and the Jesuit to win his soul for the Glory of God. But both needed possession of his body for their different purposes. The history of the Jesuit missions in South Amerca is one of compromises, clashes and war between these irreconcilable forces.

Throughout Brazil the slaving party was always strong enough to prevent the Reductions from developing to their logical conclusion, but in Spanish South America the Society found conditions far more favourable to their work. The Spanish Government went to extraordinary lengths to assist in the conversion of its Indian subjects. From the days of the conquest, enslavement of the Indians was forbidden and, when Pope Paul III pronounced sentence of major excommunication against those depriving Indians of their liberty and goods, that most Catholic Monarch, Philip IV of Spain, decreed that any of his subjects guilty of these foul crimes should be handed over to the Inquisition to be judged. The Indians themselves were treated as minors in their dealings with the law and as such found themselves outside the competence of the Holy Office.

It would be unjust to the Portuguese rulers to deny that they, too, were genuinely concerned about the conditions of the Indians, but the hand of Madrid lay more heavily on its foreign possessions than did that of Lisbon. The colonists in Brazil resented any attempts to interfere with their affairs and were easily provoked into rebellion, while the inhabitants of the Spanish Empire, after the prodigious energy that they had displayed in the conquest, relapsed into a state of torpor and seldom showed the drive, ambition or greed of the Portuguese.

Thus it was in Spanish Paraguay that the Jesuits found perfect conditions for their work. There were hordes of pagan Indians, enough space to accommodate all of them in Reductions isolated from settlers, and a friendly ruler to whom they could appeal in any trouble. The Society was given a carte blanche by Spain; no other order was permitted to convert the Paraguay Indians and no Europeans were allowed to enter their Reductions.

The first Reduction in Paraguay, which was formed in 1608, proved an immediate success and three others were started soon afterwards. But although these settlements grew steadily, the early days of the Paraguay Reductions were far from easy. The main

Indian nation, the Guarani, were close ethnic relations to the Tupi of Brazil and proved equally tractable converts, but the neighbouring Abipones often raided the early Reductions. The Jesuits had to withstand attacks from these unsubdued warriors, one of whom swore that he would not rest until he had drunk the blood of the last convert from the skull of the oldest missionary.

They had to repel raids from the Portuguese of São Paulo on such convenient assemblies of slaves; they had to fight epidemics, brought on by the congregation of their converts in unfamiliar surroundings; they had to retain the interest of savages who came in through curiosity, hope or fear, and who would leave when tired of restraint. And always they had to go out again to convert untamed tribes, which no other European would approach without an army behind him.

Such faith and devotion brought success to the Society at the cost of death to many of its members, but in Paraguay they died for a worthwhile prize. The generosity of the Spanish Crown allowed the Jesuits to create what became almost an independent country in the centre of its Empire. It was an extraordinary state, at once the most absolute and the most benevolent in human history. No subjects have ever been restricted more minutely in the conduct of their daily lives than the Guarani Indians, nor have any rulers been so obsessively concerned with the good of their people as the Jesuits who governed them.

Even the appearance of the Reductions gave an impression of order, permanence and religion. Each settlement had a square in its centre, dominated by the church, which towered far above all other buildings. In the seventeenth and eighteenth centuries church architecture in the wilderness was as advanced as in the cities. The Jesuits built their churches of stone and made some of them so vast that they looked more like cathedrals than mission chapels. Much of their grandeur was due to the Guarani, who had laboured with loving care at the stonework around their doors and windows. Their baroque towers would hold six or more bells, all of which had been cast in the mission's foundry. But their supreme achievement was the great clock of San Juan, on whose face the apostles appeared at the stroke of twelve. The churches' interiors were sumptuously decorated with pictures, sculpture, gilding and images.

The square had crosses at each corner and an image of the Virgin in its centre. The Indians' houses, which lined the remaining sides of the square, were solidly built, roofed when possible with tiles, and consisted inside of a single room. Similar streets behind and parallel to them held the rest of the converts.

Only two Jesuits would reside in a Reduction, one of whom would be an apprentice, training to become Rector of his own Reduction. All other positions of authority were held by Indians, generally by the chiefs of the relevant tribes. The settlements were visited regularly by the Superintendents and Provincial of the Society.

The economic system of the Reductions was one of communistic theocracy. The land was considered to be the property of the community and it was divided between Indian families, so that each had a plot to till. All the produce of an allotment belonged to its occupant, but he was not allowed to sell or exchange the land itself. This system soon foundered on the Guarani's indolence and the Jesuits were forced to cultivate common fields, on which all their converts were required to work when necessary. The produce of these fields financed the church, the hospital and imports of European goods, while that of the Indians' fields remained their own. Under this system the agricultural economy of the Reductions soon outstripped that of the Spanish settlers.

The Indians' lives were spent in work and prayer. After an early mass they would process to the fields with the youths carrying an image of San Isidro the husbandman. Prayers and religious songs governed every aspect of their work and recreation and, in the evening, they would return to another religious service, followed by an early curfew.

Guarani was spoken in all the Paraguay Reductions and Tupi in those of Brazil. The two languages being almost identical, a traveller who knew either of them could make himself understood throughout most of South America. In many cities Tupi-Guarani became a lingua franca even among the settlers, some of whom forgot their mother tongues.

Discipline in the Reductions was severe but just. A Brazilian Indian entered the Loretto Reduction in Paraguay, dressed in the feathers of a pajé or witchdoctor and accompanied by a man and a young woman. He began a speech to the Guarani, in which he showed some smatterings of theology through his claim to be the Lord of Death and Seed and Harvest, who had made his two companions and was himself three in one and yet one God.

But in his case a little learning proved to be a dangerous thing.

The Lord of Death and Seed and Harvest was bound by the orders of the scandalized fathers, taken to the whipping post and given a hundred lashes. After a few cuts he roared out that he was no god, but the sentence was completed and repeated on the two following days. The Jesuits insisted on his receiving triple punishment for blaspheming against the Trinity, and maintained that this would impress the true significance of the number three upon him. The witch doctor, rather surprisingly, justified them by becoming a model convert.

The Jesuits' implacable discipline must have weighed less heavily on those who were already believers, and particularly on the younger Indians who had been raised in the Reductions. The penalty for almost any transgression was the same, whether the offence was idleness, immorality, the use of fermented liquor, or breach of the curfew. The culprit, after putting on a penitential dress, would be taken, first to the church to make a public confession of his sin and then to the square to receive a public beating. Criminal cases, which were very rare in the Reductions, were punished by imprisonment and repeated beatings, followed, if the crime was a serious one, by expulsion from the Reduction.

Far from resenting such treatment, the Indians would often confess to undetected peccadillos and accept the penalty as their deserts. The transition to the rigid discipline of the Reductions was made easier for the Indians by the fact that, long before the Jesuits' appearance, flagellation had played a part in their religious and erotic lives.

But the pattern of everyday life in the Reductions, and indeed the whole concept behind them, was concerned, not with punishing sin, but with preventing it. From the earliest age children of different sexes were segregated in the fields, the church and the schoolroom. In adult life the same segregation was continued and even after death the two sexes were buried in different parts of the graveyard. Any Indian dances, songs or customs thought remotely indecorous were suppressed. On public occasions the women would appear, most unprovocatively dressed in full-length cotton cloaks, which left only the head and the throat visible. And, in case lust should rise above these handicaps, the Jesuits encouraged their converts to marry young, the boys at seventeen and the girls at fifteen.

The spiritual security of the Indians was as jealously guarded. Safely insulated in their Reductions from the contagious vices of

Europe, they were prepared for entrance into the Kingdom of Heaven, rather than into South American Society. Their education was continued up to the point where they could understand the essentials of their religion, but not beyond. From the cradle to the grave the mission Indian could live in a state of placid docility without ever needing to think or to plan for himself. His beliefs were laid down, his requirements provided by the foresight of the Jesuits. All that was asked of him was obedience.

But the Guarani Indians were never confined to lives of pious drudgery. On holidays the men would play football with a rubber ball or practice their archery, and in their spare time they would hunt and fish. Their love of music and gay colours was catered for by splendid processions on saints' days. At the celebration of the harvest the procession would make its way, singing, along a flower-strewn path under floral arches, on which birds of exotic plumage were tethered, so that they could flutter above as the Indians passed them.

All the converts would wear their finest clothes for these cere-monies and the caciques would stand out in magnificent uniforms, which they borrowed from the mission for the day. One Jesuit, who had been a dancing master earlier in his career, taught the Indians no less than seventy dances, all of irreproachable decorum.

*

The Guarani Reductions had been plagued by slave raids from their earliest moments. Those from Spanish slavers were soon stopped through the Jesuits' influence, but there was little that they could do to prevent attacks from Portuguese territory.

In the seventeenth century the city of São Paulo was isolated from the rest of Brazil and inhabited by lawless and irreligious adventurers, with an unusually strong proportion of Indian blood. Unimpressed by any authority, secular or religious, the Paulistas set out after gold and slaves on expeditions into the unexplored heart of the continent. Portuguese, half-castes and their Tupi allies were all included in these *bandeiras*. They lived off the country on journeys which often lasted for many years; they found gold and precious stones in Mato Grosso, in Goias and in Minas Gerais. They reached the Spanish Province of Quito and the Portuguese Colony of Pará and everywhere they seized slaves. Brazil today owes many of her provinces to the Paulistas but, in the seventeenth century, these inland buccaneers were the scourge of Jesuit Reductions.

In 1629 the Paulistas sacked five Reductions in Paraguay with unprecedented brutality. Churches were desecrated and Indians, too old to enslave, were tied together in groups of three or four and thrown into a great fire in the centre of the square.

The overland journey back to São Paulo was as terrible as any slave-run from Africa. Over half the Indians who began their long march into slavery would leave their bodies on the way. No redress was available from the Brazilian authorities and no assistance from the Governor of Paraguay. In 1631, having suffered a series of raids which had lost them 30,000 Indians, the Jesuits decided to move to a less accessible area.

Father O'Neill S.J. compares this exodus to Xenophon's retreat from Persia and to the flight of the Kalmuck Tartars from the Cossacks of the Empress Elizabeth. 12,000 Indians embarked on 700 rafts and set off down the Paranapane. After several days journey they reached the terrible cataracts of the Parana. They sent down empty rafts, in the hope that some might be serviceable at the end of the rapids, but all were dashed to pieces in front of their eyes. The Jesuits then led their converts through the jungle, singing hymns, until they emerged, days later, at the foot of the cataracts, where they built another flotilla. After losing many of their comrades to starvation and disease, the survivors settled in between the Parana and Uruguay rivers in a state of Argentina still known as Missiones. This heroic journey was organized and led by two Jesuits, Father Montoya and Father Maceda.

In the meantime their brothers in Europe had described the devastation wreaked by the Paulistas to the King of Spain, who sent orders to his lieutenants that the missions must be protected, that the converts should be allowed to carry arms, and that no Indians, pagan or Christian, should be enslaved or forced into service. The Pope pronounced a sentence of major excommunication on any person who enslaved an Indian. These edicts did nothing but infuriate the Paulistas, who, when the Bill was proclaimed in Santos, held a sword over the Vicar General's throat in a futile attempt to force him to revoke it. But the commands of his king and the loss of the state of Guayra to the Portuguese after the Jesuits' departure between them galvanized the Governor of Paraguay and, in 1639, an out-numbered band of Paulistas was cut to pieces by his forces. In 1642 a strong party of Paulistas and Tupi were routed in a three-day battle on the Uraguay by 4,000 mission Indians using firearms. From this moment the Reductions became increasingly able to defend themselves. Their firearms were supplemented with home-made cane cannons, their numbers had recovered and, under the Jesuits' command, they fought with the fervour of janissaries.

*

The situation in Pará and Maranhão was very different and far less favourable to the Society, hampered, at every stage, by the sullen and sometimes violent hostility of the white population. Here the Jesuits never had the freedom that they enjoyed in Paraguay and the fact that they established themselves at all on the lower Amazon can be attributed to the zeal and genius of one man, Antonio Vieyra.

As a boy Vieyra ran away from home to join the Jesuits and his subsequent career was as adventurous as he could have hoped had he pursued the more conventional course of running away to sea. After serving as a young man in missions in Angola and Brazil, he returned to Portugal, where he became the king's preacher. In this position the majesty of his language, his fire and his faith won him great influence over his ruler. But, indifferent to power, he at length persuaded the king to allow him to use his gifts where they were most needed, in Pará and Maranhão.

On his arrival in São Luis, Vieyra was shocked by the state of the country. The laws stated that the only Indians who could be enslaved were those taken in 'just' wars and those captured in tribal wars and sold to the Portuguese as an alternative to being eaten by their conquerors. The latter were known as 'captives of the cord'.

These humane laws were cheerfully and universally abused. The settlers of Pará and Maranhão were both too poor to buy negro slaves and too indolent to live on their own resources. Any Indian taken by a slaving raid was regarded as the victim of a 'just' war. Slaving expeditions would travel deep into the interior, raid the weaker Indian tribes and encourage the stronger to fight each other. The captured slaves would be penned up in miserable conditions until there were enough to send in an armed convoy to the markets of Pará. It was rare for more than half to survive the journey, and those who did could look forward to a short and wretched life on the plantations.

Indians who had voluntarily capitulated to the Portuguese were treated worse, for by no conceivable manipulation of the law could they be called the property of any man. They would immediately be pressed into service and brutally over-worked, without having had any opporunity to grow food in their new homes. The Governor of Pará, who held this office for only three years, felt it incumbent on himself to gain every possible advantage from his position. He explained to Vieyra that it was enough for him if fifty Indians survived out of five hundred, so long as the survivors could be put to some profitable use, since the death of such people was of no importance. The clerical authorities also supported the system.

Vieyra was asked to preach to the inhabitants of São Luis. His audience, accustomed to the turgid moralizing of the friars, were overcome by the eloquence of one of the greatest orators of their age. Vieyra began with the question 'What is a human soul worth?' He developed this theme with a nice mixture of passion and logic, blending his fearful threats of hell fire with subtle appeals to their good sense. He then suggested to his shattered congregation a plan which would save their souls without damaging their incomes and which at the same time would be of great benefit to the Indians. Reading it today in translation, Vieyra's sermon remains a masterpiece. But on that stifling afternoon in São Luis it must have sounded like the voice of God.

The sermon's impact was enough to make an audience of hardened slavers agree to Vieyra's plan, which involved transferring illegally-taken slaves to the king's villages, where they would be well treated. In their turn the Indians would be obliged to work for the settlers for six months of the year.

Vieyra met with less success in Belém. He reached the city in time to be told that Indians of the Pocquiz nation wished to settle among the Portuguese. The Governor suggested that Vieyra might take as many of them as he wished, so long as he had no objection to his enslaving the remainder. When Vieyra refused this disgraceful offer, he was forbidden to accompany the expedition to the Pocquiz, although he held a warrant from the king placing the reduction of Indians in his hands. The Governor, instead, sent out a blacksmith, who duly returned with a thousand slaves, most of whom were destined for the gubernatorial tobacco plantations.

Vieyra returned to São Luis on his way home to Portugal. He was depressed and convinced that so long as the civil authorities had any power over the Indians, their conversion was impossible. His humour cannot have been improved by the discovery that the citizens of São Luis had relapsed into their old slaving customs during his absence.

He brushed aside suggestions for another sermon and said that since men would not profit by his words he must preach to the fishes. He walked out to the quayside and, facing the sea, delivered an address of 'the keenest moral and political satire'.

In 1655 Vieyra returned to Belém accompanied by Vidal, a new and trustworthy Governor-General, and armed with warrants against slavery. But even with these powers he found it difficult to free Indians. By Vidal's order a special tribunal was convened to decide the fate of illegally-captured Indians, with the Governor-General, Vieyra and other lay and ecclesiastic leaders as its judges. The proceedings of this court were farcical. Less than half the number of Indians that had been summoned arrived and those who did appear had been warned that they would be flogged to death if they diverged from carefully rehearsed stories.

As an additional precaution the slavers had bribed the interpreter to suppress any unwelcome comments. Among the Indians said to have been captured in 'just' wars were twenty-eight warriors who had voluntarily travelled 700 miles to fight for the Portuguese against the Dutch invaders of Maranhão. At the end of each case Vieyra's superior logic would reduce the slave party to silence, but no argument could alter their votes. The Vicar General, who never participated in these discussions, would register his opinion by bellowing 'Slaves! Slaves!' when the case was over.

If Vieyra could do little to help the Indians who were already enslaved he could ensure that new converts were better treated. In 1655, the same year as the tribunal, two Jesuits returned from the Tocantins with a thousand Indian converts. Other missionaries paddled in their dugouts up different tributaries of the Amazon into country hitherto unknown to any European. Everywhere they went they established a reputation for kindliness and fair dealing, so that the most hostile tribes would receive them peacefully. In a few years they had overcome the hatred engendered by nearly half a century of slave raids.

In 1658 Vieyra had his greatest triumph. The island of Marajó in the mouth of the Amazon was inhabited by the powerful Nheengaiba tribe, who seem to have had an aptitude for guerilla warfare rare among South American Indians. Various attempts had been made to conquer the island, but on each invasion the Nheengaiba would vanish into the labyrinth of creeks, swamps and jungle covering Marajó, and return to torment the intruders with clouds of arrows sent from impenetrable cover. At the outbreak of war their villages would disperse, leaving the invaders nothing to attack, and every moment that the Portuguese remained on Marajó became a nightmare.

Vieyra sent Indian converts and captives from Marajó back to the island to tell the Nheengaiba that there were new laws for their protection and that he was ready to come over and meet them. The messengers left Belém prepared for martyrdom, but returned with the news that the Nheengaiba were ready to receive Vieyra and asked for time only to build him a church and a house. The submission of the tribe was conducted with every ceremony and 40,000 Indians were pacified in this bloodless conquest.

The Aldeas, as the Reductions were called in Pará, were now flourishing throughout the lower Amazon, but they were very different to the Reductions of Paraguay, where the Society had been allowed to take any measures which it thought to be in the Indians' interests. In Pará and Maranhão the Jesuits were forced to form their settlements on the principle of making the Indians serviceable to the Portuguese settlers. In São Luis and Belém the authorities kept registers of Indians containing the names of all those fit to work. These converts would be allotted to various settlers for compulsory terms of service of six months.

During these periods their spiritual education would be neglected and they would be exposed to the poor moral examples of their masters. As a result the Jesuits' influence over their Amazonian converts never approached their domination of the Guarani. In Paraguay the missionaries' lives were exclusively devoted to the good of their flock, but in Pará they had little power to protect their Indians and, at the time when forced labour was due, they were even made to seem the instrument of their oppression.

The history of the Aldeas resembles the motion of a pendulum. The Portuguese population of Pará found intolerable any restriction on the Indians' enslavement, while the Jesuits regarded slavery as the basic evil of the state. When the slavers were in the ascendant the Portuguese Crown would sooner or later become sufficiently outraged to impose its will; when the Jesuits became strong, the populace, helpless without a ready supply of slaves, would revolt. The same strength of the slave party, which made it impossible for the Jesuits to develop their Aldeas as they would have wished, sometimes worked in their favour. The choice for the Amazon Indian between slavery and conversion was more stark and immediate than for the Guarani, the Moxo, the Chiquito or the Omagua. Thus the Jesuits were able to build quickly when left alone and to survive periods of persecution.

Vieyra's conversion of the Nheengaiba was the high watermark of the first stage of the Aldeas. In 1661 the pendulum swung decisively against the Society. An infuriated mob of slave-owners sacked the Jesuit college in Belém and mistreated Vieyra when he attempted to reason with them. All the Jesuits in Pará and Maranhão were expelled in conditions of great brutality. In 1662 the Society was restored by a new governor, but in the following year a royal decree deprived them of all temporal authority in the Aldeas and pronounced that the spiritual management of the Indians should be shared with other orders. The same decree specifically forbade Vieyra from residing in Maranhão or Pará.

This pious genius deserved better treatment. In almost every way his thought was ahead of his time and he was fearless in proclaiming his views. Vieyra ran foul of the Inquisition by advocating tolerance for the Jews of Portugal; perhaps alone among the Jesuits, he recognized that the Indians must be made temporally, as well as spiritually secure. Unlike many of his order he opposed negro slavery and, if his work was mainly concerned with freeing the Indians, it was because he was shrewd enough to recognize the impossible.

Under the new system all the laws for the protection of the Indians were disregarded and the horrors of the slave hunts returned. The Aldeas deteriorated, while the friars, utterly unconcerned with their charges' welfare, complacently watched their number melt away through disease and desertion. But in 1679, after the Bishop of Maranhão had described these conditions to the king, the pendulum swung back in the Jesuits' favour. New laws were enacted abolishing Indian slavery outright, restricting the compulsory labour to periods of two months at a time and restoring their temporal and spiritual superintendence to the Jesuits.

Their triumph was short-lived, for in 1684 they were expelled from Maranhão by a popular uprising; although the Society was restored in 1687 the Aldeas of the Amazon were again divided between different orders and the Jesuit monopoly permanently broken. It had never been easy for the Jesuits to ensure that the laws in favour of the Indians were enforced, and now, with their responsibilities shared by other orders which were often prepared to connive in slavery, their task became impossible. The Jesuit Aldeas continued to flourish, but, in Pará, the battle against slavery had been lost.

*

The Jesuits of Lima and Quito were as active as their brothers in Paraguay and Pará, but the geographical difficulties facing them were more formidable. After seeing the sufferings of Gonzalo Pizarro's strong and well-equipped expedition in its passage of the Andes, one can imagine the dangers to small, unarmed parties of Jesuits. When they had reached their destinations they would be confronted with a forbidding language problem. Baraza had to learn eight languages and several dialects to convert the Indians of Moxos and some Indian languages were impossible to master.

Father Fernandez on the Beni River complained: 'In the five months that I have been here, I have scarcely learnt five conjugations, having worked and sweated day and night. . . . Of the oldest fathers, who have been twenty-five years as missionaries in these Reductions, there is not one who knows the language perfectly, and they say that, at times, the Indians themselves do not understand each other.'

It was difficult to preach Christianity in a tongue which had no equivalents for such abstract words as 'believe' and to expound on the Trinity to the Yameo Indians must have been almost impossible. The word for 'three' in Yameo was 'Poettarrarorincouroac'.

The Jesuits, with their usual energy, overcame all these handicaps and established a chain of missions across the headwaters of the Amazon, some of which were in territory which has still to be thoroughly explored. Father Samuel Fritz, a Bohemian Jesuit, was among the most heroic of these indomitable missionaries.

Fritz is described as 'a tall man, ruddy and spare in appearance, venerable and with a very curly beard'. He began his work, at the Omaguas' request, in 1686 and died in 1723, having spent nearly forty years in the Amazon system. He was personally responsible for the conversion of four Indian tribes, of which the most important were the Omagua and the Yarimagua, but tragically, he lived to see his life's work destroyed.

The Omagua,* although lacking the fabulous wealth attributed to them by Ursua, were an advanced tribe who lived on islands and the banks of the river for several hundred miles downstream from the Napo. They were proud, talkative and lazy, and never happier than when relaxing in their hammocks, with slaves at hand to serve them. They received Fritz with enthusiasm, escorted him down to their country with thirty great canoes and clamoured for baptism. Fritz established Christian settlements in twenty-eight Omagua towns and baptized the tribe when he thought that they had a proper understanding of his message.

A few years later Fritz heard that the Yarimagua, a tribe living above the Rio Negro, wished to be converted. He set off in his dugout canoe, preached to the Yarimagua and converted them. He now found himself with a monstrous parish, consisting of a thousand miles of river, with over fifty Christian villages scattered along its length. He had no assistance from any other priest and a dugout canoe was his only form of transport.

His life was spent in this canoe with brief halts for services at the Indian villages. He could never allow himself to rest, for the Omagua were always uneasy converts, liable to revert to idolatry and a race who, in Fritz's own words, 'while they are being catechized, amuse themselves and talk'. The Yarimagua, on the other hand, showed an embarrassing devotion to Fritz which verged at times on worship. 'We have no father but you,' they would say. 'You are our lover.' They thought him immortal and would attribute any natural disaster to his anger.

A life such as Fritz was leading would have undermined the strongest constitution, and, in the rainy season of 1689, he was struck down in a Yarimagua village by a disease described as being 'dropsy and worms'. He lay helpless in a hut while the waters rose daily; the Indians had departed to find food on higher ground, leaving Fritz to be cared for by one boy. Every night he was tortured by thirst, because he was too weak to move a few yards to

* The name Omagua, which means 'flat head', originates from their peculiar custom of tying up their children's heads tightly in between boards. They did so for aesthetic reasons.

the greatest body of fresh water in the world. Lizards and rats ate his food and ran across his body; the sinister grunting of alligators kept him from sleep. When the waters were at their highest, one of these 'beasts of horrible deformity' climbed into his canoe which had its prow inside the house and had it gone any further nothing could have saved Fritz and his Indian boy from a revolting death.

After three months in these terrible surroundings, Fritz realized that the only chance of saving his life lay in reaching civilization. Four weeks in a canoe brought him to a Mercenarian mission, from which he was taken down to Pará and nursed by fellow Jesuits. The pathological suspicion of the Portuguese kept him a prisoner for eighteen months, but in 1691 he was released and escorted back to his missions. He mapped the river's course on both journeys and, considering the crudity of his instruments, his chart was extraordinarily accurate. He had no means of determining his longitude and he had to rely on a wooden disc, three inches across, to find his latitude. With such rudimentary equipment and unaided by any scientific training, Father Fritz became the first man to draw an accurate map of the river.

But the idyllic stage of Fritz's missions had ended with his illness. In 1687 the transfer of many of the Portuguese Jesuit Aldeas to orders with more accommodating views on slavery had led to a revival of slave raids in Pará which, in its turn, caused a migration of Indians into Spanish territory. The slavers pursued the refugees; the Spaniards were unable to defend their part of the river and from the moment of his return Fritz was constantly plagued by slave raids, which were all too often abetted by Carmelite missionaries.*

By 1711 the perilous position of his Amazon missions forced Fritz to remove many of the survivors of the Omagua and Yarimagua to the safety of the Ucayali. He worked his last years with the Xeberos Indians of the Andean watershed and he died there in 1723 at the age of seventy.

When his body was prepared for burial, it was found to be deeply ulcerated by insect bites and, in an age when mortification of the flesh was taken as a sign of piety, he was considered the holier as a

* The Carmelites, in spite of their shameful record with regard to slavery, can claim to have saved thousands of Indian lives by introducing inoculation to their missions in 1728.

result. Fritz, content to accept any punishment that God might send to him, had never presumed to brush any insect off his body.

*

The Moxo Indians were less tractable converts than Fritz's Omagua and Yarimagua. They lived in a low plain in between the Guaporé and Mamoré rivers, which could only be reached by water, and the isolation of their home gave them a better chance of survival. They were a race of ferocious warriors, small, thickset and enormously powerful,* but addicts to bestial practices, which included cannibalism, infanticide, polygamy and the murder of any woman who had a miscarriage. Even in the early Reductions, they would steal children for clandestine feasts and, when they could steal no more, they would draw lots as to which of them should give up a child of his own.

The Jesuit Cypriano Baraza established his first Reduction among these savages at the turn of the eighteenth century. As soon as it was completed he left it in the hands of others of his order and moved on to convert new tribes. He had formed fifteen Reductions with average populations of 2,000 before his martyrdom at the hands of the Baures Indians. At the time of their conversion the Moxos were probably at a lower level of civilization than the Guarani or the Indians of the Amazon. But if the Aldeas of Pará were monuments to the Jesuits' ability to overcome handicaps, and if the Paraguay Reductions were living examples of their theories, those of the Moxos were perhaps their finest creation.

The Moxo Indians were never subjected to the same stifling discipline as the Guarani but, instead, were allowed to retain a spirit of self-reliance. All the converts had to contribute work to the public lands and herds, but a good labourer could prosper from the produce of his own allotment and some could afford to dress in silks and cloths, bought from merchants in Peru. The churches were decorated with offerings sent by supporters in Lima and by incredibly intricate wooden carvings made by the converts. Maize, manioc, rice, plantains, coffee and cacao were grown in the fields and, in perfect cattle country, the small herd brought in by Baraza multiplied.

* Colonel Church, in his book *The Aborigines of South America*, tells us that his Moxo canoists could keep up a rate of fifty-four strokes per minute for ten hours a day without tiring.

Only the climate worked against the success of the new missions. Cold, damp and unhealthy in the rainy season, it ravaged each Reduction with epidemics. The Jesuits' success in stopping infanticide, cannibalism and war slowed down the depopulation of their settlements, but they needed a steady flow of new converts to maintain their numbers.

Meanwhile, the Portuguese were advancing across the continent. While the Jesuits were establishing the Moxos missions, the Portuguese were colonizing the state of Mato Grosso on the far side of the Rio Guaporé. Even here, in one of the least accessible corners of South America, a confrontation between the two old enemies became inevitable. But when it came the meeting was conducted with such delightful manners on both sides that it stands out in the long and unhappy relationship of the Jesuits and the Portuguese.

Manoel Felix, a Portuguese explorer, in 1742 sailed down the Guaporé with a small band of Portuguese, Paulistas and negro slaves. He eventually came into the country of the Reductions, where, after being greeted by converted Indians with the cry of 'Blessed and praised be the Most Holy Sacrament', he was guided through a labyrinth of waterways to their mission. Here Manoel Felix delved into what must have been a unique cargo for the exploration of an unknown river and emerged, dressed for this historic occasion in a full dress-shirt, red silk stockings, a jacket of crimson damask lined with silk and laced with ribbons, a wig and a gold-laced beaver hat.

As he landed, accompanied by two slaves, the converts received him with awe and, mistaking him for a high dignitary of the Church, knelt down and implored him to bless them. They would not let the wretched explorer go until he had spent a full hour at this unaccustomed exercise and, as a result, could no longer raise his arm. This Reduction, although recently formed, was prosperous, but the missionary, an octogenarian German, had been unable to discipline his flock. He lived in fear of his life and complained to his visitors that the Indians mocked and beat him. Manoel Felix, after being entertained with Paraguayan tea, which he could not swallow, was sent on to an older Reduction.

Here he elected to wear a waistcoat and breeches of embroidered dove-coloured velvet, a silk-lined coat with velvet cuffs, pearl-coloured silk stockings and the same wig, hat and cane as before. He lunched on pigeon, poultry, game, meat and tongue, all seasoned to his disgust with sugar. The Reduction exuded prosperity; there were well-stocked shops, a still and gardens; it was surrounded by cultivations and by great herds of horses, mules and cattle; the church had three aisles, organs, harps and cane trumpets. Manoel Felix presented a piece of the finest brocade for use inside it, only to be mortified when the Jesuits, rather tactlessly, showed him thirty similar pieces presented by Spaniards.

After a breakfast of sponge cake and chocolate the guests were entertained by a military demonstration. A horde of Indian archers surrounded the square and with wild yells discharged their arrows into the sky so that they fell like rain on to the cross in its centre. The archers advanced again, screaming with excitement, until Manoel Felix begged the Jesuits to cancel the remainder of this exercise. They were entertained instead by an old, scarred warrior who could catch oranges in his feet.

That evening the Jesuits, pointedly if inaccurately, remarked that they could bring 40,000 archers into the field. But Manoel Felix, having now recovered his poise, held forth on the effect of cannon on such unseasoned troops.

Manoel Felix was neither a slaver nor a prospector, but a trader, anxious to open up the commercial links between the Moxo missions and their neighbours in Mato Grosso, which would have been of much benefit to both. But his negotiations for the purchase of mission cattle were interrupted by a note from the Provincial ordering him to leave the country. He continued down the Guaporé into the Mamoré, the Madeira and the Amazon. A few years later he returned to find an iron embargo laid on all trade with his nation— a decree which infuriated the mission Indians as much as it did himself.

As a result of Manoel Felix's journey a regular trade grew up between Pará and the Mato Grosso. This route was cheaper than despatching goods over land from Rio de Janeiro and safer than running the gauntlet of the water Indians of the Rio Paraguay. The new trade grew in importance with Mato Grosso, which was now in the throes of a gold and diamond boom, and Portuguese settlements, as well as Spanish Reductions, appeared on the banks of the Guaporé.

*

By the middle of the eighteenth century the missions had reached the apex of their power and prosperity. The different orders between them ringed the continent. On the Amazon the Jesuits of Quito met the Carmelites of Pará, who on the Rio Negro were close to outlying missions of Cartagena. The Moxo Jesuits communicated on one side with their brothers of Quito and on the other with those of Chiquito, whose southern boundary was adjacent to the great Reductions of Paraguay. And from Paraguay the Jesuits sent their willing martyrs out into the Chaco and the wild plains of the south.

It has been seen that the Reductions were started in Brazil and continued in Paraguay as a means of thwarting slave raids. Now, nearly a century and a half after their inception, the means had atrophied into an end. The Guarani still lived in conditions that had been designed to shake their ancestors out of barbarism. Culturally they remained in a state of suspended animation, but materially they prospered.

The plains of Paraguay were covered with vast herds of cattle, estimated at between 700,000 and 1,000,000 in numbers. Over the same plains the Reductions' army would manoeuvre. This was now a self-contained force which bred its own horses, made its own weapons and gunpowder and drove its own cattle in front of it when it went to war. It was drilled by Jesuits who had served as soldiers in their youth. The cavalry carried lances, by which they vaulted into the saddle, guns and bolas, the infantry the same weapons and slings. They had also a few pieces of artillery.

The reductions themselves were surrounded by orchards, gardens and cultivations, in which a great variety of crops were planted— cotton, tobacco, indigo, sugar cane, wheat, rice and maté. Horses, donkeys and mules were bred and the breed of cattle improved. Inside the Reductions one could find every skill. There were Guarani carpenters, joiners, wood-turners, tanners, blacksmiths, goldsmiths, armourers, bell-founders, masons, sculptors, stone-cutters, tile-makers, organ-builders and masters of many other crafts. The Reduction of Santa Maria Mayor built itself a printing press before one existed in Buenos Aires or in all of Brazil.

La Condamine tells us of the contrast between Spanish and Portuguese missions on the Amazon. 'The trade with Pará gives these Indians and their Missionaries an appearance of affluence, which immediately distinguishes the Portuguese Missions from the Spanish Missions of the Upper Amazon.' The Indians of the

Aldeas had brick houses, boxes of iron work, mirrors, knives, scissors combs and linen clothes, all obtained by selling their cacao in Pará. But the Spanish villages were forced by restrictive laws on trade to transport their goods over the Andes to Quito. Crippled by this handicap and harassed by slave raids, they existed in a state of extreme poverty. The Spanish Indians owned none of the luxuries described by La Condamine and they lived in hovels. The Spanish missionaries used dugouts for their travels, but the Portuguese added sides, cabins and masts.

In the year 1750 the Jesuit Reductions in Paraguay contained 144,000 Indians, those on the lower Amazon about 30,000, on the upper Amazon about 25,000, those in Chiquito 23,000 and those in Moxo at least 30,000. And, in addition, there were many smaller missions throughout the continent. Theirs was an astonishing achievement; to civilize, convert and administer most of an unexplored continent with only a handful of men armed with nothing but faith, must be a feat without parallel in human history.

*

But in 1753 the Jesuits' power began to crumble, for in Europe, as in South America, their influence on secular affairs was resented. Pombal, the chief minister of Portugal, had already been in conflict with the Church, the only order of which he feared was the Jesuits. In this year he appointed his brother Mendoza Furtado to be Governor-General of Pará and Maranhão and it is almost certain that Furtado was sent out with instructions to reduce the power of the Jesuits.

The new Governor collected every possible accusation against the Society, including the comical charge that they were plotting to seize power in Pará. In 1756, Pombal enacted new laws depriving all missionaries of their temporal powers; at the same time he instructed his brother to form the most populous Aldeas into townships.

The new laws were far from being mere gestures of spite against the Jesuits, nor did Pombal intend to make any concessions to the slave interests in Pará. The directions for the townships were detailed and thoughtful; they contained much abuse of the Jesuits' administration, while following their methods in most respects, and in one way Pombal's instructions were an improvement. The intention of making the Indians full and equal citizens was clearly stated and it may be that Pombal had it in mind to extend this privilege later to Negroes.

In 1758 an attempt was made on the King of Portugal's life. One of the conspirators, under torture, implicated three Jesuits as his accomplices. Pombal at once grasped this opportunity to expel the Society from the Portuguese Empire. In Pará, where the Portuguese had fought too long for an ignoble cause to win with any grace, the sentence was carried out with senseless brutality. The Jesuits were packed below decks like slaves, inhumanly used on the voyage across the Atlantic and contemptuously ejected in the Papal States.

After the Jesuits' expulsion, the new townships withered away. Pombal's intentions had been admirable, but his methods carried with them the seeds of failure. The new system, while similar in many ways to theirs, had one overriding drawback—that the administration of the Aldeas would no longer be in the hands of devoted men. The directors were extortionate, the new priests ineffective and the laws for the protection of the Indians constantly evaded. Brutal drafting killed many and caused more to desert, and there was no longer a stream of new converts to replace them. The remaining Indians suffered from the removal of any traces of moral discipline. Their houses, once so admired by La Condamine, degenerated into sties, their lives into long orgies of drunkenness. The Jesuits, in defence of the Indians, had survived rebellion, hostile governors, jealous rivals and unsympathetic rulers. It is tragic that they should have fallen to a statesman who, like themselves, was concerned with the Indians' welfare.

The Jesuits survived for a little longer in the Spanish Empire, but by the time of their brothers' expulsion from Pará, their standing both with Spain and with the Guarani, had suffered. In 1750 Spain and Portugal signed a treaty, adjusting the boundaries of their empires, one of the results of which was to place 30,000 Guarani in Portuguese territory. The Jesuits asked for three years to move their Reductions to a new home but they were told that they could not be allowed three months. At this the Indians revolted, imprisoned the Jesuits and, for a time, beat off the combined forces of Portugal and Spain, before being crushed with great slaughter. After this rebellion it seemed to the Guarani that the Jesuits had connived at their enslavement by the Portuguese, and to their enemies in Spain that they had fomented the revolt.

But the Jesuits' expulsion from the Spanish Empire in 1767 seems to have been the result of more nebulous feelings. In 1758 they had been evicted from Portugal, in 1762 from France. The power they had held for so long, and, perhaps, the arrogance with which they had wielded it, had brought them many enemies. And now ministers, merchants, Jansenists, colonists, anti-clericalists and other Catholic orders combined against them.

In Paraguay the Society could easily have resisted. The revolt of the Guarani had only involved seven Reductions; that of the Society could have set all thirty on fire. There was no power in South America capable of subduing an army of nearly 60,000 men and an army which, although poorly trained and lightly armed, knew every creek and track in its country. One has only to look back at the pathetic attempts of the Spaniards to prevent Portuguese slave raids on Fritz's missions, to see how helpless they would have been against the Guarani.*

But the Jesuits obeyed the secular authority and the cruelty with which they were shipped across the Atlantic was a measure of their unpopularity among the colonists.

The Jesuits left the Guarani Missions with a population of 100,000, reduced from its peak of 144,000 by the rebellion and by two terrible outbreaks of smallpox. They were replaced by priests of different mendicant orders, under whom the Reductions were ruined with predictable speed, and by the year 1800 their Guarani population had sunk to 45,000.

In the lands of the Moxos the converts fared better through their isolation and their training in self-reliance. But everywhere the work of the Jesuits was allowed to fall apart; the gardens and plantations were strangled by weeds, the fruit trees destroyed and the painfully assembled looms rotted away. The great herds of cattle, once the pride and wealth of the Guarani, now roamed wild over the plains of Paraguay and dwindled in numbers as swiftly as their owners.

In 1773 the Pope, under pressure from its enemies, dissolved the Society. But in Russia the Jesuits found a new protector in the person of Catherine the Great and many of the veterans of the pampas and the jungle spent their last days on the icy plains of Russia.

* The idea of a Jesuit revolt inspired a play by Hochwalder, *Sur la terre comme au ciel*, which was performed in England under the odd title of *The Strong are Lonely*.

In 1814 the Society was reformed. A bleaker future awaited the Spanish Empire. Judged on its lowest terms, the expulsion of the Jesuits was an outstanding example of failure to learn from history. The withdrawal of the Reductions from Guayra had led to the seizure of the province by the Portuguese. The failure to support Fritz's missions had resulted in the loss of much of the Amazon. After the expulsion of the Jesuits, there was no force left capable of containing the Portuguese, and the Brazilian Empire expanded with little resistance.

*

The last Jesuits left South America in 1767. Now, more than two centuries later, historians still wrangle over the value of their work. It seems presumptuous to make moral judgments on a Society which included such uncanonized saints as Nobrega, Anchieta, Vieyra, Montoya, Fritz and Baraza. And the story of the Jesuits in South America is so intertwined with that of the slave trade that we often seem to be watching a classic confrontation between good and evil. But there is a dispute about the value of their work and it is one that can never be settled for the answer depends on the judge's position. A devout Catholic can only praise the success of their proselytizing, while the anthropologist may deplore their ruthless destruction of the Indians' culture. Looking back, perhaps the two could combine to admire the fathers' courage and faith and to condemn the severity of their discipline. But the central issues will always remain in dispute. The gulf between missionary and anthropologist is as irreconcilable, if not so bitter, as that between missionary and slaver.

Before an Indian could be converted, he had clearly to be detached from the animism in which he had previously believed. In the same way he would be discouraged and then prohibited from indulging in any traditional pursuit which could be said to be remotely in conflict with Christianity. The Indians thus exchanged songs and dances, redolent with the vigour of their race, for the emasculated substitutes of the fathers. Their nomadic way of life was transformed into the dull routine of the Reduction, their naked bodies clad.

The South American Indian is one of the cleanest people in the world. The early Jesuits were astonished to find them taking as many as ten baths every day, and this was at a time when a European would be considered eccentric for taking even one bath a week. But their cleanliness disappeared when they were forced to wear clothing and they suffered skin and pulmonary diseases from the same cause. Nor could it be said that the Jesuits set them a good example in this respect. Joam d'Almeida, an English Jesuit who had adopted a Portuguese name, never removed any flea or other insect from his body and, regardless of the heat and of how much exercise he had taken, would never change his shirt more frequently than once in a week. We have been spared an account of his bathing habits.

One argument of the Jesuits' detractors is that through all these sudden and disadvantageous changes the Indians lost what Gilberto Freyre,* the eminent Brazilian historian, calls their cultural potential. Humboldt, perceiving the same result, explained it in the terms of his age, by attributing the Indians' lack of progress to the stultifying discipline under which they lived.

All these criticisms are very true, but the Jesuits could reply with equal force that they had come to win souls, not to preserve tribal customs, and that of these customs the most difficult to eradicate and therefore the most indispensable were cannibalism and polygamy, neither of which they could be expected to tolerate. They can also dispute their opponents' chosen ground by pointing out that it is a dogma of the anthropologists that, when two alien cultures confront each other, the weaker is inevitably destroyed. A confrontation in South America was unavoidable and it was as well for the Indians that it was conducted by the Jesuits.

A more potent criticism can be levelled at the Jesuits' paternalism. They disputed, with all the fervour at their command, the slave-owners' doctrine that the Indian was an inferior being, whose fate was of no importance. But in their Reductions, they themselves treated him as being incapable of self-conduct. Their harsh discipline, designed originally to tame dangerous tribes, was retained to dominate docile converts. The Indians were deliberately kept at a certain level of development when they could easily have been advanced and, in spite of a shortage of Jesuits, none of the devout Indian converts joined the Society. The isolation of the Indians,

* Dr. Freyre, although critical of many aspects of the Jesuits' administration, praises others. But when his masterly *Casa Grande y Senzala* was published, this did not prevent a Brazilian Jesuit from suggesting that an auto-da-fé should be held with Dr. Freyre in the leading role.

their excessive dependence on the Jesuits and the almost monastic severity of their lives all made them less fit to survive their masters' departure. In this way, the Jesuits' preparation of the Indians for the Kingdom of Heaven unwittingly hastened their destruction on earth.

But if the Jesuits made mistakes, the most important of which were their severity and their failure to allow the Indians to develop, their rule stands out in shining contrast to that of their contemporaries, both lay and religious. It is unnecessary to repeat stories of their individual heroism, but it cannot be emphasized too often that they were the only body which consistently upheld the Indians' interests and opposed slavery. Their spiritual triumph is beyond dispute and the acid test of their success on a temporal plane must be whether their administration was as beneficial as could be hoped for at the time, not whether it was what we would now choose for the Indians. And by this criterion the Jesuits are again successful.

The Jesuits' converts lived far better than their unsubdued cousins or than Indians employed by European settlers. Their numbers increased very little, but this in itself was a considerable achievement, since everywhere else on the continent, where Indians had come into contact with Europeans, their numbers had declined drastically.

The Guarani, in particular, lived under severe discipline, but the rules by which they were governed were benign compared to those enforced upon the European peasant of their time. It is only when one looks at Europe that the full scale of the Jesuits' achievements becomes apparent. They formed agricultural communities out of tribes of backward nomads which soon overtook their equivalents in the most advanced countries of the world. So long as the Jesuits remained in South America their converts continued to prosper. But with their removal the interrupted tragedy of the South American Indian was free to unfold.

PART TWO

THE SEARCH FOR KNOWLEDGE

Chapter Five

LA CONDAMINE AND ISABELLA GODIN DES ODONAIS

T HE SPANISH American Empire stretched from the desolation of Patagonia to California, embracing all the land between except for Brazil and a few small foreign colonies on the eastern seaboard of South America. This, the greatest and the wealthiest empire of its time, was characterized by a deep division in the attitudes of the Creoles and those of their monarchs. Most of the differences were caused by the desire of Spain to preserve her colonies in isolation from contact with any rival power and by her wish to win the Indians' souls for the Church.

The Spanish Crown passed laws for the protection of its Indian subjects that were well in advance of their time and we have seen Aguirre flogged for infringing one of them. The enslavement of Indians was forbidden and the circumstances in which they could be used as forced labour carefully defined. Indians employed by the State were generally well treated and all members of their race were declared to be outside the jurisdiction of the Holy Office.

But these well-meaning laws were evaded or ignored by the Creoles or Spanish settlers and, in many parts of the country, Indians lived a more miserable life than the openly enslaved Negroes. The very institutions which had been set up to protect them were perverted into convenient instruments for their persecution.

In other fields it was the Church or the Crown that were oppressive and the Creoles who were their victims. The Inquisition imposed its rigid censorship on all literary works entering the Indies. The Crown decided what crops and what manufactures its subjects

83

D

might undertake without threatening the prosperity of Spanish industries. Wars had been fought to prevent foreigners from trading with the Indies, but this very trade became increasingly widespread and profitable. Officials and even governors were suborned to make it possible and elaborate charades were arranged, under which foreign ships would seek refuge in a Spanish port on the pretext of having suffered some damage, and would then be free to trade although all their goods were theoretically in bond.

Understanding viceroys would hardly attempt to enforce all the royal edicts restricting local industry. But the existence of such rules and the risks and expense which were necessary to evade them infuriated the Creoles.

Spain was more successful in preventing any information about her colonies from reaching her rivals in Europe. No book or paper could be published on any aspect of colonial life without the permission of a series of obscurantist councils in Madrid, all anxious to suppress anything new. While smugglers might be welcomed by corrupt officials, the austere council of the Indies would refuse serious scientific expeditions permission to land in the New World.

*

But it was now the eighteenth century and in Europe it was the Age of Reason; every branch of science flourished in an atmosphere of scepticism and of boundless curiosity. Barrier after barrier was broken down, mystery after mystery explained. It is appropriate that it should have been a theory of Isaac Newton, the greatest scientist of his time, which led, indirectly, to Spain's misguided policy being set aside to permit the first proper examination of the Continent.

Newton advanced a theory that the Earth bulged at the Equator and flattened at the Poles. A group of French scientists, who thought it to be elongated at the Poles and attenuated in the middle, were irritated by foreign interference in a branch of science which they had always considered their own. The whole scientific world took sides in a dispute that became increasingly acrimonious and undignified until meetings of learned societies would dissolve in uproar. The French Académie des Sciences decided that the only way in which the argument could be settled was for two expeditions to make the appropriate observations, one in the Polar regions and one on the Equator.

At the time, the only suitable part of the Equator was in the Audienca de Quito, in what is now Ecuador. This geographical fact could not by itself be expected to carry any weight with the Spanish Court. But King Philip V of Spain had more substantial reasons for agreeing to any request from the French, the principal one being that he owed his throne to their support in the War of the Spanish Succession. The iron strangle-hold on the Indies, a corner-stone of Spanish Foreign Policy since their discovery, was abandoned almost casually, with the sole qualification that the expedition should be accompanied by two Spanish Officers.*

Charles-Marie de la Condamine, who was the chronicler of the expedition and its most adventurous member, had been a soldier before becoming a scholar; he specialized in mathematics and geodesy, and could also act as a cartographer, astronomer or naturalist. His portrait shows us a good-looking face dominated by a lofty brow, an aquiline nose and large hooded eyes. Accompanying him were nine fellow Frenchmen including a doctor, a botanist, an astronomer, two mathematicians, a naval captain, a draughts-man, a watchmaker and a boy, qualified to join such distinguished company by being the nephew of the Treasurer of the Académie.

It is unnecessary to give a long description of the Academicians' work, which was plagued by frustrations and tragedy. At Quito, to their astonishment, they were fêted as heroes, but after a few days their novelty wore off and the Creoles set out to discover what the Frenchmen really wanted. There was only one South American answer to such questions and that was hidden gold. The meticulous measurement of remote points and all the incomprehensible scientific equipment helped to foster this suspicion, which became a certainty when the Academicians tried to explain what they were doing. Surely no one could be stupid enough to cross half the world and spend miserable months in the icy highlands of the Andes merely in order to look at the stars and measure the earth's shape? Suspicious officials pestered them until work became impossible and La Condamine had to make the eight-month journey to Lima and back simply to procure an order from the Viceroy to allow them to continue without interference.

* The presence of these men, Don Jorge Juan y Santacilla and Don Antonio de Ulloa, proved most useful to the expedition, both being able mathematicians. On their return the two Spaniards wrote an excellent critical analysis of the workings of the Empire.

The expedition had more serious troubles. Couplet, the nephew of the Treasurer, died of fever soon after reaching Quito. Later, just as their work on the triangulations was being completed, they received the devastating news that the Lapland expedition had returned to France, having proved Newton's theory beyond any doubt. La Condamine found it hard to persuade his companions to continue.

They retired to Cuenca to rest, only to suffer the worst disaster of all. Dr. Senièrgues, a member of the expedition, became involved in a local scandal, in which he gallantly supported a girl who had been rejected by one of the town's most prominent citizens, and although he seems to have behaved honourably throughout, all Cuenca took the other side.

Senièrgues met his enemy on a street corner. After words had been exchanged Senièrgues drew his sword and the other man his pistol, in spite of which the Frenchman charged. But, too impetuous he slipped on the cobbles, fell and, before the affair could go any further, the onlookers separated them.

A few days later Senièrgues appeared in a box in the bull-ring with the girl who was the cause of the feud. The whole town of Cuenca was now openly hostile. The master of the ring, another enemy, rode up, reined in in front of them and delivered some offensive remarks to which Senièrgues replied with such vigour that the man galloped away in a panic to the jeers of the crowd. He then retaliated by announcing that, as his life had been threatened, the bull-fight was cancelled. At this the crowd rioted and, led by his enemies, headed for Senièrgues's box. He sprang out, with a sword in one hand and a pistol in the other, his back to the barrier. The mob, several hundred strong, pressed around him but were too cowardly to attack. Senièrgues started to edge along the barrier, darting his rapier at anyone who seemed too close. He had just reached the door when the mob opened fire with showers of stones. Senièrgues could only protect his head by covering it with his arms. Soon some lucky throws disarmed him and he made a wild dive for the door, but the mob engulfed him as he opened it, stabbing, hacking and stamping until he was mortally wounded. La Condamine, other Frenchmen and a few sane Creoles arrived and managed to separate Senièrgues from his murderers, place him on a litter and carry him out of the ring. The frustrated mob now stormed the box occupied by the remaining Frenchmen, forcing them to escape by a ladder.

Bouguer, the astronomer, and La Condamine were chased through the streets by the rabble, pelted with stones and forced to take refuge in a church. Senièrgues made his will that night and died four days later. To complete the expedition's misery, de Jussieu, the botanist, lost all his collection through the carelessness of a servant. The thought of the five years' privation that he had willingly undergone being wholly wasted was too much for him. Poor de Jussieu had a breakdown and never fully recovered his mental powers.

La Condamine was determined to see Senièrgues's murderers punished, but none of his efforts could alter the creaking inequities of colonial justice. At first there was an attempt to claim that Senièrgues had been killed while rescuing a prisoner from the authorities. After this contention had been dismissed, the murderers were at length identified (there were, after all, 4000 witnesses) but, although named by the courts, they were never punished.

The expedition gradually disintegrated. Couplet was dead, Senièrgues murdered, the draughtsman killed in a fall from scaffolding. Two members had gone mad, one had accepted a post at a university and two more had married, one of the latter, Jean Godin des Odonais, to a Peruvian girl of thirteen named Isabella. After seven years in South America La Condamine and Bouguer were no longer on speaking terms and the former was being sued by the Spanish members of the expedition for omitting to put their names on the pyramids which he had erected to commemorate their work.

The earth had been proved to bulge around the Equator and the arc of the meridian had been measured, but the pyramids controversy had made him universally loathed and there was nothing now to keep him in the country.

*

Even after seven years of work La Condamine's scientific curiosity was so strong that he decided to return, not by the easy way in which he had come, but by going down the Amazon to Pará and then taking a boat to the French colony of Cayenne. In this, as in the rest of his journey, La Condamine was a pioneer, the first foreigner to descend the river and one of the first scientists. He left Jean Godin des Odonais and his wife who intended later to follow the same route, promising to tell the missionaries along the river that they would be coming.

The Amazon at that time was safer than it had been in the past, or would be in the future. The hostile Indians who had fought Orellana and Aguirre had long been subdued; the missionaries still ruled the river; canoes, guides and paddlers could be obtained at their stations, spaced out all along its course. There were still unavoidable dangers, fevers, the precipitous descent from the Andes, floods, the negotiation of the great Pongo de Maseriche and raids by untamed tribes, but La Condamine's worries were more concerned with his equipment, his instruments, papers and collections, the fruit of seven years' work.

La Condamine's descent of the river was, therefore, comparatively free of dramatic incidents, but in a sense, he, as the first foreigner and the first competent scientist to make this journey, was as much a pioneer as any of the early explorers of the Amazon. His observations on matters familiar enough to its inhabitants were revelations to Europe and his work prepared the way for the horde of scientists which was to invade the river in the next century.

On the way down to Jaen, where he embarked, La Condamine had to cross the Chuchunga River no less than twenty-one times in the same day. On the last crossing his mules threw themselves in fully loaded and all his equipment was soaked although, fortunately, not ruined. His Indians built him a balsa wood raft and with it and a canoe he set out on the 3,000 mile-journey down to the sea.

La Condamine was enchanted by the Amazon. As his cumbrous raft pushed out from the bank he entered a new world, a secret inside a secret, a green maze of lakes, rivers and channels funnelling into each other to form an unbelievable inland sea thousands of miles from the ocean. He had acquired a copy of Fritz's map of the river from the Jesuits in Quito. This, the first chart of any accuracy ever made of the river, was the result of forty years' work by the priest and far more by his Order. But Father Fritz was no scientist and his instruments were rudimentary compared to La Condamine's. One of the Frenchman's tasks was therefore to take observations, find out exactly where the river was and to correct the Jesuit's map accordingly. The result was a far more accurate map of the river. There were inevitable errors; following Fritz, La Condamine made the Orinoco connect with the Caquetá as well as with the Rio Negro —but most of the mistakes were derived from what he had been forced to copy or to improvise. His own observations were accurate and his map remained authoritative for many years.

La Condamine did not content himself with finding the river's position; he measured its width and depth and those of its tributaries, the angles at which they entered and the force of their streams. He described the fauna of the river, its animals, birds, fishes and reptiles, descriptions that have now been eclipsed by those of later naturalists but which at the time gave the outside world its first glimpse of new and intriguing creatures. He experimented with poisoned arrows and the popular antidotes, salt and sugar, and came to the depressing conclusion that the poison worked but that the antidotes did not. He saw the little green stones, said to have been given by the Amazons to their lovers, and collected botanical specimens.

His most famous discovery, and by far the most important result of the entire expedition, was that of the rubber tree. La Condamine, amazed by the miraculous elasticity and resilience of its latex, brought bottles and syringes from the Omagua country to Paris where they caused a sensation in the scientific world. It is ironic that such a distinguished mathematician should perhaps be remembered best for a casual piece of botanical observation.

La Condamine's raft spun safely over the Pongo de Maseriche, where the Amazon has cut a path through a great gorge to enter the plain below. He passed through the territory held by the Spanish missionaries into that of the Portuguese, noticing as he crossed the border between them the sharp increase in prosperity. Here he transferred himself and his belongings into two forty-foot canoes, lent to him by the Portuguese, and sailed down to the sea. La Condamine had been careful to stop at every mission station to warn them that his friend Jean Godin would be following with his young wife. Confident that Godin would find the passage no harder than he had, La Condamine left for Europe and the adulation of the scientific world, quite unaware of the horrors that were to come.

Jean Godin des Odonais seems to have been remarkable mainly for his talent for postponing any decision and his inability ever to take a good one. One cannot help feeling that Isabella with her iron will would have had little trouble in dominating so ineffectual a husband.

The Godins were both determined to return to France and Jean planned to follow La Condamine's route down the Amazon; but because of Isabella's frequent pregnancies it was difficult to find a safe moment for her to make such a hazardous journey. Instead of ensuring that she was in a fit condition to travel at some specified time, or abandoning the idea and returning in a more conventional way, Jean Godin temporized from 1743 until forced into action at the end of 1748 by the news of the death of his father. His wife being once more pregnant, he arranged to go down the Amazon to Pará, travel on to Cayenne and then return with a ship to fetch her. In a letter to La Condamine he seems to realize what an odd decision he had taken:

'Anyone but you, Monsieur, might be surprised that I had so lightly undertaken one journey of 1,500 leagues with the sole object of organising a second.'

He left Quito and his pregnant wife in March 1749, and arrived in the French colony of Cayenne in April 1750. But thirteen years in Spanish territory had made poor Godin forget how fortunate he had been in being allowed to enter it in the first place and that the Portuguese were equally opposed to foreign visitors. Godin stayed in Cayenne, applying for passports four or five times every year without result or acknowledgement. La Condamine interceded on his behalf with the Portuguese Ambassador; he lobbied every influential man in both countries, but for fifteen years, an almost incredible period of frustration, fear and self-reproach, Jean Godin waited in Cayenne and his wife in Peru. At last in 1765 a Portuguese galiot arrived at Cayenne with instructions to take him up-river to the first Spanish Mission and to wait there for his return with his wife.

At this móment Godin fell seriously ill and was forced to send someone else in his place. (An alternative version of the story is that in desperation Godin had sent a plan to France of how she could conquer the Amazon. This communication never being acknowledged he feared that it had been intercepted by the Portuguese and that the ship was a trap.)

With unerring skill Godin chose the worst possible messenger, an old and trusted friend called Tristan, who disembarked at Loreto and committed what Godin called 'une bévue impardonnable qui a toute l'apparence de la mauvaise volonté'. He did not trouble to travel on to Laguna himself but gave the letters to a Jesuit priest who claimed to be going to Quito. He then returned to the Portuguese missions and began trading, well financed by the money given him by Godin for his wife's journey.

The letters never reached Isabella Godin, but rumours started to seep through the province of Quito that a Portuguese boat was waiting to take her to her husband. Her brother, an Augustine monk, managed to track down the Jesuit, who claimed to have passed the letters on to another priest. The same explanation was offered again and again and, after the third change of hands, it was clear that the documents would never be found.

It would have been insane for Mme Godin to sell all her property and set out towards a boat which might not exist. She therefore sent a trusted negro slave to find out if there was such a boat, and on his second attempt he reached Loreto, talked to Tristan and returned with the welcome news that it was still waiting there to take her to her husband.

All this took time and it was not until October 1769 that Mme Godin left for the Amazon and her husband, three years after the Portuguese boat had arrived and nearly twenty-one years since she had last seen him. Time had not been kind to her. All her children had died, including the youngest, a daughter of nineteen, who had never seen her father. The child bride had been changed by these years and their tragedies into a middle-aged woman, plump and no longer attractive except for her large brown eyes. But her over-riding desire to return to her husband was as strong as ever.

Isabella's father went down the trail, making every possible arrangement for her comfort and safety. He saw that a large, well-stocked canoe was waiting for her at Canelos, sent word that all was ready and set off downstream to arrange a suitable welcome at every mission.

Accompanying Mme Godin were her two brothers, the negro slave Joachim, her nephew, aged nine or ten, three maid-servants and three Frenchmen, who had joined at the last moment and one of whom claimed to be a doctor. They were escorted down to Canelos by thirty-one Indians.

The first part of the journey was, as always, foul. Water and mud, discomfort, heat and cold assaulted them in turn. But they were led by competent guides and until they reached Canelos fear and discomfort were their worst experiences. This should have been the hardest part of the journey. Afterwards they should have been able to sit back in their canoes and allow the current and their Indians to carry them down to a happy reunion. It could even have been quite pleasant. But in Godin's words 'quelles traverses, quelles horreurs devoient précéder cet heureux moment!'

Isabella's father had left Canelos a quiet and prosperous mission. She found it a smouldering ruin, deserted by its inhabitants. The filthy, exhausted travellers looked with disbelief at the goal where their troubles were to have ended. Smallpox, the scourge of the Indians, had laid it waste. The survivors had set fire to the buildings and fled in panic to the forest. There were no boats and a search revealed only two Indians out of the hundreds who had been there a month before.

It must have been a depressed party that made camp in the ruins of Canelos. But things were to get much worse. That night their highland Indians deserted, terrified both of the smallpox and of being forced to sail down the Amazon. It was still possible to return, although it would have been difficult and dangerous without guides, but Isabella Godin would not hear of it. The two Canelos Indians were paid in advance to build a canoe and to take them down to the next mission at Andoas, about twelve days' travel away.

The canoe was built and the travellers cast off. Now they had reached the point of no return; it would be almost impossible for such a small party, including four women and a child, to fight its way back again against the current. For two days, as they were swept on downstream, it seemed that Mme Godin's bold decision was right. The next morning they woke to find that they had again been deserted by their Indians. Still ten days from Andoas, but now almost certainly further considering their depleted forces, they were in real danger. The next day passed without incident, although none of them were skilled canoeists. The day after, they found a sick Indian in a hut by the bank and persuaded him to guide them. But three days later he was drowned while trying to retrieve the French doctor's hat from the water. They were again left alone and this time their luck ran out. The canoe upset and they were forced to swim ashore.

They were now only five or six days' journey from Andoas; soaked and miserable they built a small hut on the bank and discussed what should be done. The French doctor suggested that he, one of his companions and Joachim, the negro, who was probably the only member of the party who had ever been in a canoe before, should sail down to Andoas and send up a canoe and Indians for the rest of the party. Mme Godin wanted one of her brothers to go with them, but both had been so shaken when the canoe had last upset that neither would go near it. There was nothing left for her to do but accept the suggestion. Three men must have a better chance of success without the burden of five passengers, and those remaining on the bank would at least have a good supply of food. On the other hand, if anything happened to the canoe or to their rescuers, they were in the greatest danger, without a boat and without the skill to make one or the strength to sail it. Nor was it encouraging when the doctor was seen carefully separating all his own belongings and loading them on to the canoe.

Once the men had left, there was nothing to do except wait. Day after day nothing happened. The jungle was claustrophobic, hot, steamy, and full of insects. The unearthly voices of strange birds, frogs and monkeys alone broke the monotony. There was nothing even to look at except the same green wall behind them and the same sickeningly familiar stretch of river in front.

For the first two weeks they could not even hope to see the glorious sight of a boat slowly beating its way upstream to rescue them. Then the fortnight finished, the longest two weeks in their lives, and every eye was turned on the bend of the river. As the days passed hope turned into bitterness and despair. After twenty-five days Mme Godin decided that the canoe must have been wrecked and that their survival again depended on their own efforts. But now they were far worse off, weaker than before, with much less food, three men instead of six, and no boat instead of a large canoe. The brothers made a balsa raft, loaded it with their remaining food and belongings and cast off. It was a brave but hopeless gesture. The raft, badly handled, struck a submerged branch and capsized; Mme Godin sank twice before being pulled to the bank by her brothers. All their food and most of their belongings were lost.

But Mme Godin was a woman of sublime courage and her spirits were not broken even by this disaster. Gathering her little group together she told them that since they could no longer hope to be rescued and since they had failed to escape by water they must travel by land, following the banks of the river until they came to the mission. They soon saw that the curves and wide sweeps in the river's course made their path much longer. The wood was thick, but the going on the banks was hardly easier, with steep slopes of slippery mud covered with rushes, lianas and vegetation. They had to clamber over fallen trees to force their way through vines and bushes. They could only walk normally on the short stretches where there was a gap between the bank and the vegetation. It was so frustrating to have to follow the tortuous course of the river that on a particularly broad sweep they decided to cut the corner by heading straight through the jungle.

Once inside this gruesome place they found their progress hindered by new and terrible obstacles. There is no intermediate stage with the jungle and only a few yards inside it a traveller feels enclosed and trapped. The canopy above was like a roof, shutting out the light of the sun. To move at all was difficult. Odd plants and shrubs loomed up under their feet, meeting and interlocking with the tendrils hanging down from the trees above. It was so humid that they seemed to be breathing in steam, not air; pools and creeks diverted them from their course and clumps of vegetation far too thick to penetrate forced them to make detours. Visibility was never more than a few yards and they could seldom move in a straight line, or tell where they were going. The journey across the neck of the river-bend had seemed so short from the outside. Now it was endless.

At last, they knew that they were lost and lay down to sleep, unprotected and unfed on the floor of the jungle. Then for several days they wandered aimlessly, growing steadily weaker and becoming delirious. Their clothes had been torn off their emaciated bodies, their feet were bleeding from thorns and infected with jiggers. Totally exhausted and without any hope they lay down and one by one they died—the Frenchman, perhaps cursing his leader for abandoning him, the three maid-servants, the two aristocratic Creole brothers and the young boy—all succumbed to their agonies except for Isabella Godin.

She lay there alive beside the seven corpses, too miserable and too tired even to fight the insects that swarmed over them. She stayed there for forty-eight hours, a dying woman surrounded by the smell of death. Then she found some inner strength, raised her bruised, half-naked body off the ground, cut the soles off her brother's shoes and attached them to her feet. Leaving the putrefying bodies she stumbled off alone into the jungle.

She wandered there alone for about eight days. On the second she was lucky enough to find water, and later fruit and birds' eggs, barely enough to keep her from starvation. She could scarcely swallow, her gullet having dried and contracted in her sufferings, but somehow she survived eight days. On the ninth, continuing her aimless wanderings, she found herself back on the river-bank. A

noise attracted her attention. There were two Indians pushing a
canoe out from the bank. For a moment, frightened, she thought
of hiding in the woods, but then realized that nothing they could
do to her could be any worse than what she had already suffered.
But the Indians were friendly, they sailed her down to Andoas and
nursed her well on the journey.

She arrived in Andoas, naked, exhausted and above all in need
of rest. The Indians took her immediately to the missionary, who
had been appointed after the Jesuits' expulsion. Mme Godin
showed her gratitude by giving to each of her rescuers one of the
gold chains which she wore round her neck. No sooner had she
done so than the missionary, in front of her eyes, seized the chains
and gave instead to the Indians a few lengths of coarse cotton cloth.
This petty greed at the expense of those who had saved her life was
too much for Mme Godin and, although in no state to travel, she
at once demanded a canoe and paddlers and set off next day for
Laguna.

*

In the meantime, Joachim and the two Frenchmen had reached
Andoas. The doctor and his companion, cynically disregarding their
promises, left at once for the next mission downstream with all their
belongings. The faithful slave was left to collect Indians and canoes
and to organize a rescue party for his mistress, a task which took
longer for him than it would have for a white man. This explains
his delay in reaching the deserted hut where he had left Mme
Godin and her friends. But the Indians had no difficulty in following
the party's trail. At last, in a small clearing in the jungle, they found
a group of decomposed and unidentifiable bodies. Joachim naturally
assumed that his mistress had died there and he returned downstream in the deepest depression to Omaguas, where he handed over
the dead people's possessions to the doctor.

When Joachim returned, weighed down by his tragic news, the
doctor became terrified that he would blame him for Mme Godin's
death and kill him in revenge. He therefore sent the wretched negro
back to Quito, where he was lost to the Godin family for ever; he
waited only to collect the valuables which Joachim had brought
down river.

When Mme Godin arrived, like an accusing ghost, her hair turned
white by her sufferings, the doctor's nerve had returned. With

effusive congratulations on her escape, he presented her with the less valuable objects entrusted to him by Joachim. So it may be that his motive in sending the slave back to Quito was one of greed rather than fear and that certainly was the accusation that Mme Godin now made. Either explanation would seem consistent with his despicable character.

The head of the mission station at Laguna was so horrified at what Mme Godin had endured that he begged her to allow him to send her back safely to Quito, a request which she firmly refused. In fact, the rest of her journey was made without danger or even discomfort, apart from an abscess in one of her thumbs, ripped open by a jungle thorn.

She was re-united with her husband in Cayenne in July 1770, after more than twenty-one years of separation. Godin sued Tristan for the return of some of the money he had advanced to him and won his case. But by that time Tristan was bankrupt. The Godins eventually returned to France, but the rest of their life together must have been haunted by Isabella's terrible experiences on the Amazon.

Of all those involved in this adventure, perhaps the most extra-ordinary in the history of the river, only the doctor, its villain, emerged from it with advantage. After paying tribute to Mme Godin's extraordinary endurance, faith and courage, one must notice the patience of the Portuguese ship which waited nearly five years for her arrival and commiserate with the devoted Joachim, sent back to Quito without even knowing that his mistress was still alive.

Chapter Six

'THE GREATEST MAN IN THE WORLD'

LA CONDAMINE and his fellow Academicians had given the world a glimpse of the forgotten Continent, and Mme Godin's sufferings, which he described in his book, had made the Amazon a household world throughout Europe. But the French expeditions had mainly been confined geographically to the highlands of Quito and scientifically to the determination of the shape of the Earth. La Condamine's voyage down the Amazon, fruitful as it was, could only whet the appetite of the world of science.

Nevertheless, many years passed before much more was learned about South America. La Condamine returned to France in 1745 and Alexander von Humboldt did not arrive in Cartagena until 1799. His must be regarded as the first truly scientific enquiry into South America. For thoroughness, perseverance, curiosity, courage and sheer force of intellect it is unlikely ever to be surpassed.

Humboldt's reputation has been dimmed by the years and it is hard for us to remember that little more than a hundred years ago, when it was at its peak, he was acclaimed as 'the greatest man in the world' and even more ambitiously as 'the greatest man since Aristotle'. Today his name is probably best known through its association with the Humboldt current, which he did not discover, and the Humboldt river, which he never saw.

While he may have been over-rated during his lifetime, he deserves to be remembered on better grounds than these. His erudition was astounding; his massive intellect, his phenomenal memory and his truly Teutonic industry made him the master of all branches of science at the last moment in history when this was possible for a single human being. Even without his scientific achievements his name should still be familiar for his exploits in the fields of anthropology and philology and for his indomitable mountaineering.

Humboldt was born in 1769, the son of a baron in the Prussia of Frederick the Great. For the first twenty-eight years of his life he received a formidable education; then, after the death of his parents, he left Prussia for Paris, the centre of the scientific world.

As a young man he had an inquisitive, almost fox-like face, a suitably massive brow, grey wide-spaced eyes, light brown hair and a large nose and mouth. In his passport he wrote a whimsical multi-lingual description of himself: '*Grosses maul, dicke nase, aber menton bien fait.*' He was five foot eight inches in height, with a slim wiry body capable of great endurance and a constitution that was to survive five years in tropical South America without a serious illness. He was a man who could bear suffering with patience and boredom with resignation. He allowed himself to be provoked into sharp outbursts of bad temper only by the evils of slavery, a system for which he had an absolute loathing. In spite of his intellectual and physical qualifications, Humboldt, at first, had no success in finding interesting work.

Captain Baudin, the leader of a voyage of scientific discovery, accepted his application to join as one of the ship's scientists, but the voyage was cancelled by Napoleon. He next arranged to join Lord Bristol, the Bishop of Derry, on a yachting trip up the Nile. Lord Bristol was a delightful eighteenth-century clerical rake, a scholar and an eccentric, fortified by an annual income of £60,000. The expedition was to be made bearable by the presence of every kind of delicacy, an excellent cellar and His Grace's mistress. Unfortunately, the Bishop got not further than Milan, where, to his intense fury, he was incarcerated on the orders of Napoleon, who had other plans for Egypt. A third frustration came from Napoleon's own expedition, which Humboldt was invited to join as a scientist; but he was prevented from leaving France by the British blockade.

In Paris Humboldt had met Aimée Bonpland, a botanist who was also to have joined the expedition to Egypt. The two disappointed scientists left together for Spain, with the vague intention of taking a neutral boat to the Middle East. But friends of Humboldt's suggested that they should go to the Indies instead. An audience with the King of Spain was followed by a long memorandum from Humboldt, which succeeded in its object. Indeed he was treated with greater generosity than La Condamine. Not only was he given passports and laissez-passers under the Royal seal, but he was unencumbered by the supervision of Spanish officers. Humboldt's good fortune was only equalled by that of science in having him available for this expedition, for which he was uniquely qualified.

Humboldt and Bonpland sailed on June 5, 1799, avoided the British blockade, and arrived safely in Cumaná, on the coast of Venezuela, on July 15. As they anchored off-shore, waiting for the port authorities to come on board, they were able to enjoy a splendid sight. The air was so clear that they could see every detail of the giant cocoa trees and palms which lined the shore. Egrets and flamingoes settled on the white sand in front of them, and, on the hills in the background, pelicans moved among the cacti. 'The splendour of the day, the vivid colouring of the vegetable world, the forms of the plants, the varied plumage of the birds, everything announced the grand aspect of nature in the equinoctial regions.'

When they landed they were amazed by the fertility of the soil. Trees, shrubs and plants grew with extraordinary speed to great sizes. They found a cactus with a circumference of 4' 9" and a silk cotton, only four years old, with a diameter of 2' 6". In this favourable climate, nature had been enlisted to assist in the city's defence. The earthworks of the fortress bristled with cacti and its moat was filled with crocodiles.

A period of intense study and collection which was to last nearly five years lay before the two scientists. After a short time on the coast of Venezuela they would start their expedition up the Orinoco and across the portage to the Amazon system, returning by way of the Casiquiare. After a visit to Cuba they would sail back to South America, landing at Cartagena and travelling up the Magdalena to Bogotá. They would then make their way overland from Bogotá to Quito, and from Quito to Lima, visiting the Amazon at Jaen where La Condamine had embarked. From Lima they were to sail up to Guayaquil and then to Panama and Mexico, returning to Europe by way of the United States.

Throughout this long and hazardous journey both men showed the superb contempt for danger that can be expected only from a scientist with his mind on higher things. The city of Cumaná had been razed to the ground with dreadful loss of life only twenty-two months before their arrival. No sooner had they settled there than the tremors started again and its population fled in terror, but Humboldt's reaction was different: 'I immediately tried the atmospherical electricity on the electrometer of Volta.' Curiosity is perhaps the greatest enemy of fear. Earthquakes lose their terror if one is sufficiently interested in their mechanics; jaguars are stripped of their menace to those concerned only with their pigmentation,

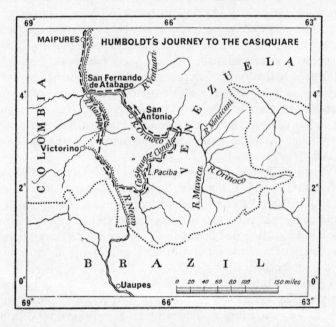

and the most resolute band of savages will flee in horror before the intrusions of an anthropologist.

When they began their journey to the Orinoco Humboldt and Bonpland were to need all their fortitude and scientific enthusiasm. Their main object was to establish the existence of a natural water-way or bifurcation between the Amazon and Orinoco systems. The existence of this link was well known to many missionaries and Indians on both sides of the border and parts of it had been visited by the Spanish expedition of Iturriaga and Solano in 1756. La Condamine had placed it on his map on the strength of conversations with Indians who claimed to have been there. It is typical of the discretion of both the Spanish and the Portuguese that in 1800 its existence should still have been a matter of controversy.

Humboldt's greatest contribution to science was not to discover the unknown, but to rediscover what was known only by a few, to subject his findings to a more thorough scientific analysis than they had received before and to sift the mass of facts, theories and non-sense through the sieve of his remorseless logic. His great difficulty was that the same missionaries, who had been aware of the properties of rubber and curare long before their rediscovery by La Condamine, believed as implicitly in such myths as the existence of a tribe known as the Rayas with mouths in their navels.

All the way up-river the two explorers were given every assistance by missionaries, one of whom, Bernado Zea, accompanied them into Brazil. But danger was unavoidable; the river itself was rough, swift and infested with crocodiles, alligators and piranha. Jaguars howled around their camp at night and poisonous snakes curled up in their hammocks. Once their boat was almost upset by a squall in a place where they could never have survived on shore, even if they had been spared by the crocodiles in the river. The gunwales were under water and their Indians had deserted; Bonpland offered to carry Humboldt, who was a poor swimmer, on his back to the shore, but at this moment a lucky gust of wind restored their balance and the crocodiles had to be satisfied with a copy of Schreber's *Genera Plantarum* which had fallen overboard during the confusion.

*

Humboldt's assessment of the Mission System is cautious and neutral, and more remarkably his moral judgments on it are entirely acceptable today. He acknowledged the selfless devotion of some individual missionaries and deplored the severity of others. Some of his hosts would deprive themselves entirely of bread and wine so that he and Bonpland could have enough, but at another mission he was woken at dawn by the screams of an Indian being mercilessly flogged with a manatee hide whip because he had refused to accompany them up-river.

He gave the missions credit for preventing tribal wars, for giving the Indians security and for allowing their numbers to increase, while criticizing them for their rigidity and for the stultifying effect of their discipline. His comments became more severe when he met missionaries conforming to the opinions of a Jesuit of the Orinoco, who had declared, 'The voice of the Gospel is heard only where the Indians have also heard the voice of arms. Mildness is a very slow measure. By chastising the natives we facilitate their conversion.' Underlying all his criticisms was the vital question—by what right are these Indians coerced?

Humboldt and Bonpland collected and dissected specimens and studied every natural phenomenon they encountered. They drank the juice of the cow tree, a distant relation of the rubber tree, without ill effects, although they noticed some coagulation; a negro, less fortunate, vomited up rubber balls for several hours. They were aware of the theory that curare could only kill if taken extravenously and to test it both men swallowed small amounts of the poison. Humboldt writes: 'Its taste is of an agreeable bitter. The Indians consider the curare, taken internally, as an excellent stomachic.' On one occasion, as he was about to pull his stockings on in the morning, he happily remembered that he had spilled curare into them and that his feet were well punctured by the attentions of jiggers. But even Humboldt and Bonpland decided that their gastronomic experiments had gone far enough when they found Indians eating earth without harming themselves. An analysis proved that they were carefully choosing soil with a high content of clay, but until there are travellers even less careful of their safety, its flavour will remain a mystery.

They rediscovered the piranha, known to them under its Spanish name of '*caribe*'. Humboldt wrote of it with a restraint which should bring blushes to the cheeks of many authors who have since described the powers of this fish in exaggerated and horrific terms: 'It attacks bathers and swimmers, from whom it often carries away considerable portions of flesh. When a person is only slightly wounded, it is difficult for him to get out of the water without receiving a severer wound. The Indians dread extremely these caribes, and several of them showed us the scars of deep wounds in the calf of the leg, and in the thigh, made by these little animals.'

They saw many alligators and crocodiles, one of which, shot by Bonpland, measured 22′ 3″, and others that escaped they calculated to be even longer. At one mission they arrived to see a crowd along the bank, who had just been the impotent witnesses of an Indian being drowned by one of these creatures in spite of his desperate efforts to gouge out its eyes. Humboldt dissected alligators and made the first analysis of their respiratory system.

But perhaps their most extraordinary experiment was with electric eels, though it was with the greatest difficulty that they persuaded their Indians to help them. Their method was to 'fish with horses' (*embarbascar con cavallos*). The Indians, armed with harpoons, surrounded the pool, then drove thirty horses and mules into it. 120 hooves broke through the mud disturbing the eels in their resting place. Soon the horses' aimless movements were changed into a sudden and horrible activity. Horses leapt out of the water, screaming with agony as the eels laid themselves underneath their bellies and discharged their electricity. They stormed up the banks, only to be forced back into the seething pool by the Indians' harpoons. Within less than five minutes two horses had drowned before the others at last succeeded in passing the Indians. The eels, exhausted, were easily taken by harpoons attached to lengths of string and were laid out on the bank for the scientists' inspection.

'I do not remember,' wrote Humboldt, 'ever having received a more dreadful shock from the discharge of a large Leyden jar, than that which I experienced by imprudently placing both my feet on a gymnotus (eel) just taken out of the water. I was affected the rest of the day with a violent pain in the knees, and in almost every joint.'

Undeterred by this accident, he 'often tried, both insulated and uninsulated, to touch the fish, without feeling the least shock. When M. Bonpland held it by the head, or by the middle of the body, while I held it by the tail, and, standing on the moist ground, did not take each other's hand, one of us received shocks while the other did not. . . . If two persons touch the belly of the fish with their fingers, at an inch distance, and press it simultaneously, sometimes one, sometimes the other will receive the shock'.

By constant and varied provocation they established most of the characteristics of this deplorable creature, using insulators, joining hands while touching its head and tail and prodding it with every sort of implement. The antics of these distinguished scientists no doubt reduced their Indians to a state of hysterical mirth. The sight of two learned men each holding one end of the gymnotus, one of them dancing in his convulsions and the other calmly taking notes, must indeed have been comical, but when we remember that a fully grown eel can discharge as much as 600 volts their perseverance becomes heroic.

As they reached the headwaters of the Orinoco and prepared to make the portage to the Amazon system, conditions became insufferable. Humboldt writes: 'When in such ardent climates, where we are constantly tormented by thirst, we are reduced to drink the water of a river at the temperature of 27° or 28° (equal to 81°–82° F), it were to be wished at least, that water so hot, and so loaded with sand, should be free from smell.' But they would have borne this affliction happily, have drunk water far hotter and utterly foul if they could have freed themselves from another curse.

The area where the headwaters of the Orinoco and Rio Negro stretch out their fingers towards each other is possibly the worst place for mosquitoes in the world. The Indians, although less sensitive to their bites than Europeans, suffered terribly. Some tribes would bury their bodies in the sand by night and cover their faces with a cloth. Others lived in what Humboldt called 'ovens', small windowless chambers, cleared of mosquitoes by a wet brush fire and battened down while the atmosphere was still too thick for the insects to enter.

Poor Bonpland, coughing like a consumptive, was forced to sort his specimens in these unappetizing quarters. It was impossible to work outside: 'We could neither speak nor uncover the face, without the mouth and nose being filled with insects.' The missionaries on this part of the river spoke of being 'condemned to the mosquettoes' for their sins; their limbs pitted as if by the most virulent smallpox, they bore a lifetime of suffering with extraordinary courage.

The portage took eleven days for their large canoe and during this time Humboldt composed a memorandum to the King of Spain setting forth the advantages of a canal to link the two systems. At length they sailed down a rivulet into the dark waters of the Rio Negro.

*

The Spanish at that time controlled a few missions on the upper reaches of the river, the rest of which was in Portuguese hands. Humboldt and Bonpland, on their hosts' advice, never went as far as the first Portuguese fort at Barcellos and it was as well for them that they did not. The Brazilian authorities, suspicious of anything that they could not understand, had given orders for their arrest and shipment back to Lisbon; the order was countermanded from Portugal as soon as it had been reported there, but this would have been too late for Humboldt and Bonpland who would have been met at Lisbon with sincere but futile apologies.

On their return journey they easily found the entry to the Casiquiare, and indeed slept their first night by a mission which was actually on this controversial stream. The Casiquiare is a geographical freak and at first sight a contradiction of the most elementary laws of gravity. Looking at a map of the watershed shared by the Orinoco and the Rio Negro one is immediately struck by the way in which these two great rivers splay out into many tendrils, like the roots of trees, but sucking in their moisture from the same soil. Often tantalizingly close, one knows that they are separated by the laws of nature because a river cannot run in two directions. Then our eye is offended by a single strand of blue connecting the two systems. On many maps it is called the 'Canal Casiquiare' on others the 'Rio Casiquiare'.

This stream, whose very existence was ridiculed by a scholar of one clerical order well after its banks had been settled by members of another, does exist and it is no turgid natural canal offering a navigable path through the swamps of the watershed. It is on the contrary a swift stream, with a current measured by Humboldt at speeds as high as 11′ 8″ per second or 8 m.p.h., and even here in the headwaters of the system it was, he estimated, two to three times as wide as the Seine near the Jardin des Plantes. Technically the Casiquiare presents no difficulty, being in fact simply an arm of the Orinoco which flows south instead of north and joins the Rio Negro instead of returning to its own parent.

On its banks the travellers, to their disgust, found the mosquitoes waiting for them in as great numbers as ever. The Rio Negro, like most black water rivers, is comparatively free from these pests. But crocodiles and alligators were there too and one night Humboldt's dog, a big brute of a mastiff, was taken by a jaguar.

The Casiquiare successfully charted, the two travellers made their way slowly down the Orinoco. On their return they all suffered badly from fevers, Bonpland being on the point of death for many days. Humboldt, with his iron constitution, was less severely affected and was able to spend much of his time nursing his friend. During his illness Bonpland exhibited the same courage as he had shown on the Orinoco and his cure can be attributed in part to the herbal remedies which he himself prescribed.

On their recovery the two scientists found themselves in possession of 12,000 specimens of plants, including duplicates, many of which were new to science, and this was in spite of heavy losses because of the rain. Their experiences increased the world's knowledge of many species of animals, of Indians and of the social and physical structure of the region, but perhaps their greatest achievement was made through Humboldt's sextant. The course of the Orinoco, the Casiquiare and the Upper Rio Negro were now known more accurately than ever before. He was to continue this process throughout his South American travels, taking in all 700 observations, which together formed a framework on which to base new maps of the Continent.

*

Humboldt and Bonpland intended this to be their last expedition in South America. They sailed off to Cuba hoping to meet Captain Baudin there and then to accompany him around the world. But he, at the last moment, had decided to sail round the Cape of Good Hope instead of Cape Horn and they returned to Cartagena disappointed.

Instead of being wafted out to the South Sea Islands and the Philippines on a naval ship, Humboldt and Bonpland found themselves in an unstable canoe battling once more up a river—in this case the Magdalena—the main highway to Santa Fé de Bogotá, where they made the acquaintance of Dr. Mutis, the celebrated botanist. From Bogotá they took the high mountain trail to Quito, a dangerous road so narrow and precipitous that even mules were unable to negotiate parts of it. The bare slopes of the Andes were swept by wind and rain; the air was icy; they lacked shelter at night and food by day. When they met other travellers they had either to retreat or to clamber up the side of the precipice hanging on to roots and rocks until they had passed by.

Their boots were cut to pieces by what Humboldt describes as 'reeds of bamboo'. At one point when his feet were bleeding and his last boots had been thrown away he was offered a ride on an Indian's back until they recovered. The Indians of the Andes were employed as 'caballitos', or little horses, to carry their enervated masters uphill. Humboldt writes: 'Every morning they allow themselves to be saddled, and leaning on a short stick they carry their masters on their backs. Some of them are recommended to travellers as being sure-footed and possessing an easy and even pace; it really makes one's blood boil to hear the qualities of a human being described in the same terms as would be employed in speaking of a horse or mule.' He refused this degrading offer and walked doggedly on to the next village, bare-footed and bleeding but un-contaminated. The brutal journey to Quito lasted for over four months.

Quito itself was sadly changed since the days when the French Academicians had stayed there. In 1797, four years before Humboldt's arrival, the whole province had been convulsed by an appalling earthquake. The ground opened everywhere, spewing out sulphur. It was almost as if the whole country had been sucked into the mouth of an erupting volcano. So terrible were its effects that 40,000 people were killed and the climate of the province utterly changed. Bouguer had noted the mean temperature to be around 67°F, but after the disaster it varied between 41° and 54°.

But the inhabitants of the city had fully recovered from this catastrophe by the time of Humboldt's arrival and gave the travellers a most enthusiastic welcome. The Marquis of Selvalegre lent them a house in which to recuperate after their journey and they found the city living in 'an atmosphere of luxury and voluptuousness' brought about, Humboldt thought, by the knowledge that any day another tremor might engulf them all.

On the plateau of Quito, the two scientists continued their collections and observations and spent much time examining the neighbouring volcanoes, climbing the peaks of Pichincha, Cotopaxi, Antisana and Ilinica and gradually acclimatizing themselves to extreme altitudes. Eventually they felt prepared for their greatest challenge—the ascent of Chimbarozo, then thought to be the highest mountain in the world. In fact Chimbarozo is only 20,561 feet in height and in South America alone there are nineteen mountains of over 21,000 feet. Nevertheless, a climb still considered formidable by mountaineers was almost foolhardy when undertaken with little organization or equipment.

At 15,600 feet the path became steep and narrow and their Indians predictably deserted them at the very moment when their help would first have been useful. Humboldt, Bonpland, Carlos Montufar the younger son of the Marquis de Selvalegre, and a half-caste Indian were left alone. The mist came down and they fought their way up almost blindly towards the hidden summit. The ridge they were following narrowed down until it was often no wider than eight or ten inches. On one side there was a sheet of ice at an angle of about 30°, smooth and shining like glass, on the other a sheer drop of 1,000 feet. They favoured the side of the path next to the precipice, hoping to be able to clutch a projecting rock if they fell. In places the rocks were so sharp that they cut their hands on them and as they climbed higher they all showed the symptoms of 'soroche' or mountain sickness—bleeding from the gums and nose and violent nausea.

At last they reached a ravine 400 feet deep and sixty feet wide; on the far side of this impassable obstruction they could see the ridge continuing towards the summit, but they could go no further. Humboldt set up his barometer and took a reading which showed them to be 19,286 feet above sea level, by far the greatest height climbed by any human being at that time. On the way down they were nearly overwhelmed by a violent snowstorm, which, if it had found them any higher, would certainly have killed them. Chimbarozo defied many other expeditions before being scaled in 1880 by the great Edward Whymper, conqueror of the Matterhorn.

This achievement, regarded by Humboldt himself as the greatest of his expedition, was a fitting climax to it. He set sail for Mexico, after a brief but productive period on the coast, where he re-discovered guano, speculated on the affect of the Humboldt current on the weather of the Continent and ascertained the position of Lima and various islands. His time was literally divided between taking equally accurate observations of the heavens, the ocean, and the volume of an adult cormorant's daily excretions. Thus his scientific work in South America ended with the same admirable catholicity as it had shown throughout.

*

Humboldt returned to Europe a hero, the recipient of honours from every learned society. But no flattery was allowed to divert him from his work and his output was prodigious. He and Bonpland had been in the New World for four years, an adventure which he crammed into thirty-three volumes, illustrated by 1,425 maps and plates, a life's work for any ordinary man. Humboldt had an incredible memory, and a devouring curiosity in every natural phenomenon. Perhaps there was also a corresponding weakness for enlarging in his books on everything he found, so that they contain many longueurs, and do not make easy reading today. We can no longer endure digressions of several hundred pages on some esoteric point of science, but in their day Humboldt's massive volumes electrified the world. Everything in them, theory, fact and narrative, was new and tantalizing. It is exclusively through Humboldt that South America, the lost continent, was found again.

The years and too much adulation turned the adventurous youth into a somewhat pontifical old man. Even in his writings dignity replaced the zest of Humboldt's early letters from South America. Universally honoured, seldom contradicted and never married, he lived on until May 6, 1859, when he died in his ninetieth year. His life had bridged two ages. Born in the same year as Napoleon and Wellington, he survived both; the young subject of Frederick the Great lived on almost into the age of Bismarck. Throughout this time he knew the most famous men of three continents, Frederick the Great, Napoleon, Goethe, Schiller, Metternich, Bolivar, Chateaubriand, Franklin, Jefferson, Canning, Cavour, Beethoven and Walter Scott.

Bonpland's end, although not so distinguished, was nearly as protracted. On their return from South America, Humboldt obtained for him a pension and a position as Superintendent of the Empress Josephine's gardens. His nature was, however, better suited to collection than to authorship and in 1816 he returned to South America to continue his work. But the Continent had changed since they had last seen it and what had been an empire was now a series of independent and sometimes hostile states.

In 1820 Bonpland, when making scientific collections on the Rio Paraguay, was attacked by cavalry troopers and wounded in the head by a sabre. His servants were butchered and he was carried into the interior of Paraguay, a prisoner of its mad dictator, Dr. Francia. There he remained for nine years, well-treated but unable to leave, in spite of the efforts of Humboldt and the French Government to obtain his release. When Bonpland was at last freed, Europe combined to shower him with honours, but he was content to settle down in South America in a small shack with a vast and growing brood of coffee-coloured children. He corresponded regularly with Humboldt and their friendship remained unimpaired until Bonpland's death in 1858, a year before that of his companion.

The journey of Humboldt and Bonpland is a model for any scientific expedition and its success was as much due to the characters of the two men as to the wealth of material which awaited them in South America. No problem was left unstudied, no danger or discomfort could deter them. Humboldt's fine intellect and prodigious memory were allied to a formidable appetite for work, exceptional physical stamina and exemplary courage. Few men could have written his *Personal Narrative* and fewer still could have come so close to conquering Chimbarozo. It is unlikely that anyone else could have done both.

Bonpland, although not so gifted, was perfect in his role of Humboldt's lieutenant. While inferior to his leader in intellect and diligence, he displayed the same courage, endurance and enthusiasm. Five years of hardship would be enough to destroy most friendships, but it cemented the relationship between these two men. Bonpland, when an old man, suffered from occasional twinges of jealousy at his companion's greater fame, an offence for which he has been savagely punished by Humboldt's biographers, but otherwise their friendship remained unimpaired for sixty years.

Father Zahm, the traveller and priest who later accompanied Theodore Roosevelt to the Mato Grosso, reports that he found a small village in Argentina named Bonpland. It is pleasant that he, too, should have his memorial.

Chapter Seven

THE NATURALISTS

FROM 1823 to 1840 a series of revolutions and civil wars prevented foreigners from visiting the Amazon. Even after Brazil won her independence in 1823 all offices of importance in Pará were held by Portuguese. For twelve years the Portuguese and Brazilian factions conducted a feud against each other which sometimes erupted into riots and massacres. Then in 1835, when the peasants of Pará revolted, seized Belém and slaughtered their enemies, a political dispute became a racial war.

The rebels were called the *cabanos* after the huts they inhabited and the war against them the *cabanogem*. Within months the *cabanos* controlled almost all territory by the banks of the Brazilian Amazon, while the Imperial fleet remained in command of the river. A short but merciless war ensued, disfigured by atrocities on both sides. Belém fell to a naval blockade in 1836, but slaughter of the *cabanos* continued until 1840 and only in this year did it become possible for new scientists to follow in Humboldt's footsteps. And Humboldt's publications, by creating a wave of interest in South America, were directly responsible for the expeditions undertaken by these distinguished men—Darwin, Spix, Martius, Bates, Wallace, Spruce and the Schomburgk brothers.

Nothing can show the power of his reputation more clearly than the reverence with which his name was mentioned by the most distinguished of his successors. Richard Spruce, in the Casiquiare, roused himself from a cloud of mosquitoes that gave his cabin the appearance of a beehive, to record with awe that he was entering 'Humboldt's country'. Charles Darwin, a far greater scientist than Humboldt, wrote of his *Personal Narrative*: 'This work stirred up in me a burning zeal to add even the most humble contribution to the noble structure of Natural Science.' Darwin was later to use the expression 'second only to Humboldt' as his highest form of praise. Wallace, the discoverer with Darwin of the principle of Natural Selection, corrected one of the master's less accurate measurements of altitude with embarrassed diffidence, although Humboldt himself had confessed that at this point his thermometer had been useless.

However intensive Humboldt's work had been and however accurate his conclusions, there was far too much raw material for research in South America to be exhausted by one man. There were gaps in his descriptions as well as in his travels; he had for instance spent only a few weeks in the Amazon system, although he made important contributions towards the fixing of its position. Science was now becoming more specialized than in his day in South America and the profusion of every form of life demanded the work of specialists.

In the Amazon valley alone there were more species of insects than in any other part of the world, more kinds of fish than in the Atlantic Ocean and great numbers of unknown birds, reptiles, mammals, plants, shrubs and trees, many of them peculiar to the area. Henry Walter Bates's collections show what could be achieved by a highly dedicated and skilful man. Bates spent eleven years in the Amazon Valley, during which time he amassed specimens of 52 separate species of mammals, 360 of birds, 140 of reptiles, 120 of fishes, 14,000 of insects, 35 of molluscs and 5 of zoophytes, making an incredible total of 14,712 different species of which no less than 8,000 were new to science. This total represents an average of nearly four species for every day of his time in South America, including those on which he was ill, travelling or observing.

While Bates's collection was probably the most impressive, it was not out of all proportion to those of other naturalists. Wallace, who never specialized to the same extent, and who spent only four fever-racked years in South America, gathered 800 species of butterflies, 500 of birds and, in the Rio Negro alone, 205 of fishes. Spruce returned with over 7,000 botanical species, a figure which he could have increased by including more common specimens; Agassiz collected 2,000 species of freshwater fish and Spix and Martius, in less than three years, amassed 2,300 animals and

6,500 plants—a collection so vast that a full generation went by before it was properly catalogued.

But if the prizes on the Amazon were vast its discomforts were on the same scale and the naturalists needed extraordinary patience and enthusiasm to gain their successes. They came, for the most part, at the worst possible time, after the removal of the missions and before the inauguration of the first steamboat service up the river. From the traveller's point of view the missions had offered two great advantages: they controlled the area, keeping it in a fairly law-abiding state, and they would give strangers any assistance they might need, whether food, shelter, guidance or the loan of paddlers. While missions were established at regular intervals along all the main rivers the dangers and discomforts of travel were reduced, but once they were abolished chaos returned. The Indians melted away into the jungle; any form of law vanished and villages were rapidly depopulated. The remaining Indians had little use for money and less for exercise and in the absence of authority, canoes and paddlers were almost unobtainable. It was enough to disillusion the most liberal-minded of travellers.

Trade had dwindled with the missions that had cultivated it. Isolation on the upper reaches was so complete that, when Spruce was staying in San Carlos on the Venezuelan Rio Negro, the first news in that town of the fact that there was a new president of Venezuela broke through a copy of *The Times* sent up-river to him. The news could cross the Atlantic twice, travel a thousand miles up the Amazon, wait for a boat going to Venezuela and then be carried another thousand miles over the cataracts of the Rio Negro, in less time than it took to be circulated in the country which it concerned.

Even on the mainstream communications were abominable. In the dry season, when the current was slack and the Trade Winds strong from the east, a sailing boat might travel the thousand miles from Pará to Manaos in forty days, but in the rainy season the same journey would last for three months, or as long as a fast tea-clipper run from England to Australia. Once Spruce took sixty-three days for the five hundred miles from Santarem to Manaos. When the current was strong and the wind too weak to sail against it, sailing ships had to be hauled upstream by cables paid out and attached to trees. The first steamboat service, inaugurated in 1853, took eight days to reach Manaos from Pará.

Some dangers of the river were constant; navigation was hindered by floating islands, compact masses of grass up to several acres in size and up to thirty feet in depth, cut out by erosion. The Pororoca, the famous tidal bore of the estuary, could easily be ridden out in a canoe and was only harmful to those who tied up their boats in shallow water, but the floods when the silted-up entries to lakes were burst open by the rising river, the massive landslips, when the foundations of the bank had been eaten away and giant trees were sent tumbling down into the water, and the sudden squalls in mid-stream, were more serious dangers.

Food was so scarce that the naturalists were sometimes forced by necessity to eat dishes as odd as those which Humboldt had consumed for Science's sake. The alligator was found excellent eating by both Waterton and Edwards, but the former was made sick by wasp grubs and the latter described electric eel as 'too fishy in taste to be agreeable without strong correctives'. To Bates the giant ant-eater tasted 'very good, somewhat like a goose in flavour', but he could not eat 'the execrable salt fish which Brasilians use'. Spruce drank the 'milk' of a tree and all of them agreed on the delicacy and excellence of monkey's flesh.

Then there were the pests of the river, large and small: jaguars, alligators, vampire bats, sting-ray, piranha, candiru, bushmaster, fer de lance, parrot and coral snakes, anaconda and a bewildering number of poisonous or irritating insects, from the mygales spider whose bite is fatal for a human being, to the Saüba ant which can destroy his belongings with surprising speed. In between these extremes there were poisonous ants, centipedes, caterpillars and scorpions, painful wasps, piums and motúca flies, jiggers and bêtes rouges and, responsible for far more deaths than the rest combined, the ever-present, unidentified killer of the tropics, the mosquito.

All the naturalists who stayed for any length of time suffered from malaria or yellow fever. There was a terrible epidemic of yellow fever in Pará in 1850 which carried away ten per cent of the population, including Wallace's younger brother. Fevers were attributed to various causes, exposure to the night air, cold and miasma. There were also epidemics of smallpox, the scourge of unvaccinated Indians, and leprosy was rife.

In this uncongenial setting resilience and enthusiasm were even more important than professional skill, as was shown by Charles Waterton, the first naturalist of any note to follow in Humboldt's

MEN AND HORSES CROSSING A MOUNTAIN STREAM

LAKE GUATAVITA, THE REAL EL DORADO

A MOJOS INDIAN DANCING
BEFORE THE ALTAR

THE JESUIT EXPLANATION
OF THE TRINITY

THE REDUCTION OF SAN JOSE IN CHIQUITOS

Photo: British Museum

THE RUINS OF A JESUIT SEMINARY NEAR BELÉM
OVERGROWN BY CREEPERS

THE MURDER OF DE SENIÈRGUES

Photo: British Museum

CABALLITOS IN THE ANDES

CATCHING AN ALLIGATOR WITH LASSO

VICTORIA REGIA IN A LAKE BY THE AMAZON

PIRANHA

THE OPERA HOUSE IN MANAOS

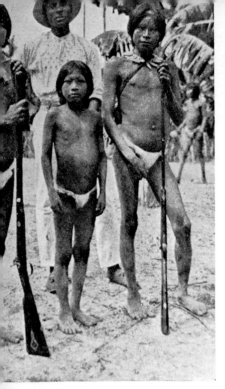

PUTUMAYO MUCHACHOS
WITH BARBADIAN
OVERSEER

LATEX BEING TAPPED

Photo: Botting

Roger Casement
April 17. 19

ROGER CASEMENT

THEODORE ROOSEVELT
AND COLONEL RONDON

COLONEL FAWCETT

CUILI (CENTRAL FIGURE ON LOG) WHO CONFESSED TO THE
MURDER OF FAWCETT'S PARTY

ORLANDO VILLAS BOAS

Photo:

KALAPOLO WOMAN PREPARING MANIOC

footsteps, who, although amateurish almost to the point of lunacy, was deterred by nothing at all.

Even in his native Yorkshire, Waterton's custom of sleeping on bare boards with a block of wood for a pillow was regarded as eccentric. He was a member of a wealthy Roman Catholic family, so Jacobite in its sympathies that his love of all animals was qualified by a violent detestation of the brown or 'Hanoverian' rat. He was a teetotaller in an age of excess and an opponent of shooting for sport at a time when such an attitude was unknown in a man of his background. Waterton's book, *Wanderings in South America*, is extraordinarily well named, his geographical references being so vague that it is impossible to follow his course. One can say that he made four expeditions to South America, the first in 1812 and the last in 1824, in the course of which he travelled extensively in the three Guianas and occasionally in Brazil and Venezuela.

His geographical vagueness is matched by an equally casual approach to biology; indeed his main skill as a naturalist seems to have been in the field of taxidermy, if one can judge from the long and tedious treatise on stuffing birds which disfigures his last chapter. The rest of his book, although peppered with Latin quotations and classical allusions, still reads well and it is impossible not to be affected by his own ebullience and enjoyment of every episode. Much of what he saw was new and he had a gift for describing animals and a natural impetuosity which landed him in ridiculous and often incredible situations.

The luxury of a hammock after the cold boards of his Yorkshire home seems to have forced Waterton to indulge his Spartan affectations in the daytime. He invariably walked barefoot in the jungle, even though this habit led to lacerations by stones, thorns, branches and insects which often incapacitated him for days. Every evening he carefully exposed his flesh in the vain hope that he might be bitten by a vampire bat, in order, he explains, 'that I might have it in my power to say it had really happened to me'. On one occasion he allowed a jigger to eat its way into his hand for half an hour through a desire to study it at work. His disgust at the vampires' timidity vanished when one of his companions, 'a Scottish gentleman', was bitten. The Scotsman, irritated both by the bite and by Waterton's amusement, retired to the latrine only to have the more serious misfortune of sitting on a swarm of soldier ants which happened to be crossing it at the time. For once Waterton found himself at a loss for an apposite quotation.

Waterton relates the story of his ride on the giant cayman with more gusto than conviction. He had been fishing for alligator using shark hooks without any success, until some Indians advised him to try barbs hung above the water and baited with the flesh of a rodent called the agouti. A giant alligator was soon secured by this method and with some difficulty Waterton persuaded his Indians to pull it in. As it was drawn up, struggling, into the shallows, Waterton sprang on to its back, seized its front legs 'as a bridle' and remained there, in spite of all the reptile's efforts to dislodge him, until it had been subdued. He wrote of this episode, 'Should it be asked how I managed to keep my seat, I would answer I hunted some years with Lord Darlington's foxhounds.'

On another occasion when he encountered a small boa-constrictor, although alone and unarmed, he seized it with his bare hands and after a desperate struggle defeated the snake. Its jaws were secured with Waterton's braces and it was tied up until the morning when, like the alligator, its throat was cut and its carcass turned over to his rather aimless dissections.

Waterton's book received violently hostile, if rather unfair reviews, but in Humboldt's shadow his graphic descriptions and inconsequent charm could not expect to be appreciated. One can, nevertheless, sympathize with the reviewers who infuriated him by ridiculing the cayman and boa-constrictor stories, and still more with the critic who impaled two of Waterton's failings so succinctly with the words 'Latin, Latin everywhere and not one Latin name'.

*

The work of the Anglo-Prussian Schomburgk brothers, Robert and Richard, was undertaken almost entirely to the north of the Amazon system and, although their discoveries included the magnificent Victoria Regia Lily and many other forms of life found in the Amazon Valley, their place lies in the history of Guyana and Venezuela rather than that of the Amazon. This distinction is always difficult to draw. Neither Humboldt nor Waterton spent much time on the Amazon, but one can include them in any history of the river on the grounds that Humboldt's journey had an immense effect on the entire continent and that Waterton's main value lies in his description of the wild life found throughout tropical America.

William Edwards, an American naturalist, spent eight months on the Amazon in 1846. He could scarcely be expected to make an important collection in so short a time, but on his return he wrote a delightful book about his experiences. It is through his *Voyage up the River Amazon* that Edwards can claim a place in its history, for it inspired Bates and Wallace, two of the greatest naturalists of the nineteenth century, to go to the Amazon Valley and not to some other part of the tropics.

Neither Bates nor Wallace had the private means of La Condamine, Humboldt or Waterton and they were dependent on selling duplicates of their collections to finance their expeditions. They arrived together in Pará in 1848, both young men full of enthusiasm, Wallace then being twenty-five and Bates twenty-three. They separated in 1850, Bates continuing his study of the creatures of the main river and Wallace pressing on into the unknown headwaters of the Rio Negro and its tributary the Uaupés. Both men were eventually forced to leave South America by failing health, Wallace in 1852 and Bates in 1859. While their relationship seems to have been friendly enough throughout, their separation was made inevitable by differences in their ambitions.

Bates was a collector and his success in this respect was probably greater than that of any other naturalist. He would settle in a promising place and remain there until he had exhausted its resources or until it was clear that he would do better elsewhere. While he had all the gifts necessary for a collector, he was also capable of profound study and able to describe the life of his subjects, and in particular the ants, in the most vivid manner. Bates spent the greater part of his eleven years on the Amazon in three places, Pará (now Belém), Santarem and Ega (now Teffé). He managed to merge himself into the life of each of these communities without acquiring any of their idolence and without losing his scientific drive. He is one of the few naturalists who never complained of the lack of civilized society and he is one of the very few who could be said to have liked the people of the Amazon Valley as well as the country itself. His analysis of their character goes well beyond the standard complaints of drunkenness, broken promises, idleness and dishonesty.

Unlike many travellers Bates never courted hardship nor danger, but he could endure both without complaint when they were necessary to his work. He had several adventures with dangerous reptiles. On one occasion when he and some friends were camping on a sand bank, he was woken in the middle of the night and looking under his hammock, was startled to see a large alligator a foot below him, which had stolen on shore to seize a poodle belonging to one of his companions. The bathing place at Teffé was infested with these creatures, but after a time he became resigned to their presence and wrote: 'I used to imitate the natives in not advancing far from the bank and in keeping my eyes fixed on that of the monster, which stares with a disgusting leer along the surface of the water . . . when a little motion in the water was perceived behind the reptile's tail, bathers were obliged to beat a quick retreat.' Whenever an alligator became too bold the men of the village would hunt it down in canoes and kill it with harpoons.

Once, in the forest, Bates had an almost miraculous escape after treading on a deadly fer de lance. The snake struck at him and hit the slack of his trouser leg, and before it could recover itself an Indian boy who was with him resourcefully cut it in half. Another snake, fortunately harmless, fell from a tree on to Bates's head, as unpleasant an experience as one could imagine. He survived the assaults of the insects which he collected so assiduously, even finding time to note their techniques of attack, but the insects won the last battle. Bates cured himself of Yellow Fever but later he became so weak after several bouts of malaria that he was forced to return to England.

Bates's book, *The Naturalist on the River Amazon*, is the finest ever written on the area. He had a mystic communion with the forest, of a kind more normally associated with the desert or the sea, and he is able to transfer enough of his feelings on to paper to make his the best of all descriptions of the Amazon Jungle. The passages telling us of the habits of the insects are masterly, but although he specialized in this branch his touch is as certain when he writes about toucan, alligators, turtles, or monkeys. His account of the Indians' predicament shows that he might have been equally successful as an anthropologist. He made one grim prophecy which has come tragically close to being fulfilled: 'The inflexibility of character of the Indian, and his total inability to accommodate himself to new arrangements, will infallibly lead to his extinction.'

This invaluable book is ours by chance, since Bates, modest to a fault, had no intention of writing about his experiences. It was only when Charles Darwin, impressed by a lecture of his on Protective

Mimicry, urged him to write, that he agreed. He was fortunate enough to gain the post of Assistant Secretary to the Royal Geographical Society, which gave him financial security for the rest of his life, but it was a small reward compared with the honours heaped upon Humboldt and La Condamine.

While Bates spent nine years in only three different places, Wallace, after separating from him, explored the lesser known parts of the Rio Negro for two years and collected while he travelled. On his first expedition he ascended the Rio Negro, passed by the entry of the Casiquiare and made the crossing into the Orinoco system by the Pimichim river, a short walk away from the village of Javita on an affluent of the Orinoco, where Humboldt had stayed before him.

After returning to Manaos he set off again on another expedition combining exploration with Natural History. He intended to ascend the great western tributary of the Rio Negro, the Uaupés, which lances its way deep into Colombia, and there he hoped to find the white umbrella bird, a mythical creature which travellers claimed to have seen on this river. When Wallace reached the mouth of the Uaupés he was prostrated with malaria, a disease which afflicted him many times. He made two journeys up this river and on both occasions he was hindered by bad health. On his return to Manaos he was so weak that he had no alternative but to leave the country.

Wallace's travels were marred by tragedy; his constitution seemed to have been ruined; his younger brother had died of yellow fever in Pará and his troubles accompanied him even after he had boarded a ship for home. One day the captain appeared in his cabin and with admirable phlegm observed, 'I'm afraid the ship's on fire. Come and see what you think of it.'

Wallace could not be expected to think much of it. The ship, carrying almost all his hard-won specimens, was clearly doomed; the nearest land was 700 miles away and he was in no state to endure a long passage in an open boat. As the passengers circled the burning wreck in the boats they saw Wallace's monkeys run out on to the bowsprit, hesitate, refuse to jump and return to be engulfed by the flames. Only one parrot fluttered down into the ocean to be saved.

After ten days in the boats the passengers' position seemed to be equally desperate, for their food and water were almost finished and they were still 200 miles from land, but at this critical moment their luck turned and they were rescued by a passing ship.

Wallace was still too young and too brilliant to be crushed by these misfortunes. After the publication of his interesting book, *Travels on the Amazon and Rio Negro*, he left again for the tropics, this time for Malaya, where his work outshone his earlier achievements in South America. He is remembered now mainly as the author of the authoritative *The Malay Archipelago* and as the co-discoverer, with Darwin, of the principle of Natural Selection. Wallace's great scientific ability was occasionally betrayed by a strain of credulity in his nature. He thus diverged from Darwin's views on the origin of man by maintaining that there was a divine purpose behind man's evolution, although this same purpose had been brought about by the forces of Natural Selection.

He became a bitter enemy of vaccination, a treatment which he considered to be always useless and often harmful, an advocate of land nationalization and spiritualism, and a passionate amateur economist. Although the fevers of the Amazon seemed to have broken his health while he was still in his twenties, he survived until the age of ninety. As Professor Cutright has pointed out, the fact that Bates, Wallace, Spruce and others were forced home by disease had no effect on their life expectancy. He produces an impressive table to reinforce this point:

> Humboldt   (1769–1859) lived to the age of 89.
> Waterton   (1782–1865)   „   „   „   „   „ 83.
> Schomburgk (1811–1891)   „   „   „   „   „ 80.
> Wallace   (1823–1913)   „   „   „   „   „ 90.
> Bates   (1825–1892)   „   „   „   „   „ 67.
> Spruce   (1817–1893)   „   „   „   „   „ 76.

Thus six men, who between them spent nearly fifty years in South America and suffered from most of her fevers, lived to an average age of eighty-one years. It could only be added that General Rondon, who must have spent far longer than any of them in tropical South America, died an active ninety-two.

*

Richard Spruce, although delicate throughout his life, spent no fewer than fifteen years in tropical South America. As a botanist he showed the same devotion to his plants and mosses as Bates to his insects and he was so long about his work that he rivalled both Bates's collecting feats and Wallace's explorations. Thus he was

able to build up an awe-inspiring record of travel and at the same
time to stay as long as was profitable in the best collecting grounds.
He spent eleven months in Manaos and a year and three-quarters
at Tarapoto (a village on the Huallaga river in Peru). He ascended
the main river as far as Canelos and, after various expeditions in the
Andes, crossed the Continent to the Pacific. He explored the
Trombeta, the Uaupés, crossed to the Orinoco and followed it
down as far as the old Maypures mission just south of latitude
6°N. He became the first European to ascend the Pacimoni and
Cunucunúma rivers in Venezuela.

Spruce's practical and patient nature is well illustrated in the
story of how, soon after his arrival, he became lost in the jungle in a
thunderstorm. The experience of being lost in the limitless forest is
enough to drive most people into a suicidal panic, even without the
deafening accompaniment of a tropical thunderstorm. But Spruce
calmly sat down and waited until the sun emerged enough for him
to determine its course and then walked straight out to safety. His
sensitivity was jarred by unnecessary destruction and it took him
some time to find the solution to the problem of flowers found only
in the forest canopy, far out of reach of the most nimble Indian:

'At length the conviction was forced upon me,' he wrote, 'that
the best and sometimes the only way to obtain the flowers or fruit
was to cut down the tree, but it was long before I could overcome a
feeling of compunction at having to destroy a magnificent tree,
perhaps centuries old, merely for the sake of gathering its flowers.'

Spruce's tragedy is that, in spite of keeping voluminous notes
throughout, he never wrote a full account of his travels. After his
death his papers were edited most ably by Wallace, and there is
enough in them to make one feel that he could have written as
good a book as Bates and one drawn from greater experience. He
shows such enthusiasm for his subject that the sight of a rare moss
could rouse him from the deepest dejection; he had a dry humour,
a gift for description and narrative and a fine analytical mind.
Through no wish of his own he became involved in dramatic
incidents and was even forced to defend his life against drunken
Indians, mutineers, and once against a compatriot.

This Englishman, a deplorable character attracted to the Amazon
by rumours of a gold strike, nevertheless succeeded in impressing
Spruce as 'a very quiet fellow' and was engaged as his assistant. The
quiet fellow, who had recently been imprisoned in Lima for murder,

was unable to keep his violent instincts subdued. Spruce was shocked when he broke an Indian's jaw in a trivial quarrel and horrified when he launched a murderous attack on a Brazilian with a pick-axe. His victim's only offence had been to make an innocent remark in Portuguese to Spruce, which the other Englishman, ignorant of the language, took as an insult. Spruce soon found evidence that his assistant intended to rob and murder him. For several nights he lay in his hammock with a loaded revolver in his hand, until a safe opportunity came to dismiss him. Spruce heard afterwards that the Englishman had been murdered in his turn by two Indians, presumably after some provocation.

Spruce was not always fortunate in his choice of employees. On the Orinoco when he suffered one of his worst bouts of fever, his Indians seemed more interested in his liquor than in his health and he was forced to hire a nurse at the next village they reached. For several weeks, while he lay at the point of death, this woman ignored him and held parties in his sickroom, occasionally turning to curse him for not dying so that she could spend his money.

On another occasion an Indian working for Spruce was bitten by a parrot snake while gathering specimens in the forest. Spruce succeeded in saving his life against all precedents and was startled afterwards to hear that in doing so he had also saved his own. His patient had many relatives in the village, in all of whose eyes natural death was non-existent. If the Indian had died it could only be because someone had encompassed his death and they would have reasoned that Spruce had 'willed' him to go into the forest and must have 'willed' the snake to bite him. Justified by such impeccable logic they would have felt a moral obligation to kill Spruce in his turn.

Spruce's journey ended with a commission to prepare seeds of the cinchona tree, from which quinine is derived, for export to India. He fulfilled his role, gathering and packing the seeds with skill, and nursing them on a raft down the Guayaquil River to the Pacific. On their arrival in England the delicate seeds germinated and were successfully planted in India and Ceylon, but the sites were poorly chosen and the trees never grew freely. Spruce had lost his life savings of $6,000 in the failure of a Peruvian bank and the pension of £50 a year given him by a grateful government for this service must have been useful, if not overwhelming in its generosity.

Spruce was the last of a group of great naturalists whose courage, industry and genius contributed so greatly towards knowledge of South America. For some reason, perhaps because so much information needed digesting, there were few distinguished naturalists from the time of Spruce's departure until the beginning of the twentieth century, when the American naturalists started their southern migration and the age of Darwin, Bates, Spruce, Hudson and Wallace was succeeded by that of Cherrie, Miller, Beebe and Chapman. But it is the earlier period, when every day brought its own discovery, when the new families of animals, birds, insects, fishes and plants were first identified, studied and collected, that must have the greater interest.

Chapter Eight

THE ANIMALS

THE GREAT naturalists were fortunate enough to visit the Amazon before commercial hunting had reduced its animal population. This is not to say that the numbers of animals in the Amazon Valley ever rivalled the endless herds of untouched Africa. Orellana, the earliest explorer of all, could only find enough to eat by raiding Indian villages and when there were no villages his men went hungry, chewing the leather of their saddles and rooting up grubs and lizards. It is fair to say that no Indian would be reduced to the same straits either then or now, so long as he had a bow, a blowpipe or the means to make either.

The Indians' primitive weapons were perfect for their purpose. The nature of the country made long shots rare; the bow would kill fish underwater as well as monkeys in the trees and the blowpipe was utterly silent. La Condamine tells us that although he and Maldonado were armed with guns, almost all their food throughout their descent of the river was provided by their Indians' blowpipes. If one of them fired at a group of monkeys they could, at the most, kill one before the others disappeared, but if their Indians fired the monkeys, hearing no noise, would wait until several had been killed.

If there were some areas where game was scarce and hard to find, there were others where food of a sort was amazingly abundant. Alligators filled the rivers and lakes in numbers which astounded almost every traveller. Spruce gives us an account of the strange plague that sent thousands of their bodies floating down the Tapajós, so that all the boatmen of Santarem were called out to keep the rotting corpses in midstream and to relieve the town of their foul stench. Bates describes the waters of the Solimoes as being 'as well stocked with large alligators in the dry season as a ditch in England is in summer with tadpoles'. Spruce saw equal numbers in the lakes and rivers around Villa Nova. Turtles swarmed in countless thousands and in the dry season the surface of the water boiled with fish.

There were other species, now scarce, which were common in those days. The feathers of the cock of the rock and the heron, like the hide of the alligator and the pelt of the otter, had still to be coveted by the outside world and jaguar skins were of such low value that Spruce would acquire them in exchange for a handkerchief, and so easy to replace that he allowed his dog to use them for a bed and did not complain when it chewed three of them to shreds. Other hides were as worthless and in the absence of any incentive the Amazonians' natural indolence restricted their hunting to enough to provide themselves with food and the means to barter for essentials. At this time commercial hunting threatened only one creature, the turtle, and it was perhaps the most common of all the inhabitants of the Amazon.

The turtle was made vulnerable by its habit of laying its eggs in vast numbers on sandbanks well above the level of the water, and valuable by the oil contained in its eggs. Bates has left us a vivid description of the gathering of these eggs from a sandbank near Ega.

When the laying season arrived there would be two mass migrations to an otherwise deserted strip of sand, first of the turtles to deposit their eggs and then of the human beings to remove them. The first would perhaps be more impressive, for the turtle is by nature a shy creature and so difficult to see in its own environment that, at any other time of the year, a traveller might feel that there were few of them in the river. But when the time came for them to lay their eggs they would swarm up on to the sandbanks in such multitudes that for over a mile their jostling shells would hide even the sand on which they lay. The latecomers would sometimes have to leave their eggs on top of those of the earliest arrivals, but as if warned by some subtle instinct, the first turtles would excavate a hole about three feet deep, lay its eggs there and cover them with a layer of sand, leaving room for others to drop theirs on top. Each turtle would lay around one hundred eggs of roughly the size and shape of a billiard ball, an astonishing feat. (It is impossible to fit so many eggs back into the turtle's shell without removing all its flesh.)

When the turtles started to come out of the water, the inhabitants of the nearest village would post sentinels to warn off intruders and to tell all passing boats to keep their distance. Even after the laying had started, any disturbance would cause a slow motion stampede of the 'Cattle of the Amazon'* back to the safety of the water.

Once the turtles had finished—and they took a full fortnight for their work—the villagers would occupy the sandbank in their turn, men, women and children, with their hammocks, canoes, dogs, baskets and calabashes. The thorough organization of the gathering of the eggs was one of the few legacies of order preserved from the days of the missions. An elected official, with the quaint title of 'The Commander of the Royal Beach', would divide the sandbank into sections reserved for different families. Humboldt tells us that in the days of the Jesuits, a part of each sandbank was always left untouched, to prevent the number of turtles decreasing in the future, but this wise precaution lapsed after their expulsion.

Each family would excavate its area and pile up mounds of turtles' eggs as high as their own heads. After putting aside some for food, the rest would be taken to canoes, pulped and the oil extracted from them. In Bates's day 8,000 jars of oil were known to be produced in the Amazon Valley every year. As 6,000 eggs were needed for each jar, 48,000,000 were turned into oil every year, the total produce of at least 400,000 female turtles. But even this figure is an underestimate, as the calculation made by Bates of 120 eggs for each female turtle is probably too high; the animal production figure of 8,000 jars is conservative and his calculations make no allowance for the eggs set aside for food or for the young turtles wastefully destroyed. It would probably be nearer the truth to say that the entire produce of half a million female turtles was removed every year. It is not surprising that, even in Bates's time, their numbers were shrinking and nothing can illustrate more vividly how numerous they once were than the fact that they have survived at all.

While the Amazon never boasted any animals which could compare in size with the giants of other continents, it has the dubious distinction of harbouring a number of creatures so horrible that they have become legendary. Almost all the villains of the Amazon live in its waters and it is worth pointing out at the beginning that the alligator, the piranha, the sting-ray, the electric eel and the candiru

* So called because they are often preserved in underwater stockades.

do not between them offer the same danger as, for instance, the African crocodile. They may occasionally claim a human life, but their main victim is the human imagination.

We have already seen through Humboldt's and Bates's eyes the alligator at its most menacing, lying in wait for the unwary or drunken Indian. Wallace embellishes their accounts but Spruce gives us the corrective. He was watching the pirarucu fishermen of the lower Amazon, who harpooned their quarries in lakes swarming with alligators, and he noticed that when one of the fish was speared the men would jump into the water alongside the alligators to land it, although it was often pumping out blood at the time. There seemed to be a gentlemen's agreement under which the alligators never attacked the fishermen and in return were always given the offal when the fish were cleaned. Even when attacked by an alligator a man had some chance of survival. Humboldt records instances of Indians having freed themselves by digging their fingers into the reptile's eyes and Bates tells us of a far less likely escape near Ega. An Indian boy was seized by the leg when bathing and pulled under water. His father dived into the river, caught up with the alligator and gouged its eyes until it released its victim. The boy still carried the scars at the time when Bates saw him. There are far too many impeccable accounts of attacks made by them to deny that alligators were often dangerous, but when one recalls that villagers throughout the Amazon and Orinoco systems bathed regularly in their presence, they hardly seem to have made the most of their opportunities.

As has been seen, the Amazon River and its tributaries contain more varieties of fish than the Atlantic Ocean, and Professor Agassiz collected over 2,000 separate species. A quotation from his book, *A Journey in Brazil*, gives an even more striking illustration of their abundance: 'All the rivers of Europe united, from the Tagus to the Volga, do not nourish one hundred and fifty species of freshwater fish, and yet in a little lake near Manaos, called Lago Hyanuary, the surface of which covers hardly four or five hundred square yards (an area smaller than a tennis court and its surrounds), we have discovered more than two hundred distinct species, the greater part of which have not been observed elsewhere.' It is perhaps to be expected that some, among so many species, should be harmful and of these by far the most common and famous is the piranha.

The piranha, perhaps more than any other fish in the world,

personifies greed, savagery, remorselessness and every other malignant quality. The mind that can accept the idea of being drowned by an alligator, dismembered by a shark, knocked unconscious by an electric eel or even struck by a poisonous snake may well recoil from the thought of being stripped to the skeleton by a swarm of minute fishes. The alligator can be attacked through its sensitive eyes and a strong man can easily hold its jaws together, but no one can gouge out a thousand eyes or hold shut a thousand greedy jaws.

The piranha never grows longer than two feet and specimens of eighteen inches are rare. It is a flat fish, innocuous at first sight and even, in the vermilion variety, rather beautiful, but it seems harmless only until one notices its jaws, powerful, deep-set and slightly retracted, and its heavy triangular, razor-sharp teeth. For its size, its bite is exceptionally powerful and a piranha only six inches long can sever a man's finger or toe in one snap.

Humboldt was the first of the naturalists to notice the piranha and we have already heard his restrained account of its habits. Schomburgk, in British Guiana, came into closer contact, one of his Indians being severely bitten in the foot. Schomburgk was able to find three separate species of piranha, all of them with the same essential physical characteristics and the same revolting habits. Waterton, Edwards, Wallace and Spruce omit all mention of the piranha and Bates's description of it goes no further than that of Humboldt:

'Piranha, a kind of Salmonidae (tetragon-opterus). Piranhas are of several kinds, many of which abound in the waters of the Tapajós. They are caught with almost any kind of bait, for their taste is indiscriminate and their appetite most ravenous. They often attack the legs of bathers near the shore, inflicting severe wounds with their strong triangular teeth.'

It is probable that the early naturalists rather underestimated the malice of this fish and the dangers of bathing when it was present, but none of them except for Schomburgk had seen it do anything more menacing than quarrel over offal. Only when they began to be bitten themselves did their accounts of its habits become more sensational. Wickham, the exporter of the rubber seeds, lost a finger when spitting a piranha which he thought was dead. Cherrie, the American naturalist, had a narrow escape when he fell into a stream when fishing for piranha. But their reputation did not reach the general public until Theodore Roosevelt's *Through the Brazilian Wilderness* was published in 1914.

Most of Roosevelt's companions had already suffered from the piranha's attacks. Cherrie and Miller, the two naturalists who accompanied him, had both been bitten and Colonel Rondon, the greatest explorer in the history of Brazil, had lost a toe while bathing. Rondon also told Roosevelt how, on one of his expeditions, he had to dynamite a stream to provide food. His party waded in after the explosion to collect the stunned fish floating on its surface. One of his lieutenants, having his hands full, stuffed an extra fish in his mouth. Unfortunately, the last fish was a piranha and, as he climbed out of the stream, it revived and bit a large section out of his tongue. The wretched man had a severe haemorrhage and nearly died.

Another of Rondon's men had ridden out of camp on a mule and when it returned alone the rest of the party followed its tracks back until they found him, fully clothed, but with every bit of flesh stripped from his bones. It was impossible to tell whether he had been killed by the piranha or merely drowned and then devoured. Just before Roosevelt's arrival a boy had been eaten alive at Corumba, the capital of the State of Matto Grosso, and on his way up the River Plate and Paraná he saw with his own eyes the results of their work.

'They are the most ferocious fish in the world', he wrote:

even the most formidable fish, the sharks, or the barracudas, usually attack things smaller than themselves. But the piranhas habitually attack things much larger than themselves. They will snap a finger off a hand incautiously trailed in the water, they mutilate swimmers ... they will rend and devour alive any wounded man or beast; for blood in the water excites them to madness. They will tear wounded wild fowl to pieces, and bite off the tails of big fish as they grow exhausted when fighting after being hooked. Those that we caught sometimes bit through the hooks, or the double strands of copper wire that served as leaders, and got away. Those that we hauled on deck lived for many minutes. Most predatory fish are long and slim, like the alligator, gar and pickerel. But the piranha is a short deep-bodied fish, with a blunt face and a heavily under-shot or projecting lower jaw which gapes widely. The razor edged teeth are wedge-shaped like a shark's and the jaw muscles possess great power. The rabid furious snaps drive the teeth through flesh and bone. The head, with its short muzzle, staring malignant eyes and gaping, cruelly armoured jaws, is the embodiment of evil ferocity. The actions of the fish exactly match its looks. I never witnessed an exhibition of such impotent savage fury as was shown by the piranhas as they flapped on deck. When fresh from the water and thrown on the boards they uttered an extraordinary squealing sound. As they flapped about they bit with vicious eagerness at whatever presented itself. One of them flapped into a cloth and seized it with a bulldog grip, another grasped one of his fellows, another snapped at a piece of wood and left the teeth marks deep therein.

Later in his journey Roosevelt came to a small lake inhabited by piranha and alligators. It was clear that the alligators preyed off the piranha, but when he shot one their positions were reversed. The wounded alligator made instinctively for the water and Roosevelt was astonished to see it turn round and return to land with even more desperation. The piranha had started by chewing at its wounds and then, maddened, they tore out chunks of hide and flesh, until the alligator finally regained the shore.

As many travellers who took them for dead discovered to their cost, the piranha fights until the last. Their insatiable hunger, the incredible strength of their bulldog jaws and their ravenous courage all inspire us with horror, but their size prevents them from being as lethal as they would wish. Cherrie, who fell bleeding into the middle of a school of piranha, was able to escape, although not without injury. The scarred bathers seen by Roosevelt on the banks of the Paraguay had all survived attacks, which might have been fatal if made by larger creatures. We have innumerable complaints of fingers and toes removed by these repulsive creatures and of gashes made by them in the legs and thighs, but Colonel Rondon's story of the boy killed at Corumba is the only reliable account of a human being dying from their attacks. There were doubtless others, but not enough to have come to the attention of the naturalists. The inhabitants of the Amazon Valley have never hesitated to bathe where there are known to be piranha and they will tell any enquirer that the fish seldom attack unless there is blood in the water.

*

Another dangerous fish found by Roosevelt was the piraiba or cat-fish. The one he caught, which was three and a half feet long, had the semi-digested remains of a monkey in its stomach. The Brazilians with him swore that around the mouth of the Madeira catfish grew far larger, and would even prey on men. The expedition's doctor had seen a monstrous piraiba which had lunged over the side of a canoe at two men and had been defeated only by their machetes. Colonel Rondon told him that on the lower Madeira villagers would build stockades in which to bathe, for fear of the catfish and the cayman. Of the two the piraiba was the most dreaded, since its habit was to lie, invisible, on the bottom of the river until the moment came to pounce. None of the other naturalists seem to have run foul of this formidable creature.

The Madeira river has little to recommend it, even if one disregards the presence of the giant catfish. Its waters are clotted with silt and mud; its banks, abominably hot, act as havens to hordes of malarial mosquitoes, as the builders of the Madeira–Mamoré railroad were to discover. Its size exceeds that of the greatest tributaries of other rivers by a suitable margin for the main affluent of the Amazon, the water passing its mouth being only slightly less than that carried by the Mississippi and over twice the volume of the Nile in flood. Its use as a waterway, however, is affected by a chain of dangerous rapids 200 miles in length. In addition to the catfish and the mosquito it harbours one other pest worthy of attention, the candiru, which can reasonably claim yet another title for the Amazon System, that of the most unpleasant fish in the world. A thin fish, seldom more than two inches in length, it is found in many parts of Amazonia and is common in some tributaries of the Madeira. Its body is covered with swept-back quills. If anyone is rash enough to bathe in its presence it will enter a natural orifice of his body and by preference the penis, and once it is inside it can be extracted only by an agonizing operation. Some observers have attributed the bark guards worn by the Indians over their private parts to fear of this loathsome fish.

After the candiru the electric eel and the sting-ray must seem innocuous. We have already followed Humboldt's and Bonpland's heroic experiments with the gymnotus and although the researches of other naturalists have unearthed new material on the nature of the creature's organs, its habits and distribution, Humboldt's description of it in action remains the best. The sting-ray, as feared by the Indians as any other creature, is dangerous mainly because of the difficulty of seeing it as it lies, perfectly camouflaged, on the bed of the river. The ray will not attack unless molested, but it is often trodden on accidentally by users of the river and the punishment for disturbing it is frightful. The barbed stinger lances into the intruder's flesh and leaves a jagged wound when withdrawn, but the pain is quite disproportionate to the wound alone. Its victims roll about on the ground, convulsed with agony and screaming aloud. The pain is accompanied by intense cold in the wounded part and in the groin. The sting is seldom fatal but it is often as long as a week before the victim can set his foot on the ground again.

The river has many strange inhabitants, some of which are remarkable through their presence in fresh water and others through their astonishing habits. Shark have been caught as far upstream as Iquitos, 2,300 miles from the Atlantic and other salt water creatures are found nearly as far from their proper habitat; the largest of these is the twenty-foot-long sawfish. There are extraordinary mammals—the manatee or sea cow, the freshwater dolphins and the gigantic Amazonian otter—which can grow up to seven foot in length.

Some fishes possess unusual gifts; the Colombian catfish can climb vertical walls by using the suckers on its body; the lungfish hibernates in mud for the dry season and survives for several months with scarcely any moisture; the charucin, when alarmed, travels along the surface of the water in a series of long low leaps, so that it seems to be planing; some families are viviparous and many have partially developed lungs. This ability to survive exposure to an alien element seems to be characteristic of the creatures of the Amazon Valley, perhaps because, over the years, animals have adapted themselves to being marooned by water and fishes to being stranded in ever-decreasing pools. Thus almost all the animals can swim well and some, like the capybara and tapir, are almost as much at home in water as on land; even the giant sloth, which loathes water, is an adept swimmer which can survive submersion for half an hour.

The denizens of the forests of the Amazon are, mercifully, less formidable than those of its waters. There is the normal tropical quota of poisonous snakes, amongst whom the bushmaster, the fer de lance and the cascabel are the most deadly, but the only mammals that can be of any danger to a human being are the jaguar and the white-lipped peccary, a wild hog. The jaguar prefers the flesh of dogs to that of men and will only attack when cornered or when desperately hungry. There seem to have been no rogue jaguars to rival the bloody records of man-eating tigers, lions and leopards in other continents and the peccaries' ferocity has probably been

over-estimated, although a herd of them could destroy any adversary
with ease. The anaconda, the king of snakes, may also be less vicious,
as well as a great deal smaller, than has been maintained.

Waterton was the first to describe the anaconda and he did so
with a characteristic lack of restraint:

> The camoudi snake (as it was called in British Guiana) has been killed
> from thirty to forty feet long; though not venomous, his size renders
> him destructive to the passing animals. The Spaniards in the Oroonoque
> positively affirm that he grows to the length of seventy or eighty feet
> and that he will destroy the strongest and largest bull. His name seems
> to confirm this; there he is called 'matatoro' which means literally
> 'bull killer'. Thus he must be ranked among the deadly snakes, for it
> comes to nearly the same thing in the end whether the victim dies by
> poison from the fangs, which corrupts his blood and makes it stink
> horribly, or whether his body be crushed to mummy and swallowed
> by this hideous beast.

Books on the Amazon abound with stories of monstrous snakes of
a similar size seen, and sometimes even measured, by their authors.
In the first case one must make some allowances. The anaconda
is a thick snake with, as Bates puts it, 'a most hideous appearance,
owing to its being very broad in the middle and tapering abruptly
at both ends'. It is difficult to judge the length of a snake, especially
one of such a peculiar shape. Dyott, the American explorer, is
properly realistic when he describes an encounter with an anaconda
by moonlight. It looked, he wrote, 'every inch of forty feet, which
meant that he must have been nearer twenty'.

Every traveller to the Amazon has heard stories of gigantic
snakes anything from forty to eighty feet in length, but these
monsters have consistently eluded the naturalists. Even when authors
claim to have killed such formidable serpents, there has always been
some pressing reason why they could not bring the remains back
with them to prove their point. Thus Colonel Fawcett said that he
had shot one of sixty-two feet, which he did not regard as being
exceptional, and Algot Lange wrote that he had killed one fifty-six
feet in length and over two feet in diameter.

It was, however, left to Father de Vernazza, a nineteenth-century
missionary, to give the most extravagant account of the anaconda's
size:

> The sight alone of this monster confounds, intimidates and infuses
> respect into the heart of the boldest man. He never seeks or follows

the victims upon whom he feeds, but, so great is the force of his inspiration, that he draws in with his breath whatever quadruped or bird may pass him, within from twenty to fifty yards of distance, according to its size. That which I killed from my canoe upon the Pastaza (with five shots of a fowling piece) had two yards of thickness and fifteen yards of lengths; but the Indians have assured me that there are animals of this kind here of three or four yards diameter, and from thirty to forty long. These swallow entire hogs, stags, tigers and men, with the greatest facility.

Wallace believed in the existence of huge anacondas through reading Dr. Gardner's account, although he himself had never seen one greater than twenty feet. When Gardner, a botanist, was travelling in the province of Goias near the headwaters of the Araguaia River, his host's favourite horse was discovered to be missing from its pasture and all their efforts to find it were fruitless. At length a vacquero saw the body of an enormous bloated snake stuck in the fork of a tree. 'It was dragged out to the open country by two horses and was found to measure thirty-seven feet in length; on opening it the bones of a horse in somewhat broken condition, and the flesh in a half digested state, were found within it, the bones of the head being uninjured; from these circumstances we concluded that the boa had devoured the horse entire.' Gardner does not make it clear whether he was present when the anaconda was measured, but one must either accept or reject his narrative as a whole, without quibbling about the length of the beast, as thirty-seven feet would surely be the smallest size at which a snake could swallow a horse.

Various travellers, starting with Waterton, have recorded their astonishment at seeing a pair of antlers projecting out of a tree or over the top of a bush far higher than the tallest deer. The perpetrator of this grisly practical joke was of course the anaconda, who having swallowed the deer's body would be forced to wait for decomposition to free it from the projecting horns.

Theodore Roosevelt did much to dispel the myth of gigantic serpents by offering a reward of $5,000 to anyone who could produce the skin and vertebrae of an anaconda of over thirty-feet in length. The reward, although an incalculable fortune in the debris of the rubber boom, was never claimed. In the absence of any specimen of such modest dimensions we can safely conclude that the anaconda seldom, if ever, grows longer than thirty feet and that if this is so, accounts of monsters over twice this length must be nonsensical.*

But the best anaconda story has nothing to do with its size. Im Thurn, a nineteenth-century English naturalist and colonial administrator, had a friend living in a secluded part of British Guiana, whose cook would rise before dawn every day and strike a match on the same wooden post in the kitchen. One day the matches failed to strike and after wasting several on her usual post she was forced to light them elsewhere. As the match flared up she was terrified to see a huge anaconda curled around the post, apparently undisturbed by having its skin scraped.

*

The macabre chronicle of Amazonian horrors could not end with a more appropriate monster than the vampire bat. These creatures are repellent at the best and at their worst an insidious menace. The traveller will awake in the morning, having slept normally, and find the end of his hammock and the ground underneath it soaked with blood. On further examination he will find a small conical hole in his body, usually on one of his extremities, a toe, a finger, or the tip of the nose; this wound, which is likely still to be bleeding, will clot with unusual slowness. The entry of the vampire's tooth should be painful enough to awaken its victim and why it fails to do so is an unsolved mystery, in spite of a number of ingenious suggestions. Naturalist after naturalist has bled without waking, even when the wound was in as sensitive a part of the body as the lip or the nose.

This ability to attack without being noticed makes the vampire bat difficult to study, and it was not until Darwin discovered one bleeding a horse that its species was correctly identified. Earlier naturalists had assumed that they were being attacked by a large and hideous bat with a peculiarly sinister appearance, which was in fact quite harmless and which suffered much persecution as a result of the mistake. The real culprit was far smaller and looked comparatively benign.

There were places where life became almost unsupportable because of the vampire's raids. One blood-letting would do little

* Marston Bates in *The Land and Wildlife of South America* gives 37.5 feet as the greatest recorded length of an anaconda, but he does not disclose his source.

harm to a big mammal the size of a horse, an ox or a man, but the cumulative effect of regular attacks would debilitate and eventually destroy the strongest creature. Thus Wallace on Mexiana Island, in the mouth of the Amazon, found that hundreds of cattle had been bled to death and Spruce at São Gabriel on the Rio Negro saw one miserable soldier with eight separate wounds in his big toe. While the vampire could be a serious menace, its attention could always be avoided entirely by moving a few miles away and it could often be thwarted by elementary precautions. Both Spruce and Wallace escaped unscathed in areas infested by vampire bats through wrapping up well at night and leaving no flesh exposed. A light left on all night was a fairly efficient deterrent and one used with apparent success to keep the bats away from the horses in the cavalry barracks in Pará, but the most effective counter-measure was found by the only family in São Gabriel that was never bitten. For a time the children in the household, like everyone else in the village, suffered terribly each night, until one evening by a happy mistake their cat was allowed inside. The next morning they found that no one had been bitten but that there were several dead bats on the floor. After this, the cat was kept in every night and a vampire bat had only to alight on a hammock to be struck down at once.

There are many unpleasant ways of being woken in the Amazon Valley, but the most startling is to be deafened at dawn by a blast of sound, which it seems must have been torn from the throat of some gigantic carnivore. It starts as a reverberating growl which bursts out into a series of tremendous booms, but the creature responsible for this noise is a harmless and rather small monkey. The howler, as it is aptly named, is able to produce such volume through the extraordinary construction of the hyoid apparatus in its throat, which is nearly twenty-five times as large as that of other monkeys of its size. The howler uses its voice, with true Brazilian abandon, to herald the dawn, to give warning of its enemies, to command its clan and to mark out its territorial limits. In the last case two bands of howlers will bellow at each other from the edges of their borders until one party withdraws.

There are many species of monkey in the New World, almost all of which are represented in the Amazon Valley. They inhabited South America before the formation of the land bridge at the Isthmus of Panama and evolution in isolation has brought about several differences between them and their cousins of the Old World.

THE ANIMALS

There are no gigantic apes, no gaudy rumps to be found in South America. Instead some species have long prehensile tails, which serve them as a fifth limb and which are unique to the species of the New World. The formation of their teeth and the structure of their nostrils also differ from those of other monkeys.

One must mention, as being among the most interesting monkeys of the Amazon Valley, the pygmy marmoset, an enchanting creature, which, without counting its tail, is only three to four inches in length, the red uakari, which blushes a vivid scarlet when disturbed, the acrobatic spider monkey and the brilliant capuchin. At the University of Chicago a hungry capuchin was tethered out of reach of a banana; a rat with a piece of string attached to it was then placed in the same cage. The capuchin caught the rat, threw it over the banana and, having kept hold of the string, reeled in rat and banana together. When the experiment was repeated without any string, the capuchin achieved the same result by holding the rat's tail.*

As we have seen, the size of the Amazonian monkey is comparatively small, but de Castlenau, the meticulous French scientist, once thought that he had found an exception to this rule. 'When I was descending the Amazon', he wrote, 'I saw near Fonteboa a black Coata of enormous dimensions. He belonged to an Indian woman, to whom I offered a large price for the curious beast, but she received me with a burst of laughter. "Your efforts are useless," said an Indian who was in the cabin, "that is her husband." '

Lieutenant Herndon, when recalling this incident, comments in his uninhibited Confederate way, 'These Coatas are a large, black, pot-bellied monkey. They average about two and a half feet in height, have a few thin hairs on the top of their head, and look very like an old negro.'

*

No traveller in the Amazon Valley can avoid meeting the Saüba or Parasol Ant, to the naturalist a delightful and subtle insect but to the cultivator an unrivalled menace. One sees first a long thin line of vegetation meandering along the ground, but on closer examination one recognizes that each piece of leaf is carried by an ant a fraction

* The experiments took place in Dr. Heinrich Klüver's laboratory and are described in Dr. Bates's *The Land and Wildlife of South America*, one of the best modern books on the subject.

its size. So vast are the numbers of the Saüba, and so great their persistence, that they can strip an entire plantation of its foliage in the course of a single night. They are a blight to agriculture and the despair of every farmer. After the collapse of the rubber boom, their relish for young trees was one of the greatest obstacles to establishing plantations on the Malaysian pattern.

Anyone following a line of Saüba will eventually arrive at their dwelling place, a mound sometimes as large as forty yards in circumference and four or five feet in height. But this impressive erection is only an outcrop of a vast and intricate maze beneath the earth's surface. In the Botanical Gardens at Pará Bates saw a French gardener attempting to exterminate what he thought to be a small colony of Saüba. With some ingenuity he used bellows to blow sulphur fumes down their holes. After a time the smoke started to re-emerge from other entrances and, to Bates's astonishment, he saw it rising from the earth out of holes as much as seventy yards away. The walls of a reservoir near Pará were once burst by the ramifications of this ant's tunnelling and Bates quotes the Reverend Hamlet Clarke as saying that the Saüba of Rio de Janeiro excavated a tunnel underneath the bed of the Parahyba River at a point where it is as broad as the Thames at London Bridge.

Perhaps the most extraordinary, and for a long time the most mysterious, habit of the Saüba is precisely what it does with the tons of foliage that it takes back, piecemeal, to its nest. The first theory, logically enough, was that the ants ate the leaves, but Bates, after examining their nests, declared that they used it as thatching for the entrances to their domes. For once in his studies of insect life Bates was wrong and their real purpose is far more remarkable than either of these explanations. The ants, the greatest scourge of cultivation, are planters themselves, rogue farmers who steal men's harvests to grow their own. The leaves are used as compost on which the ants grow the fungi that act as their food. Each variety of Saüba ant has its own duties, as Professor Cutright tells us:

> Even though the chamber has been opened to the light of day the medium-sized workers continue their job of bringing in the leaves. That apparently is their sole function, for as soon as they reach the underground rooms the leaves are immediately attacked by the small workers or minims. They take complete charge of the leaf material now and at once chew it to bits and shape it into small pellets. These in turn are placed at advantageous points in the crevices of the fungus

where they may best serve to fertilize the mycelium. It is the role, too, of these tiniest workers to feed the larvae. They do this by regurgitation. They may also feed some of the adult workers which are too busy to do their own eating. And it is their task to carry away the leafy material after it has served its purpose as a compost.

It has been observed that the real owners of the Amazon Valley are its ants, and if this is so the masters among the ants must certainly be the Ecitons, the Foraging or Soldier ants. When their formidable armies start to march, every living creature must remove itself from their path. There is no danger to any mammal, unless it is totally crippled, but the ecitons will attack anything that they encounter, regardless of its size, and naturalists attempting to study their habits have described their aggressive tactics from personal experience.

The ants will climb up an intruder with surprising speed, fasten their powerful jaws in his flesh, then, using this grip as a fulcrum, they will double their bodies round and sting him with their tails. They are merciless to other insects, the spiders, caterpillars, maggots cockroaches, scorpions, lesser ants and any larvae, all form part of their diet. They will not hesitate to plunder the nests of the most formidable wasps and they will overwhelm colonies of vicious fire ants.

Bates made the first classification of this insect (he found ten different species, eight of them new to science, differing amazingly in their habits). Some, quite blind, would carry out their depredations through long tunnels just beneath the surface of the earth. Others would climb into the forest canopy. Their only common characteristics were their utter greed and immaculate organization, as is shown by this description of a raid on the home of another kind of ant, the large but harmless Formicae.

The ecitons

were eagerly occupied, on the face of an inclined bank of light earth, in excavating mines, whence, from a depth of eight or ten inches they were extracting the bodies of a bulky species of ant, of the genus Formica. It was curious to watch them crowding round the orifices of the mines, some assisting their comrades to lift out the bodies of the Formicae and others tearing them to pieces on account of their weight being too great for a single Eciton; a number of carriers seizing each a fragment and carrying it off down the slope. On digging into the earth with a small trowel near the entrances of the mines, I found the nests of the Formicae with grubs and cocoons, which the Ecitons were thus invading, at a depth of about eight inches from the surface. The eager free-booters rushed in as fast as I excavated, seized the ants in my fingers as I picked them out, so that I had some difficulty in rescuing a few entire for specimens. In digging the numerous mines to get at their prey, the little Ecitons seemed to be divided into parties, one set excavating and another set carrying away the grains of earth. When the shafts became rather deep, the mining parties had to climb up the sides each time they wished to cast out a pellet of earth; but their work was lightened for them by comrades, who stationed themselves at the mouth of the shaft, and relieved them of their burdens, carrying the particles, with an appearance of foresight which quite staggered me, a sufficient distance from the edge of the hole to prevent them from rolling in again.

Bates on his insects is eminently quotable and one can ask for no better account of the termites than that given in his great book. The termitariums are a common sight in South America; often a plain will be pock-marked with their castles as far as the eye can see, the smallest and most fragile-looking being as hard as stone. This ubiquitous pest is similar to the ant only in some of its habits and physical characteristics, for it belongs to a different family of insects and is not even subject to metamorphosis. But in order and adaptation to their needs the two species are alike.

The wonderful part in the history of the Termites is, that not only is there a rigid division of labour but nature has given to each class a structure of body adapting it to the kind of labour it has to perform. The males and females form a class apart; they do no kind of work, but in the course of growth acquire wings to enable them to issue forth and disseminate their kind. The workers and soldiers are wingless and differ solely in the shape and armature of the head. This member in the labourers is smooth and rounded, the mouth being adapted for the working of the materials in the building of the hive; in the soldiers the head is of very large size, and is provided in almost every kind with special organs of offence and defence in the form of horny processes resembling pikes, tridents, and so forth. Some species do not possess these extraordinary projections, but have in compensation greatly lengthened jaws, which are shaped in some kinds as sickles, in others as sabres and saws.

These ready-made soldiers had the courage to match their armoury. When Bates broke into one of the termites' archways, at first there were only workers to be seen, scurrying for safety, but then the soldiers came out to protect their retreat and exhibited an absolute lack of fear, thrusting their grotesque weapons up towards the intruder. When one rank is destroyed it is replaced with another, and when a soldier bites his jaws will never let go, even if his body is torn into pieces. The timidity of the worker and the suicidal fury of the soldier are both essential to the colony's survival, for the workers' role is to tend the larvae, and the soldiers, who have no other function, must act both as guards and, if necessary, as offerings for the general good. It seems amazing that creatures should have evolved with such advanced and specialized characteristics, simply in order to be sacrificed when their more important fellows are in danger.

The same profligacy continues when the winged termites, the prospective monarchs of new colonies, leave their homes. Bates describes them, attracted by the light, swarming indoors and even extinguishing lamps by their numbers; but the next day their natural enemies will have taken their toll and it will be hard to find a single one. It is poignant that so much devotion, self-sacrifice and unrewarded labour should go towards producing thousands of winged termites, all but a handful of which will be destroyed within twenty-four hours of their departure.

Insects grow to staggering sizes in the Amazon. Spruce found a centipede eleven inches long and one inch thick; Brown and Lidstone caught a spider which covered a space of ten inches by eight inches with a body two and a half inches by one inch. *Titanus giganteus*, the greatest beetle in the world, grows as long as six inches; the beautiful morpho butterfly has a wingspread of up to at least seven and a half inches and there are moths larger even than this. But more remarkable than the insects' size is their abundance. Bates found, within an hour's walk of Pará—an area of about thirty square miles—over 700 species of butterfly; there are sixty-six species in Great Britain and 390 in the whole of Europe. Some kinds of South American butterfly are amazingly numerous. Bates and Spruce observed their migrations at about the same time when, for two days, they swept in an uninterrupted flow over the river.

*

Even the conquistadores of Orellana, the hardiest of men, were defeated on occasions by the mosquitoes, and we have seen the same happen to every traveller since his voyage of discovery. Colonel Rondon, after giving Theodore Roosevelt a blood-curdling description of the habits of piranha, alligators and anacondas, added the warning that the inconvenience and suffering caused by these pests were as nothing compared to the work of the insects. Indeed, reading accounts of their numbers and virulence, one is forced to wonder why anyone should ever go to this river of misery, let alone live there. The answer is that there are many parts uninfested by any irritating insects, and more where they are present in perfectly bearable numbers. The traveller builds up a tolerance towards their bites and develops the reflex action of a sharp slap towards the bitten part of his body, without interrupting whatever he is doing at the time. But in the most pest-ridden parts of the river, where conditions are truly murderous and neither acclimatization nor nets give any noticeable relief, the only solution is to surrender and move elsewhere.

The worst insects are sometimes harmless enough in isolation and only made unbearable by their great numbers. The tick's attentions are scarcely painful, but anyone who has walked through the grass where they live will find his legs covered with their repellent bodies, puffed up with his own blood, and unless they are most carefully removed they will leave sores. The motúca fly also causes little pain with its punctures, but it opens up such gashes in the flesh that the blood runs out in rivulets. The Pium fly is more serious and Bates describes its distressing habit of relieving the mosquito at sunrise with the utmost punctuality. He continues:

> In places where it is abundant it accompanies canoes in such dense swarms as to resemble thin clouds of smoke. . . . They alight imperceptibly and squatting close, fall at once to work, stretching forward their long front legs, which are in constant motion and seem to act as feelers, and then applying their short broad snouts to the skin. Their abdomens soon become distended and red with blood, and then, their thirst satisfied, they slowly move off, so stupefied with their potations that they can scarcely fly. I once travelled with a middle-aged Portuguese, who was laid up for three weeks from the attacks of the Pium; his legs being swelled to an enormous size, and the punctures aggravated into spreading sores.

There are the mosquitoes, always present and often deadly, although it was to be many years before it was recognized how dangerous they could be. There are jiggers, bêtes rouges, red wasps, hornets, fire ants and other, less common pests, like the strange insects which Bates saw only once, but whose bites, through his thick clothes, made him cry aloud in pain.

There are birds of almost every kind, some like the egrets, the scarlet ibises, the trogons, the humming-birds and the kingfishers, bewildering in their beauty, others sporting the grotesque beaks of the toucans, the cocks of the rock, the macaws and the roseate spoonbills. Parrots of every size thrive in the forests, from the majestic macaw to fluttering clouds of parakeets, smaller than the great morpho butterflies of the Amazon.

There are birds with exotic names like cotinga, tanager, pava and tinamous, and others with strange nesting habits like the oven bird which builds its oven-shaped nests in the forks of trees, or the cacique which hangs its nests downwards from their branches. There are vultures, eagles, jabiru cranes in great colonies and a number of waterfowl. The plains between the Beni and Mamoré are frequented by the Rhea or South American ostrich and the headwaters of the Andean tributaries by the king condor.

One of the least known, and certainly the most extraordinary, of all the Amazon's birds is the hoatzin, a bird which, although found in the middle of a continent, has difficulty in either flying or walking. The hoatzin's attempts at flight are so futile that it often fails to reach a tree as little as fifty feet away, slumps on to the ground and has to rest before it can raise itself once more into the air. On the ground they trip over their own feet in a dismal fashion, but they are at home in trees and in the water. The young are born with curved claws projecting from the joints of their wing, with the assistance of which they can clamber about freely, like lumberjacks with pitons. The hoatzins invariably nest in trees on the banks of rivers and, when there is any danger, a saving instinct impels the young to hurl themselves into the water beneath. They dive without hesitation or appearance of fear and once in the river, they use their wings to swim long distances underwater at an astonishing speed.

In the absence of any other means of self-protection it is surprising that so defenceless a creature has survived in the midst of so many predators. Bates wondered if the hoatzin's continued existence might owe something to an unfortunate characteristic of this ugly, raucous and fascinating bird. The hoatzin is sometimes called the stinkbird, as a just tribute to its foul and penetrating odour, and he speculated that if its smell was as repulsive to animals as it was to human beings, its natural enemies might often be content to seek a less distasteful meal.

PART III

BLACK GOLD

Chapter Nine

THE RUBBER BOOM 1870-1911

IN ITS time the Amazon had been many things to many men, a
cruel wilderness and then an executioner to Orellana, a battleground for lost souls to the early missionaries, a slave-bearing
area for the bandeirantes to raid, a mirage to the seekers of El
Dorado, a paradise to the naturalists, a magnet to explorers and a
graveyard to many.

Now, as the last quarter of the nineteenth century began, it was
to become important and soon vital to the outside world; for nearly
forty years it was to be prosperous and indispensable, flamboyant
and arrogant, before sinking back into an even greater poverty than
before. For two and a half centuries now men had dreamed of the
untapped treasures of the Amazon, of gold, jewels and lost cities.
But when their dreams were realized the wealth came flowing, not
in the form of precious gems, but as latex from the flesh of the tree
called the *Hevea brasiliensis.*

There was nothing new about rubber except its value. The
Indians of the New World had always known its properties.
Columbus found them in Haiti playing with rubber balls, a pastime
that they were soon forced to change for others more productive
but not so pleasant. In Mexico Cortes's men used the latex to water-
proof their garments. Father Fritz's Omaguas made pouches, bags,
syringes and even crude shoes from it. But the scientific world did
not become interested until Charles Marie de la Condamine's
return from the Amazon in 1744, and it was not until far later, in
1823, when Macintosh took out his patent for the manufacture of
rubber-proofed fabrics, that its commercial development began.

Even then the material had many drawbacks, the greatest being

F
147

its tendency to become soft and sticky in hot weather and hard and brittle in cold. In 1839 this handicap was overcome by Charles Goodyear's discovery that if rubber were mixed with sulphur and heated it would become stronger, more elastic and more resistant to heat and cold.

With this discovery of vulcanization, rubber was firmly established. Brazil, by far the largest producer, made only 388 tons in 1840, the year following Goodyear's breakthrough. By 1860 this figure had swollen to 2,673 tons and it continued to grow, as new industrial developments created demand for rubber in many different processes. But the momentous day for the industry came as late as 1888 when a patent was taken out by a Scottish veterinary surgeon called John Boyd Dunlop for 'A hollow tyre or tube made of India-rubber and cloth, or other suitable materials, said tube or tyre to contain air under pressure or otherwise and to be attached to the wheel or wheels in such method as may be found most suitable.'

The bicycle and then the car precipitated what had been a profitable but unexciting industry into a wild commodity boom.

*

Rubber existed elsewhere, in Central and South America, Northeast Brazil, South-east Asia, Africa, Madagascar, Mexico and Russia. It could be derived from several trees, vines, shrubs and even herbs. But the quality, the yield and the abundance of the *Hevea brasiliensis* were unique and it grew only in the Amazon Valley.

The mechanics of collecting rubber were simple enough. The Patrão (or proprietor) would borrow money from a bank or merchant, and with it engage labour, and set up an establishment on some river. Land titles were easy to come by, if ill-defined, and there were often fights over a promising group of trees. The owner would send in matteiros, expert and highly paid labourers whose task it was to find the trees and cut paths connecting them. A few shacks would be set up on the river bank, for the rubber, stores and administration. Then the rubber could be gathered. The owner generally installed a manager at considerable cost and sometimes never visited his own estate.

Labour was the industry's most urgent problem. The Indians had no desire for money and would often run away or fight if they were enslaved, and the population of the Amazon Valley was in any case too small to exploit the rubber trees. Imported labourers from Europe sickened and died and Chinese coolies were politically unacceptable. The work was hard and unhealthy, and payment was by results.

The seringuero, as the gatherer was called, started his day at 4 a.m. with two rounds of his estrada. He would set off carrying a gun, machete and a crude tapping hatchet known as a machadinho. There would be anything between fifty and two hundred trees to visit, depending on where the estate was. For much of the year the ground would be waterlogged, the streams in flood and the paths connecting the trees overgrown, and always insects abounded. The seringuero would cut an incision in each tree, tie a cup underneath and go on to the next.

After half an hour's rest he had to repeat his round, this time collecting the latex from the trees. The liquid rubber would then be carried into a small conical hut with a hole in its roof. If the seringuero was married his wife would have gathered nuts from the Urucuri tree to burn in the hut. When the fire reached the right heat, an open cone was put over it to concentrate the smoke. A pole would be revolved where the smoke was thickest and a little latex poured on to it until a base of coagulated rubber had formed. The fire was kept up and the pole revolved for the two or three hours that the smoking would take. By the end, the atmosphere in the hut would be thick with smoke and the carbonic acid gas exuded by the nuts, but there would be a broad 'biscuit' of rubber round the pole. The next day the new latex would be added to it.

The seringuero had to build his hut in his own time. This miserable shack would normally have mud floors and would some-times even be flooded in the rainy season. No effort would be made by his patrão to encourage him in any hygienic habits. His sewage would too often be thrown on the river bank close to where he washed and drew his water. In the rainy season it was impossible to tap rubber and he would moulder in his hut, eking out his life on the rotten food supplied at grotesque expense by his master.

Malnutrition, carbonic acid gas and disease combined to make his life a short one, and it was never easy for him to leave. His journey from his old home, his expenses en route, all his equipment, gun, tapping materials, food and clothes were provided by his patrão and debited to his account. As seringueros were generally illiterate and their employers seldom over-scrupulous, they started their working lives something like £100 in debt. They could discharge this debt only by bringing in rubber and receiving in return fifty per cent of its value. The growing of food was discouraged and in any case the seringuero had little time for anything outside his estrada. All the necessities of life had to be bought from the estate store. From this fact and from the seringuero's original indebtedness there sprang an iniquitous system designed to deprive the labourer of his share of the profits and to keep him in a condition of slavery.

*

The merchants in Manaos, Pará or Iquitos, where the cost of living varied between two and four times those of London, Paris and New York, would sell goods to the aviadores at large profits, who in their turn would ship them up to the rubber districts and sell them again at even larger profits to the managers of the estates. The manager, when selling to the seringuero, would take a final profit of anything from 50 to 200 per cent, leaving the wretch with no choice except to buy what he needed to keep himself alive at many times its true value. In the case of the distant estates food was usually rotten and sometimes swarming with maggots by the time it reached the workers. But they had no choice. They bought it at the manager's price or starved. The inflated prices that he had to pay and a little legerdemain with the books were usually enough to keep the seringuero in debt. But when rubber prices were high there was often something left over for him and an annual migration of labourers came in from the poor eastern states for the rubber season.

In Brazil there was no legal obligation on the seringuero to remain, even if in debt, although he could be sued in a civil court for his debts if he ran away. But the law has never been much respected in the Amazon Valley and most managers made sure that their labour force stayed where they were. In Peru and Bolivia any fugitive could be arrested and made to return to his master until he had liquidated his debt. He could alternatively be sold to another master for the amount of his debt or for an agreed proportion of it. The purchaser's power over him would then become as complete as the seller's had been and his condition was slavery in everything except name. The state of the indebted seringuero was known as peonage and the means used to keep him in debt as the Truck System.

In normal circumstances and in a more advanced part of the

world, it would have been difficult to find labour willing to work in such conditions. But Brazil was fortunate in being able to draw on the parched wildernesses of the north-east, in particular on the cattle state of Ceara. Every few years there is a *secca* or drought in Ceara so severe that all animals die, and the human beings who wish to survive have to move. Even now they come trekking down, penniless, burnt and emaciated, to the labour markets of São Paulo. During the rubber boom agents would circulate with stories of the wonderful money waiting to be made in Amazonas; of how they could go there for one season and come home to Ceara and live like lords for the rest of their lives. Even if they did not believe the stories anything was better than Ceara in a *secca*. They came to the Amazon in shiploads, thousands of tough, desperate men, inured to hardship and squalor.

*

Production was now booming, and each decade between 1880 and 1910 Brazilian output rose by 10,000 tons. In 1911 alone it increased by another 6,000 tons to a record figure of 44,296 tons. Prices soared under an insatiable demand from the new industries of America and Europe. Until the early years of the twentieth century the price per pound stayed around 3/- to 4/-, on which the producers thrived. By 1910 it had risen to a peak of 12/9 and fortunes had been made.

One effect of the boom was to give impetus to the settlement of the Amazon Valley; another was to strike its Indians the most destructive blow that they had received since the expulsion of the Jesuits. Indeed the depredations of the early Portuguese slavers were half-hearted and piecemeal compared to those of the rubber collectors, and their worst atrocities insignificant when judged by the terrible standards of the Putumayo.

As the boom continued all the rich stands in the accessible parts of the Valley became occupied and new arrivals had to fight their way up unknown rivers to find rubber, but the lure of 'black gold' was strong enough to make them disregard any danger. Thousands of small expeditions set out in canoes, stopped by a promising stand and began their work. Soon another wave of seringueros would surge past them into the unknown headwaters of their river. As there are estimated to be over 100 million rubber trees in the Amazon Valley, there was always a good stand available for the next arrival.

The rubber gatherers were hard men, as ruthless in their search for wealth as the conquistadores had been before them. The European seringuero was in debt to his patrão, who in turn owed money to his suppliers. None of them were too scrupulous in their dealings with the Indians, who involuntarily formed the last link in a chain of exploitation. Entire tribes were rounded up and forced to work on rubber plantations, often in horrifying conditions. Many Indians resisted slavery and, in retaliation for raids on their villages, killed their oppressors. In the golden years of the rubber boom (1890–1911) small wars erupted throughout the Amazon Valley. Massacres and atrocities were committed by both sides, but, in almost every case, it was the white man's attempt to enslave the Indians which started the fighting.

The white man's superior weapons won most of these skirmishes. Thus the Indian tribes were pushed away from the main rivers, where they had always lived, and forced to take refuge in the heart of the forest. It was impossible for a large village to support itself off such poor country and as a result their tribes fragmented and many sub-tribes were formed, generally based on a one to five family unit.

It was the same process which had started with the conquest, had been temporarily stemmed by the Jesuits, and had continued ever since. It was a stronger race chipping away at the land, the liberty and even the existence of a weaker. But now it was intensified by greed for rubber. War, murder, slavery and dispersion exterminated more than a score of Indian tribes in these twenty abandoned years.

The boom transformed Manaos from an unimportant group of shacks in one of the poorest parts of a poor country into a boomtown which put the Klondyke and the Rand to shame. The Rubber Barons, unlike the Coffee Kings and other commodity tycoons thrown up by Brazil, lived in the cities and not on their estates. Thus a small town like Manaos for the first time saw an extraordinary and sudden concentration of wealth.

Loading and unloading was difficult in the harbour. To overcome this an English firm was hired to build a floating dock, then the largest in the world and capable of dealing with a sixty foot rise and fall in the level of the Rio Negro. Trams were operating in Manaos before any city in South America and indeed before Manchester or Boston. There is no stone in that part of the Amazon and, as the streets of hard packed mud did not look sufficiently elegant, ships were chartered to sail over to France and come back loaded to the Plimsoll line with cobblestones.

Prices inside the city became ridiculous, one American visitor estimating that the cost of living was three to four times that of New York, but the rubber barons were undeterred by cost. Their palaces were built of Italian marble, furnished with the finest pieces from England and France, and festooned with crystal chandeliers. Their linen came from Ireland and unused grand pianos littered their salons. At their parties champagne at $50 a bottle flowed like latex off a virgin tree. No extravagance, however absurd, deterred them. If one rubber baron bought a vast yacht, another would install a tame lion in his villa, and a third would water his horse on champagne.

Nor were the public works neglected. The massive Customs House was prefabricated in England, a model of that in Delhi, shipped out and reassembled on the spot. Telephones and telegraphs and electricity were installed and a magnificent Palace of Justice was built. Gardens were laid out and filled with ornate fountains, crammed with gilded cherubs. Such was the wealth of the city that even a sewage system was installed.

Every luxury was on sale; jewellery was imported in bulk from Minas Gerais and diamonds were lavished on the armies of harlots which came stampeding in from every bordello in Europe. At one stage vice in Manaos had reached a point when the police estimated that two out of every three houses were brothels.

But the crowning glory of Manaos in ambition and beauty was its opera house, built from imported materials in 1896. It still rears its extraordinary dome above the city. Even for the Manaos of today it is incongruous and out of scale, dwarfing the modern buildings nearer the river bank. In the days of the rubber boom its presence must have been as overwhelming as that of a great Gothic cathedral towering over some English market town.

For the opening night the most famous performers in Europe were engaged at vast fees to brave yellow fever, beri-beri and malaria, and to give up all other engagements for several months in order to make a few appearances at the Theatro de Amazonas. Tradition says that Caruso sang in this fantastic building and that Bernhardt starred there, but it is unsupported by the opera house's records. Pavlova was invited, but it is thought she never came. And amid its baroque splendour sat flamboyant, if slightly raffish, audiences, perspiring in their unaccustomed jewels and white ties.

The house itself was a worthy setting for the finest artist, but the operas cannot have run for very long. The theatre holds nearly 2,000 while the population of Manaos at the turn of the century cannot have been more than 40,000, not many of whom had the necessary wealth and perception to become patrons of the arts.

The rubber barons seemed to have every reason for their prodigality. No other kind of rubber could challenge the supremacy of the *Hevea brasiliensis*, in quality, in volume or in cost. Demand was soaring and the technology of the time was incapable of producing synthetic rubber at any price. Nor was there any chance of demand falling off, with the motor car industry growing at such a rate.

While there seemed no limit to demand for rubber its supply appeared in practice to have a ceiling. Although there are estimated to be 100 million rubber trees in the Amazon Valley, only a minute fraction of which have ever been tapped, all the easily accessible trees were already being worked and the more remote seringas could be exploited only at a greater cost and by importing more labour. In these circumstances the barons started in 1909 and 1910 to withold rubber from a market shrilly demanding it, allowing the American and European buyers to fight among themselves for an inadequate supply. It seemed that, even if production in the Amazon Valley rose only slowly, the rubber barons' profits must continue to soar.

Nothing seemed impossible. Rubber was now representing nearly half the value of all Brazil's exports. Surely a few more years would see it up to three-quarters, and all this was being done by an area holding only one per cent of the country's population. Perhaps the capital would have to be moved up to Manaos and the country would be ruled by a plutocracy of rubber barons. El Dorado had been found.

*

At this very moment, that of their greatest wealth and arrogance, the ruin of the rubber barons was already certain. As early as 1872 Sir Clements Markham, the great South American historian and geographer, decided that attempts should be made to cultivate rubber in the East. The early results were not very successful. In 1873 a Mr. Farris delivered 2,000 *Hevea* seedlings, only a dozen

of which germinated, an inadequate supply with which to start a
new industry. Two more expeditions were sent out under Cross
and Wickham. Cross brought back to Kew Gardens 134 *Castilloa*
seedlings from Panama and 1,000 *Hevea* and 42 *Ceara* from Brazil,
but Wickham had the greater success.

It was he who had originally suggested the idea to Sir Joseph
Hooker, the head of Kew Gardens, and Hooker had interested
Markham. But by 1876 Wickham had almost abandoned the plan
and was planting experimentally on the Tapajós plateau near
Santarem, to the derision of the local rubber men. As one seringuero
said later, 'If God had intended rubber trees to grow in rows he
would have made them like that.' Then Wickham heard that an
English ship, the *Amazonas*, which he had seen passing upstream,
was now stranded in Manaos without a cargo. He cabled at once,
chartering it for the Indian Government, and at the same time
hired every Indian he could find to scour the forest for *Hevea* seeds.
By the time that the *Amazonas* had returned, Wickham had collected
70,000 seeds of the white *Hevea*, second in quality only to those of
the black. Lovingly packed in banana skins, the most valuable cargo
ever to leave the Amazon steamed down to Pará.

The popular story of what happened there is well known. By a
combination of bribery and smuggling, ending in a lavish banquet
on board, Wickham is said to have persuaded the Customs Officers
to allow his 'delicate specimens' to pass uninspected, it being then
illegal to export live rubber plants. This entirely credible story was
allowed to go uncontradicted until June 7, 1939, when the
Commercial Museum at Belém (as Pará is now called) issued a
statement maintaining that at the time of Wickham's expedition
there was no law forbidding the export of rubber seeds from Pará.

There grew up little by little a legend in which Sir Henry A. Wickham
was pictured as a common adventurer who audaciously and surreptitiously stole seeds of the rubber tree, carrying them hidden in a fantasy
ship after having lessened the zeal of the Customs of Belém by a
banquet which he gave on board at the time of sailing. In as much as
there was no illegality in this—and the best proof of this is the fact
that there were shipped in this same period many hundreds of young
stalks of Hevea that there were no means of hiding when they were
carried on board. . . . It was in relatively recent times that the exporta-
tion of the Hevea seeds was prohibited in the State of Pará, and years
afterwards in the State of Amazonas, a measure totally useless since

none was adopted either in the State of Mato Grosso or in Bolivia
where the richest rubber stands are found.

Wickham's own account of the episode does not help. He refers
to 'bluffing' the officials in Pará but goes into no details. It seems
likely that there is some truth in both stories. Rubber seeds do not
keep their life for long, except when planted under expert care. The
one thing Wickham could not afford was delay and as it was, only
some 2,000 of his 70,000 seeds survived. The officials might well
have to be squared to allow a quick clearance to the most innocuous
cargo.* There is on the other hand no reason to doubt the official
version, but Wickham may have declared his seeds as 'botanical
specimens' to avoid inspection for mature rubber, on which there
was an export duty of twenty per cent.

An interesting point about the story is that none of those involved
can have had any real idea of the value of the *Amazonas*'s cargo.
Wickham and Markham no doubt thought of it in the same terms
as Markham's early coup when, with Spruce, he removed cinchona
seeds from Peru. It would be at least another twenty years before
the shrewdest observer could forecast that rubber was to become
one of the world's great industries.

There have been other stories of the guile of British seed collectors,
one of whom was said to have arrived in Pará announcing to the
Governor that he had come on behalf of Queen Victoria to add to
her collection of orchids. All the local botanists busied themselves
gathering specimens while he appeared to pass his time in idleness.
At last his ship left loaded down with the rarest plants, but when
the next tide brought them floating back sodden and wilted past the
town, they realized that they had been tricked and that he had been
quietly amassing rubber seeds the whole time.

Two thousand of Wickham's *Heveas* germinated in the orchid
houses of Kew and were duly sent out to the East, mostly to Ceylon
and Malaya. Experiments made in the '80s and early '90s led to the
predictable conclusion that the *Hevea* was the most suitable kind
of tree for plantations. But even by 1900 only 5,000 acres had been
planted. It was, above everything else, the boom in prices that drew

---

* The 1968 scientific expedition to the Mato Grosso, organized by the Royal
Geographical Society and the Central Brazil Foundation, had to wait for seven
months for clearance of its instruments by these notorious Customs officers,
who finally released them only on the insistence of the Federal Government.

capital into the plantation industry and thus it was also the greed
of the rubber barons that hastened their ruin.

By 1905 the planted acreage had increased to 150,000, by 1910
to 1,000,000 and by 1911 to 1,500,000. Since a rubber tree should
not be tapped until it is about six years old, the production of
plantation rubber inevitably lagged behind the planting programme.
As late as 1906, thirty years after Wickham had removed the seeds,
world-wide plantation production was only 510 tons, just over a
third of what Brazil had produced in 1830 and less than one per
cent of world production. Considering their distrust of any innova-
tion it is no wonder that the rubber barons were so confident. Even
in 1910, when plantation output had risen to 8,200 tons, there
was no cause for alarm, but two years later it had risen to 28,518,
and after another two years, in 1914, to 71,380, exceeding the
production of wild rubber for the first time.

The effect of this new source was first to bring supply and
demand back into equilibrium and later to produce a state of over-
supply. Prices slumped from the 12/9 per pound reached in 1910
to averages of 5/3 in 1911, 4/9½ in 1912, 3/4 in 1913 and 2/7 in 1914.
The industry was transformed from a monopolist's paradise into a
battleground for survival. There were still many experts in the New
World and the Old who thought that the Amazon Industry could
continue to expand, and some who forecast that a period of low
prices would see, not its death, but that of the Plantation industry.
They pointed in particular to the superior quality and price of Fine
Hard Pará from the black *Hevea*, they contrasted the heavy capital
costs, inevitable delays and unavoidable overheads involved in
planting, with the unlimited supply of virgin trees in the Amazon
Valley ready for immediate tapping.

The hard facts of economic life pointed the other way. In the
golden years geographical and botanical inconveniences had been
unimportant, as had gross inefficiency and destructive greed. But
when the great slump came the Amazon Industry was in no condition
to meet it.

The very truck system, designed to mulct the seringueros of their
share of the profits, ended by contributing to their masters' ruin.
When prices were high the system worked to the employers'
advantage. It was true that the merchant in Manaos or Pará made
an unnecessarily high profit, and the owner of the boat that brought
the goods up-river an even higher one, but the cream was taken off

by the owner of the estate, who would at the same time be buying rubber from his workers at half its price and paying for it in goods for which he charged them many times what he had paid himself.

The break in this circle of extortion came when the price of rubber fell and the seringuero's debts became swollen to an impossible extent. A stage was reached as early as 1913 when the seringuero's food alone cost more than he could hope to repay by his deliveries of rubber. When the owner now bought goods he was paying over twice their value without having any chance of recovering the seringuero's debt. His paper profits still looked as good as ever but he was falling into bankruptcy himself. The ripple of insolvency would spread out to engulf traders, merchants and bankers in their turn.

The truck system alone was not enough to bring the Industry down. It simply ensured that a large part of the producer's costs remained high when they should have been reduced. Compared to the new plantations of the East, the Amazon Industry was riddled with weaknesses, some unavoidable, some easily corrected but never, as it happened, put right.

The first and greatest difference was that between growing trees in plantations and tapping wild trees. In spite of the heavy capital costs of clearing, planting and finance the plantation system was greatly superior. Under scientific supervision the plantation tree grew faster and yielded more; after five years it would be the size of a twenty-year-old Amazon tree. Experimental breeding, both direct breeding from known high yielders and the grafting of high yielding clonals on to young trees, led to increasing returns per acre, a process which has continued in a most impressive manner ever since. With the labour force concentrated on the plantation, proper management and supervision were possible. Tapping was a science in the East, butchery on the Amazon. Plantation rubber was coagulated chemically and in bulk, but in the Amazon the seringuero wasted much of his time preparing the biscuit over his fire, and through his carelessness and lack of skill, many impurities would be added to the rubber and the latex of different species be mixed. The plantation coolie could move easily down his line of trees, while the seringuero had to force his way through the jungle. One would spend most of his day in working on his trees, the other in getting from one tree to the next.

The East too was fortunate in having a cheap and almost limitless pool of labour. The Amazon labourer had to be imported and to feed him cost far more than the coolie's wage. Transport to the many ports of the Dutch East Indies and Malaya was cheap, but the freight rates on the Amazon were inflated by over-manning and dear fuel. Malayan rubber had to pay a tax of 2½ per cent on leaving the country, Brazilian rubber about 20 per cent and also a 2½ per cent commission on sale as well as the heavy costs of grading and storage.

The result of these contrasts was that in 1913 rubber on the Amazon cost 2/4·3 per pound to produce and export, compared to 1/10 for plantation rubber. The difference was soon to be far greater. Most of the plantations were new and yielding less than they would when mature. The planters could see their costs coming down to 1/3 in a few years time. In a real slump they were more flexible, being able to trim their labour forces and fall back on selective tapping of their best trees. A few Brazilians in desperation tried to plant, but without success. For some reason the *Hevea* can be cultivated far more effectively in the East than in its homeland. Saüba ants stripped the young trees; the survivors grew slowly and many developed leaf mould. The capital, knowledge and perseverance to fight an uphill battle were all absent. As prices fell, year by year, the rout of the Amazon Industry became complete.

Its utter ruin can be appreciated from a few statistics. In 1910 the output of wild rubber was 62,000 tons and that of plantation rubber 8,000 tons or about one eighth of that figure. In 1920, only ten years later, the position had been precisely reversed, the output of plantation, at 360,000 tons, being eight times that of wild rubber. By 1928 wild rubber was outnumbered by twenty times. Now it is wholly insignificant. In 1892 Brazil accounted for 61 per cent of the world's trade in rubber, and in 1910 rubber represented nearly half of the total value of her exports. Now she cannot even produce enough for her own requirements.

The electric lights went out in Manaos. The opera house was silent and the jewels which had filled it were gone. The whores trooped back to their own countries. The champagne ceased to flow, and fewer ships called. Vampire bats circled the chandeliers of the broken palaces and spiders scurried across their floors. In the forest seringueros starved when their masters were ruined. El Dorado receded again into the jungle mist.

Chapter Ten

THE MADEIRA-MAMORÉ RAILWAY
1873–1912

MANY OF the richest rubber trees in the Amazon Valley stood in Bolivia, above the rapids of the Madeira and Mamoré rivers. But, even at the height of the rubber boom, the dangers and expense of transport limited their commercial value.

There were two trade routes. In the first case the rubber would be ferried upstream, transferred on to mule-back (and a mule in this country could carry no more than 150 lb.), taken 16,000 feet up into the Andes and 16,000 feet down again to the Pacific, where the surviving 'biscuits' could be loaded on board a ship. But this was still the beginning of their journey, for the ship would have to sail round Cape Horn before turning north towards the great markets of Europe and North America. In ideal conditions the movement of a consignment of rubber from its seringa to the nearest buyer would take four months, but six months would be a more normal time.

The alternative was to transport the rubber down the Mamoré, Madeira and Amazon to the ocean vessels waiting in Manaos. This method, while offering every advantage of cost and time, had one overwhelming drawback. The greater part of the Madeira river is navigable for quite substantial vessels, but where it receives the waters of the Mamoré, it forms a series of rapids and falls, which stretch over 200 miles in length. Some of these rapids can be shot by skilful boatmen, but others have to be portaged. The area is also one of the most fever-ridden in the Amazon Valley, and any delay in passing through it would lead to sickness among the crew. The losses of life, rubber and boats deterred most of the patrones from using this route.

The use of some sort of by-pass to the rapids had been canvassed for many years and the various merits of a canal, a road or a railway were disputed. But the rapids were in Brazilian hands, while the rubber stands above them belonged to Bolivia. A man gifted with imagination, drive and enthusiasm was needed, to persuade the Bolivians and Brazilians of the advantage of a by-pass to both nations and the financiers of the Western world of the feasibility of such a project. Fortunately such a man was available in the person of Colonel George Earl Church. A biography of this man of many talents would be out of place in this book; it is enough to say that he excelled as a soldier, engineer, explorer, geographer, author, adventurer and anthropologist; he had fought with distinction in the Civil War, for the Mexicans against Maximilian and his French allies, and in many smaller clashes in South America. Although an American he was a vice-president of the Royal Geographical Society and a member of the Council of the Hakluyt Society; his book *The Aborigines of South America* remains a classic of its kind.

Colonel Church soon obtained the consent of the Bolivian and Brazilian governments to the construction of a railway and when, with more difficulty, he raised the necessary money in England,* work on the railway could begin. The first contractors, an English firm, left for the Madeira in 1872. But by the following year they had already returned to England and served a writ for the voiding of their contract, on the grounds that the project was impossible. Colonel Church at once signed a fresh contract with P. & T. Collins, an American engineering concern. We are fortunate enough to have a complete record of their work on the railway through the memoirs of one of the American engineers, Neville B. Craig.

At this time American railway engineers were probably more expert than any others in laying tracks across a wilderness. The development of the West had given them experience of working in the hardest conditions and the same work had brought together gangs of tough and skilful labourers, who were mainly of Irish extraction. On their arrival in San Antonio, at the lower end of the rapids, the Americans immediately settled down to their job. This

* The loan unfortunately coincided with the news that a Bolivian minister had been buried alive by the La Paz Indians—an announcement which did little to encourage investment in that country.

performance provoked a comment from a Brazilian customs officer, which still has all too much significance. 'When the English came here,' he said, 'they did nothing but smoke and drink for two days, but Americans work like the devil.' Their organization however was less than diabolical; within a few weeks they had run out of food and medicine. They carried on, begging food off neighbouring rubber gatherers and ignoring the absence of quinine.

Nothing in the Wild West had prepared them for the difficulties of work on the Madeira-Mamoré railroad. In the thickest woods of the United States three expert axemen could clear a three-foot path for about 1,450 yards in one day's work, but they were pleased if they could cut 200 yards through this rain-forest in the same time. A massive hard-wood, when cut through at its base, would often still stand, held in place by thousands of vines. And when one of the labourers sank his axe into the trunk of a tree, he would frequently bring down on his own head hundreds of the fire ants that lived in its branches, each one with a bite like a red hot needle. Every tree and every bush seemed to hold virulent ants.

The labourers were absolutely ignorant of the animal and insect life of the region. They respected the jaguar as an obviously formidable beast, but they identified the peccary, which is a more dangerous animal, with their native ground hog, and there was much hilarity when one of them, returning to the camp late for his supper, confessed that he had 'been treed by ground hogs'. They discovered the dangers of the water when Craig put his finger inside the mouth of a small piranha which he had landed, and after this episode, however unbearable the insects on its banks, they never took refuge in the river.

An engineer owned six brightly coloured silk handkerchiefs, of which he was inordinately proud. One evening he hung them up to dry and the next morning he found them missing. A search soon revealed a trail of small patches of silk, each apparently moving of its own volition along the floor of the jungle, but all, in fact, carried by the Saüba ants, which had cut them up and removed them during the night. On other nights their camps would be disturbed by armies of eciton ants and the men would leap out of their hammocks and dance around in bare-footed agony until they had found enough fire to divert the army.

One of the most obnoxious pests was an insect which Craig called the 'sweat fly', but which must, by his description, have been a stingless bee. These creatures are drawn to sweat with the same suicidal obsession as a moth to the flame. 'Through little rents made in our clothing,' Craig wrote, 'they would get in close contact with the flesh and fill our flannel shirts until distended to their utmost capacity. They would cover our hands, faces and necks and get into our eyes so persistently that it often required two men to keep them out of the eyes of a transitman during the few seconds required to line a point ahead. ... It was difficult to eat unless at least half a dozen flies accompanied every bite that entered our mouths.'

But by far the most dangerous of the insects was the mosquito. With quinine always in short supply and often unavailable, it was not uncommon for half the total labour force to be incapacitated with malaria. Before the piranha incident one of the engineers tried to bathe in a stream, but as soon as he had removed his clothes little rivulets of blood started to course down his body from a hundred punctures where the mosquitoes had attacked him. Malaria, even at this time, was not usually a fatal disease, but the conditions in which the Americans were forced to live made it lethal. Feverish men would be routed out of shelter by eciton ants in the middle of a thunderstorm; they would run out of medicine and be given no quinine; they would run out of food and be given whisky or cachaça; they would be bled by vampire bats and robbed of their sleep by insects.

Halfway through their work they discovered a new horror and one that was far more terrifying than any disease. John King, an American cook, was left alone in camp and when the workmen returned they found his body lying in the middle of the clearing, transfixed by three long arrows. The railwaymen were not afraid of a fight, but they had already learned that their own Indian labourers could approach them unseen and unheard through the thickest jungle, and there was horror in the thought that a naked warrior, as silent and as deadly as the jaguar, could be stalking them at any moment. Against his jungle craft all their knowledge and guns would be useless. Under this menace the Americans moved about only in groups and their work suffered greatly as a result. The Indians, in their turn, had a superstitious dread of firearms, so that clashes between the two were rare.

Their cup of misery became full when they discovered that they could expect, at the best, to be paid only a fraction of the wages due to them. The Madeira-Mamoré Company was under an injunction forbidding it to pay out any cash pending a suit from its bond-holders, and P. & T. Collins, in the absence of any payments from the Company, were on the verge of bankruptcy.

Under these intolerable conditions some Italian labourers made an unsuccessful attempt at mutiny. Soon afterwards seventy-five deserted and set off on foot for Bolivia. They were never seen again. Several of the Americans left at the end of their contracts and, unable even to afford their fares downriver, set off instead in canoes and rafts, but few of them reached the safety of Pará. New labourers were brought in to take their place from America and Ceara, but the latter did not prove satisfactory.

In the end it was neither disease nor any of the appalling difficulties surrounding their work that killed Colonel Church's railroad, but a particularly squalid speculation. After the failure of the English contractors in 1873, the bonds which the Bolivian Government had issued to finance the project sank to sixteen per cent of their face value, where they were bought up by unscrupulous gamblers. The new bondholders, by laying out £27,000 in bribes, then persuaded the Bolivian Government to revoke Colonel Church's concession. They also brought an action claiming that the project was impossible on the resources available to the company, and demanding that the money held in trust should be distributed among the bondholders. In the meantime no payments were made to the contractors and men died for want of supplies on the railroad. The English Courts had no alternative but to approve the action, since the company's resources were inadequate and it no longer had a valid concession. The speculators received a payment of 52 per cent; the surviving railwaymen were repatriated; and P. & T. Collins were bankrupted.

*

The Americans had made a fine start to the construction of the railway. They had surveyed and cut through 320 miles of jungle; they had settled the course of the rails for sixty-seven miles, cleared a swathe a hundred feet wide for twenty-five miles, and laid four miles of track up which an engine, 'the Colonel Church', steamed each day. Without including Cearese and Indians, this achievement had cost them 221 lives out of a total labour force of 941. Their fatalities were therefore 23·6 per cent, compared with a figure of 10·5 per cent for the Union Army in the Civil War. The courage and esprit de corps that they showed in performing such dangerous work in such abominable conditions were beyond praise, particularly when one remembers that they were receiving no reward for all their sufferings.

The last Americans left San Antonio in 1879. Four years later a confident team of Brazilian surveyors was sent to the scene of their labours. The new arrivals, as always in the story of the Madeira-Mamoré Railroad, despised the efforts of their predecessors and boasted that they would give the Americans a lesson in railway-building. But after a few months of malaria they accepted the Americans' surveys and plans without even checking them. The next year the Brazilians returned to complete P. & T. Collins' survey but, apart from cutting across one great loop of the Madeira, their line clung to the river bank for almost all of its course, regard-less of any considerations of cost, distance or topography.

Little more was done until 1903, when by the Treaty of Petropolis Brazil agreed with Bolivia to build the railway in exchange for con-cessions of land in the Acre Territory in the headwaters of the Purús and Juruá. Aided as they were by all the resources of the Brazilian Government and all the technical advances of thirty years, the new contractors were in a very different position from P. & T. Collins. A railway company was formed with a capital of eleven million dollars and a leading firm of American railway engineers employed. In 1907, when work began, the engineers found 'the Colonel Church', removed a tree which had grown up through its smoke stack, and restored it to working order.

An average of 10,000 labourers were engaged for each of the five years that it took to build the railway; agents scoured Europe and North America and even lured workmen away from the comparative safety of the Panama Canal. But there were never enough men fit for work. They were bitten by mosquitoes and infected with malaria; they drank the water of the Madeira and contracted typhoid and amoebic dysentery; their very numbers helped to spread infection and their casualities were so frightful that between 1908 and 1911 their hospital treated over 30,000 cases.

Only in the last years of the project, when the grim lessons of the Panama Canal* were applied to the railroad, did the death rate fall. Quinine was made a compulsory first course to every meal and the

* The Panama Canal was opened in 1914, but the battle against malaria and yellow fever had been won in 1905, when William Gorgas was allowed to begin his campaign against its mosquitoes.

men were forbidden, literally on pain of death, to drink unboiled water. Stagnant pools were sprayed with petrol, swamps were drained and doors and windows screened. The new methods proved as successful on the Madeira as they had in Panama and Havana and in 1912 the railway was completed. But in terms of money and of suffering it must have been the most expensive 228 miles of track ever laid. Some macabre mathematician has calculated that for every crosstie laid on the Madeira-Mamoré Railway, one man died.*

By a savage irony all these sacrifices were in vain. As the first trainload of Fine Hard Pará raced down the tracks to the new Brazilian terminus at Porto Velho, the long fall in the price of rubber had already begun. Within a few years it became uneconomical for rubber producers to use the efficient but expensive services of the railway. The site was abandoned again to the ghosts of its workmen and the roar of the rapids.

In 1931 the Brazilian Government bought up the railway company for a nominal sum and traffic was resumed. But it is now a very different kind of traffic from the bustling trains that brought down their cargoes of black gold from Bolivia in 1912. Two trains leave Porto Velho each week and amble along at some 15 m.p.h., stopping for the night halfway along the track. On Wednesdays an Express roars out of Porto Velho, and arrives eight hours later in Guajará Mirim, having achieved a miraculous average of just under 30 m.p.h. But even on Wednesdays the train is seldom full. The Madeira-Mamoré Railroad carries little from nowhere to nowhere—a sad end to a project which, in Colonel Church's words, was to open up a land 'as fair as the Garden of the Lord'.

* This much-repeated story is inaccurate. There are some half million crossties on the railway and no more than 30,000 men ever worked on it.

Chapter Eleven

THE PUTUMAYO AFFAIR 1903–1916

IT IS not easy for us to understand the mood of militant outrage with which our ancestors reacted to atrocities, whether they were in the Balkans, the Congo or the Amazon. Tribal massacres as frightful as any of these are now dealt with briefly, almost apologetically, by the Press. But in the nineteenth and early twentieth centuries the European Powers, and in particular England, felt with the fervour of moral superiority that the world could be civilized and that any blot on it was a challenge.

The Putumayo river is one of the main northern tributaries of the Amazon. Its course now marks the boundary between Peru and Colombia, except for a short stretch where Colombia has access to the main river, but until the beginning of the rubber boom neither country showed any interest in the area.

The Indians who lived there were allowed to continue their tribal ways of life without any interference from outside. They had a complex religion, with their own version of The Flood. The moon to them was an evil spirit. They were animists who believed that God was incarnated in the form of the anaconda and they venerated the great snake as a result. They would even decorate their bodies with the marks of a snake skin, or with the skins of lesser snakes.

They were poor warriors, who, unlike most South American tribes, had never discovered the use of the bow, but they poisoned the tips of their spears when they went to war. Tortoise shells served them as drums and when beaten vigorously these instruments were audible over a distance of twenty miles. They were a primitive race, without even any skills in weaving and adept only in the use of natural drugs. The coca leaf gave them energy and a hallucinatory plant, yagé, enhanced the magical exhibitions of their witchdoctors.

These Indians belonged to four closely related tribes—the Huitotos, the Boras, the Andokes and the Ocainas. The early travellers in their country describe them as docile and almost embarrassingly friendly.*

At the end of the nineteenth century collectors found a poor kind of rubber growing in great abundance between the Putumayo and Caquetá rivers. This rubber was known in the trade as weak-fine, or more colloquially as 'Putumayo tails'. By the beginning of the twentieth century there were several rubber posts, mainly Colombian, but in 1903 a powerful Peruvian rubber company, J. C. Arana Hermanos, entered the area. Its owner, Julio Arana, had been supplying the Colombian collectors for several years, shipping their goods up from Iquitos, which, although 1,000 miles away by water, was a far more convenient base than anywhere in Colombia.

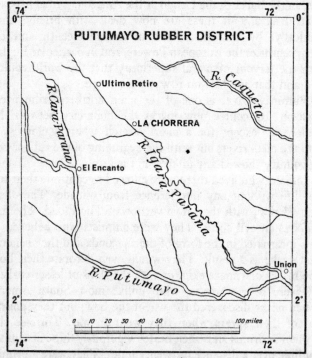

* I am much indebted to Señora Iriarte of Bogotá for a lengthy and authoritative study of the Putumayo Indians, from which I have extracted these few facts.

Arana first appeared in Iquitos in the 1880's, barefooted and hawking Panama hats, but his natural talent for commerce and his utter ruthlessness soon led to more profitable activities. His boats began to trade with rubber gatherers on the Putumayo River and its tributaries. After he had built up a monopoly in supplying the Colombians he started entering into partnerships with them, buying them out when they wished to leave, and forcing them out when they did not. By 1908 he was in control of most of the area and he kept a small army of cut-throats to enforce his will.

On December 6, 1908, the shares in Arana's rubber company were offered to the British public. The company's auditors, the august firm of Deloitte, Plender & Griffiths, had sent a representative out to the Putumayo, who returned with an idyllic description of the life led by the Indians and a promising report of the possibilities of the region for mining, agriculture, and other profitable pursuits. A number of acceptable, but dim-witted Englishmen were co-opted on to the board. The company was valued at £1,000,000 but only £130,000 of Preference Shares were offered to the public, all the Ordinary and most of the Preference shares remaining in the hands of Arana and his partners.

The issue was a failure, ninety per cent of the stock remaining in the underwriters' hands. The prospectus itself was fraudulent and false from beginning to end. It described flourishing trading establishments in Manaos and Iquitos, where there were in fact only individuals trying to collect bad debts. The book value put on the assets was laughable, the profits declared had never been made, and the company had no legal title to any of its rubber estates. The mineral and agricultural potential was also non-existent. The description of the methods of rubber collecting, and even of the sort of rubber collected, was incorrect. A handful of speculators, the forerunners of those who now invest in pig farms and racing systems, subscribed for the shares, for the word 'rubber' was still magic. Otherwise few people noticed the offering and those who did had probably forgotten about it when the storm broke a year later.

*

In December 1907 two young Americans by the names of Hardenburg and Perkins were making their way down the Putumayo. They were told stories of Peruvian atrocities by Colombians and Indians, who advised them to make the portage to the Rio Napo to avoid the Peruvian rubber-gatherers and soldiers; but they pressed on down the river and soon found themselves involved in a miniature war. They were captured by a launch returning from a raid on a Colombian post. Several Colombians had been killed, their women captured and raped, regardless in one case of advanced pregnancy, their Indians and rubber stolen. The raiding party was accompanied by an army contingent under the command of a Peruvian officer.

The Americans were beaten and insulted and their baggage was stolen, but they were eventually released. Hardenburg went to Iquitos, where Perkins joined him later after a vain attempt to recover their belongings. The two men were staggered by the barbarities inflicted on the Indian rubber-workers of the Putumayo. They had seen the bodies of men, women and children carrying the ghastly scars of the lash, known already as the 'Marca d'Arana', and after Hardenburg had left him, Perkins had seen Indians shot like animals on trivial and frivolous pretexts. When they made further investigations in Iquitos they found still more degrading evidence of atrocities, and collected sworn statements showing conditions so frightful as to overshadow even the inhuman Belgian rule in the Congo.

Armed with this evidence, Hardenburg made his way to London and at first found it difficult to sell his story. Well documented as it was, its horrors were incredible. At last he gained the ear of the Editor of *Truth* magazine and the Anti-Slavery and Aborigines Protection Society, a powerful organization which played a leading part in exposing conditions on the Putumayo and in the Congo, and the first of a series of articles was published in *Truth* on September 22, 1909.

It would be hard to imagine a less appropriate setting. The article, 'The Devil's Paradise', subtitled 'A British-Owned Congo', was sandwiched in between an atrocious jingle on Captain Scott's forthcoming expedition to the South Pole and an editorial entitled 'International Press Junketing'. One of its columns rested on a footnote advertising Fortnum & Mason's 'Perfection' tea, 'A choice afternoon tea at a moderate price'. The rest of the magazine was equally out of character, full of snippets of news and gossip and of lamentably facetious poetry. But 'The Devil's Paradise' was electrifying. It started with a quotation from *La Sancion*, an Iquitos newspaper.

This article alleged that it was the practice of the agents of the company to

> force the pacific Indians of the Putumayo to work day and night at the extraction of rubber without the slightest remuneration; that they give them nothing to eat, that they rob them of their own crops, their women and their children, to satisfy the voracity, lasciviousness and avarice of themselves and their employees, for they live on the Indians' food, keep harems of concubines, buy and sell these people wholesale and retail in Iquitos; that they flog them inhumanly until their bones are laid bare; that they do not give them any medical treatment but let them linger, eaten by maggots till they die, to serve afterwards as food for the chief's* dogs; that they mutilate them, cut off their ears, fingers, arms and legs; that they torture them by means of fire and of water, and by tying them up, crucified head down; that they cut them to pieces with machetes; that they grasp children by the feet and dash out their brains against walls and trees; that they have their old folk killed when they can no longer work and finally that to amuse themselves, to practice shooting, or to celebrate the sabado de gloria, as Fonseca and Macedo† have done, they discharge their weapons at men, women and children, or, in preference to this, they souse them with kerosene and set fire to them, to enjoy their desperate agony.

After this Hardenburg's and Perkins' account of their own experiences inevitably paled, but they did at least show that the atrocities were not confined to the Indians. They also mentioned that there were Barbadians working on the plantations as slave-drivers. The English registration of the company was pointed out and the article ended with the testimony of different individuals, as horrifying as the passage quoted from *La Sancion*.

A question was at once tabled in the House of Commons, asking whether the Foreign Secretary's attention 'has been called to the proceedings of an English company called the Peruvian Amazon Company; whether any report as to the alleged ill treatment of British subjects from Barbados has been made by the English consul at Iquitos; and whether he will call for a report on the doings of this company from the local English consul at Iquitos.'

This unwelcome enquiry came as an appalling shock to the Foreign Office, few of whose officials seemed to have any clear idea of where the Putumayo was, still less of the grisly events that were

* The Chief of Section, i.e. the European in charge of the station.
† Fonseca and Macedo were two of the most depraved Chiefs of Section.

taking place there. Harassed minutes were circulated revealing an almost pathetic helplessness:*

'We know nothing about the Peruvian Amazon Co., neither do the commercial or consular departments.'

'The Consul (at Iquitos) is an unpaid official and if it is a fact that he is also a rubber collector he might be unwilling to say much.'

He had indeed failed to say much in the past, the only letter of his entered in the political files from the beginning of 1907 until the article in *Truth* being a somewhat humourless account of a riot in the city over, of all things, a shortage of soap.

Cazes, the British Consul in Iquitos, was an unpaid official, a merchant dealing mainly in rubber, but although he had business relations with the Peruvian Amazon Company he was an honest man. Cazes was on leave at the time of the *Truth* articles and was thus able to call on the Foreign Office, but he was able to add little. The only knowledge he had of the *Truth* allegations came from *La Felpa* and *La Sancion*, both papers 'of little standing or reliance', and from rumours of hard methods. Barbadians had complained to him of ill-treatment, particularly of being forced to join armed expeditions to collect native labourers by force, but Arana maintained that all the West Indians had been repatriated except for those who wished to stay. The Consul could see from their appearance that they had been well treated. His firm had agents who traded regularly with the Putumayo and they had brought down no bad reports. He admitted the existence of a system in Iquitos tantamount to slavery, but maintained that the Indians were not oppressed. Telegrams asking for more information were sent from London to Lima, Barbados and Bogotá.

In the meantime *Truth* published its second article, together with angry letters from the company and the Peruvian Legation, both denying that the atrocities could have taken place, and, in the case of the company, adding that if they had, it was not their responsibility. This article contained ten sworn statements from Peruvian eye-witnesses, piling horror upon horror.

In the meantime, the Ambassador in Lima had discovered that a Captain Whiffen had recently visited the area. After some confusion, for against all probability there were two Captain Whiffens

---

* The quotations in this chapter, unless otherwise specified, are taken from the very full Foreign Office file on the Putumayo, now in the Public Records Office, and none of which has previously been published.

in the Army List, he was found and his testimony bore out that of
Hardenburg. Whiffen, an officer of the 14th Hussars, had been
placed on half pay after a wound in the groin in the Boer War. In
spite of his injuries he had been exploring the upper reaches of the
Javari and had passed through the company's territory twice, where
he had engaged one of the Barbadians, John Brown, as his servant.
For some reason the rubber-collectors mistook him for a representative of the company so that places were cleaned up before he
arrived. Nevertheless, he reported that 'it is very common to see an
agent with twenty concubines, or even thirty, many of them children
of but 10–12 years of age'. He found a girl of nine tied up in the air
by her hands, which were lashed together behind her back, cut her
down and found out that her offence was to have stolen two eggs
when she was starving. He discovered that Aguero, the man who
had ordered this punishment, had also shot a woman for contracting
venereal disease.

After he had engaged John Brown, Whiffen learned of even
worse atrocities. Another woman had been executed for being
raped by a diseased Brazilian employee. 'In 1906 or 1907 Jiménez
and Aguero* had a shooting match after a drunken orgy. An Indian
was tied to a tree and the first to excise his penis was judged to be
the winner.'

From Bogotá the Colombian Government confirmed that
Colombian rubber-collectors had been murdered by Peruvians, and
specifically endorsed every detail of Hardenburg's account of the raid
in which he had became involved. In the United States, the State
Department, while confirming that Perkins and Hardenburg had
been awarded £500 by the Peruvian Government for the loss of
their belongings, was cautious in its estimate of their personal
character. They wrote to the Foreign Office: 'The two men are
prospectors and the State Department would not care to guarantee
their trustworthiness, but Perkins belongs to a thoroughly respectable family.'

There now seemed to be enough evidence with which to confront
the company. In reply to a letter from the Foreign Office, Arana in
a circumstantial manner accused Whiffen and Hardenburg of blackmail. The depositions quoted in *Truth* were said to have been made
up by criminals dismissed by the company and in many cases the

* Jiménez and Aguero were two of the vilest servants of the Peruvian Amazon
Co. Their names occur frequently in Casement's Report.

jails which they now occupied were named. The company's auditor, Mr. Gielgud of Deloitte, Plender & Griffiths, was quoted on the Indians' good state of health and friendly relationship with the Europeans. The letter was reasoned and calm, with just the right undercurrent of distaste. Arana was a brilliant liar, calm and logical in England, and in Peru the embodiment of misunderstood patriotism. At the next company meeting on January 1, 1910, the Chairman admitted that Arana was the only director who had ever been to the Putumayo, and in February Gielgud, until then Auditor of the Peruvian Amazon Company, became its Secretary.

We must note the role played by this man. Before the Company was quoted in England he was sent out by Deloitte's to examine its properties in South America, including the rubber estates of the Putumayo. The report which he wrote on the condition of the Indians portrayed them as happy, well-fed and on the best of terms with their genial superiors. In the mornings they would greet their employers with welcoming cries of 'Ho Normand' or 'Ho Jiménez'. When Gielgud returned to England there was one entry in his accounts that caused some embarrassment. This was shown as 'Gastos de Conquistacion £22,000', which means costs of subjection or expenses of conquest, an item that Arana was unwilling to allow the English directors to see. The two men went over the accounts for a long time and the item was absorbed into 'estates including development expenditure', and by the time it reached the Balance Sheet, into 'Rubber and Agricultural Estates'.

At the lowest possible level this was hardly sound accounting practice. Gielgud was employed by the company at £1,000 p.a., and £2,000 when in Peru, a welcome change from the niggardly £150 he had been drawing from Deloittes. He always swore that he saw no evidence of atrocities until he returned with the Company's Commission of enquiry in 1910, and when he did he was as outspoken as anyone. Roger Casement, whose great Report on the Putumayo atrocities was soon to reveal the truth to a horrified world, at first disliked him for his familiarity, but grew closer to him afterwards. None of the Commission seems to have doubted his good faith.

*

The correspondence between the Foreign Office and the company continued, with persistence on the one side and truculence on the other, but without any real progress being made. Whiffen denied the blackmail charge and his boy, John Brown, supported his version of the atrocities from Montserrat, his native island, to which he had returned. Public opinion was whipped up by the Anti-Slavery Society; petitions flowed into the Foreign Office, and questions multiplied in the Commons. The Dean of Hereford was forced to retract, under threat of litigation, an attack on the Company's treatment of the Indians made at the annual general meeting of the Temperance Society in Caxton Hall. On June 8 the Company gave way to pressure, made a *volte-face* and announced that, at the urgent request of Sr. Arana and the accused employees, they were sending a Commission to the Putumayo. An English Consular Officer was to be appointed to accompany them, on the pretext that British subjects were involved. On July 13 it was decided that this Consul should be Roger Casement, the Consular Official who had already exposed the atrocities in the Congo.

The Commission left in the middle of August, composed of Colonel the Hon. R. H. Bertie, Mr. Barnes, a tropical agriculturalist, Mr. Fox, a rubber expert, Mr. Bell, a merchant, and Gielgud, the Company's Secretary and until lately its auditor. It had been arranged that Casement was to join them in Iquitos. On September 7 Colonel Bertie was forced to return through ill health. Back in England he put the Foreign Office in possession of his views, but as he had not even reached Iquitos, let alone the Putumayo, he came back with more gossip than facts. 'Hardenburg is undoubtedly a forger—very little is known of Captain Whiffen or his reasons for leaving the country. He disappeared in rather a suspicious way. His black boy is apparently a villain.'

On September 14 the Commission left Iquitos for the Putumayo, but before going Casement sent a letter back to London giving the results of their interviews in Iquitos. They had seen six Negroes and a Spaniard, all employed at some time by the Company, and their evidence indicated that something in the Putumayo was badly wrong. There was a long interval without any news, during which the Foreign Office discovered to their intense annoyance that Casement had also been sending reports directly to the Anti-Slavery Society. He was not well; his last letter (to his friend Spicer, an official in the Foreign Office) finished, 'My stay here will depend on my health. Since coming to Iquitos I have been ill and my eyes are very weak. The heat has been stifling up here and mosquitoes day and night . . .

'Au revoir and I shall be very glad to see your face again, this place is appallingly depressing.'

On December 4 a telegram was received in London: 'Consul General Casement has returned from Putumayo. Mission has been accomplished. Expects to arrive Manaos December 9, Pará week after.'

Casement's visit had confirmed almost all of Hardenburg and Whiffen's accusations, and the Company's Commission had also been convinced. But Casement's report went much further than his predecessors' in its revelation of the frequency of the atrocities. Even today and to a generation numbed by the horror of the Nazi concentration camps, it makes terrible reading.

The first part of the Report, dealing with the Barbadians, was comparatively mild. It should be emphasized that it was only because of their presence on the Putumayo that the Foreign Office had been able to send Casement out there. Most of his evidence on the terrible state of the Indians came from interviews with Barbadians.

Nearly 200 Barbadian labourers were engaged by Arana Brothers in 1904-5. The wages that they were paid, although good by Barbadian standards, were only half the rates normal on the Putumayo, and almost all fell into the Company's debt. They soon discovered that their duties were those of slave-drivers rather than labourers. Some of them heard this when they had reached Manaos and tried to get the British Consul to have them sent home, but he turned them over to the police and they were forced to continue.

When they arrived at La Chorrera, the main station on the Putumayo, they were armed with Winchester rifles and sent on expeditions to capture Indians and then to force them to work rubber. Like the other salaried employees they did no work themselves. They were paid in trade goods of the lowest quality, valued at prices far higher even than those ruling in Iquitos, where the cost of living was estimated to be three times that in London. They were badly fed and the victims of occasional brutality.

One of their number, Clifford Quintin, quarrelled with a Colombian and was flogged by Sanchez and Normand, two of the worst villains. His wrists were fastened behind his back and he was tied up by them to a crosspole and given fifty lashes with a whip of twisted tapir hide. When Casement saw him, over five years later, he still bore the marks. Alexander Walcott, another Barbadian, was battered **nearly** to death with machetes for protesting over the execution of two Indians. Joshua Dyall was accused of seducing one of a white employee's concubines. He was hung up by his neck, beaten with machetes and then put in the stocks. In Ultimo Retiro, where Dyall was confined, these implements had such small holes for the victim's feet that it was torture even for an Indian. Dyall was a big-boned Barbadian, so that two men had to sit on the upper beam to make it close. Three years later both his ankles were deeply scarred and when released he could not even stand upright. Edward Crichlow was imprisoned in special stocks designed by himself which held the victim's arms and neck as well as his ankles. On one occasion his two ankles were held in holes five feet apart for several hours.

The Negroes were given Indian 'wives' but were made to change them when they moved their place of work, and were not permitted to take them away if they left the Putumayo. They had to pay for their wives' food and clothes, although the women spent much of their time working for the company without reward.

Perhaps more serious than the atrocities practised on the Barbadians, was the brutalizing effect on them of life on the Putumayo. On the whole they were punished only when they were unwise enough to quarrel with one of the Company's employees, but they were forced to witness and to commit atrocities with sickening frequency and to flog Indians so often that most of them lost count. On the slave-hunting expeditions which they often made they had to stand by and watch the most abominable cruelties, knowing that any protest would only lead to a flogging. Most of the Barbadians interviewed by Casement had been living in these conditions for over five years, with little prospect of leaving. It is greatly to their credit that so few of them were corrupted, though Armando King was as bad as most of the Europeans, Dyall after his experiences in the stocks obeyed Normand's cruellest orders, and a certain Hilary Quales worked for Abelardo Aguero. Once several Indians were strung up by their arms, tied in the usual way behind their backs. Quales, to amuse his master, swung them violently to and fro. He then began nibbling their legs and buttocks. One of the Indians kicked him in the face. Quales seized the man's foot and bit off a toe, an incident which caused Aguero much amusement.

*

If the Barbadians were cheated, corrupted and harshly treated, the condition of the Indians was infinitely worse. Before the rubber-gatherers moved into the area, it had a native population of between 40,000 and 50,000. When Casement visited the Putumayo it was thought to be between 8,000 and 10,000, over three-quarters of the population having been wiped out in six years. Disease no doubt played its part, but most of the decrease can be directly blamed on a system of starvation and murder.

There were four principal tribes, the Huitotos, Boras, Andokes and Ocainas; split by inter-tribal and civil feuds, docile by nature, and pining pathetically for shoddy trade goods, they were easily subdued and enslaved. Once they had been set to work gathering rubber they found themselves the victims of systematic brutality. If an Indian failed to bring enough rubber he was flogged, the severity of the flogging varying with the amount of rubber by which he was short. If he ran away he was hunted down like an animal and either shot or brought back and tortured before being killed. If he hid successfully in the forest, his wife or children would be tortured to find out where he had concealed himself. Even if he stayed in his section and always brought in his quota of rubber he was allowed, at the most, just enough food to keep alive. If he brought in an exceptional amount he might receive worthless trade goods. Regardless of how well he did the job which had been forced upon him, his life was at his master's whim. He might be killed or mutilated in reprisal, for sport or through sadism. He might starve through neglect or by intent. Whatever he did his life would be miserable and short.

Only the *muchachos*, the Indian quislings who helped the Peruvians, and the Europeans' concubines could avoid this condition, the former by inflicting it on others. Every system of tyranny needs its collaborators, and for a commercial organization the muchachos had the added advantage of being very cheap and entirely ruthless. Their loyalty was absolute, for only the company stood between them and a well-deserved death at the hands of their own tribes. The muchachos were particularly useful for tracking down Indians who had run away, a job which they could do far better than any European. They carried Winchester rifles, weapons never allowed into the hands of any other Indians. The concubines, forcibly removed from their fathers or their husbands, found themselves living a life not unlike that in a harem of an exceptionally cruel and jealous Sultan. A smile to another employee could and did lead to agonising death if your master was Normand. Many Europeans had twenty concubines, some as young as nine or ten, who were given away or killed, like the slaves that they were, when their masters tired of them. Occasionally an Indian woman of strong character would raise herself to the position of wife, sometimes, as in the case of Jiménez's Indian wife, by debasing herself to the same level of cruelty.

When the rubber was brought in each Indian would eye the scales in terror as his load was weighed. 'The Indian is so humble that as soon as he sees that the needle of the scale does not reach the 10 kilogram mark, he stretches out his hands and throws himself on the ground to receive the punishment. Then the chief or subordinate advances, bends down, takes the Indian by the hair, strikes him, raises his head, drops it face downwards on the ground and after the face is beaten and kicked and covered with blood the Indian is scourged.'

Flogging was the mildest punishment inflicted, but it could be fatal and it was earned by the most trivial offence and sometimes by no offence at all. The whip used was made of tapir hide, five strands being twisted into one whip. It was not as murderous, Casement thought, as the hippo-hide whips he had seen in the Congo, but in the hands of a strong man like the chief flogger, a Peruvian Negro named Simon Angulo, it could cut deep into the flesh with every lash and make the blood pour down the victim's sides. Thirty lashes or more were usually fatal because, unless salt water was poured over the victim afterwards, maggots would appear in the wounds, the man would start stinking and be shot, if he had not died already. One of the Barbadians was confined in the stocks between two Indians in this terrible state and the stench soon had him screaming for mercy.

Flogging was so common that Casement was told that ninety per cent of the population bore scars of the lash, women as well as men. Some of the worst-marked were children of ten or twelve. If a very young child was short of its quota of rubber, its mother would be flogged in front of it. Sometimes the stocks were used in conjunction with the lash, sometimes to facilitate the act of rape; and sometimes the Indians in them were left to starve to death, reaching such a desperate condition before they did so, that they would eat the maggots out of their own wounds and dirt off the ground.

G

Men and women would be tied up, suspended by their arms, often twisted behind their backs. They would be battered with the flat sides of machetes or mutilated by their cutting edges. They would be held under water until they were on the point of drowning. They would be strung up by chains around their necks and left with their toes just touching the ground.

These punishments were to terrorize the Indians and spur them to collect more rubber, and were common in most stations. When an Indian had rebelled, attempted escape, or in any way irritated his superiors, or when the chief of section was unusually depraved, they could be far worse. Murder was a matter of whim.

The Barbadians' simple language enhances the horror of the atrocities. Augustus Walcott described to the Commissioner what justice was like when administered by Aurelio Rodriguez:

Question: And you say you saw Indians burnt alive?
Answer: Alive.
Question: How do you mean? Describe this.
Answer: Only one I see burnt alive.
Question: Well, tell me about that one.
Answer: He had not work caucho.* He ran away and he kill a 'muchacho' a boy, and they cut off his two arms and legs by the knee and they burn his body.
Question: And he still living?
Answer: Yes, he still living.
Question: Did they tie the body up and burn it so?
Answer: They didn't tie him up, they drag the body and they put plenty of wood and set fire to it and throw the man on it.
Question: Are you sure that he was still alive and not dead when they threw him on the fire?
Answer: Yes, he did alive I'm sure of it. I see him move—open his eyes, he screamed out.

Another Barbadian, Sealey, accompanied Jiménez on an expedition after fugitives in 1908. This is his story as pieced together by Casement:

On the first day's march from Morelia, about five o'clock in the afternoon, when they were some one and a half days distance from the Caquetá, they caught an old Indian woman in the path. Jiménez asked the old woman where the rest of the Indians were. Sealey states

* i.e. Rubber.

she was a bit frightened. She told him that the next day at 11 o'clock
he would get to the house where some Indians were. She was an old
woman not able to run. They did not tie her up. They went on with
her, keeping her all night in camp until about two o'clock of the next
day, and then Jiménez asked her 'Where is the house, where are the
Indians?' The old woman stood up and said nothing. She could not
speak, she kept her eyes on the ground. Jiménez said to her:

'You were telling me lies yesterday, but now you have got to speak
the truth.'

With that he called his wife—he had an Indian woman, the woman
who is still with him—and he said to his wife:

'Bring me the rope off my hammock.'

She took the rope off and gave it to him, and with that he tied the old
woman's hands behind her back. There were two trees standing just
like that—one there and one there. He made an Indian cut a post to
stretch across between the two trees then he hauled the old woman up,
her feet were not touching the ground at all. He said to one of the boys
—'a muchacho'—'Bring me some leaves—some dry leaves,' he said,
and he put these under the feet of the old woman as she hung there,
her feet about a foot or so above the ground; and he then take a box of
matches out of his pocket and he light the dry leaves and the old lady
start to burn. Big blisters I see on her skin up here' (he pointed to her
thighs) 'all was burned; she was calling out. Well sir, when I see that,
Sir, I said "Lord have mercy!" and I run ahead that I could not see
her no more.'

'You did not go back?'

'I stayed a little ways off to where she was. I could hear him speaking.
He say to one of the boys "loose her down now" and they loose her,
but she was not dead. She lay on the ground, she was still calling out.
He tell one of the Indians: "Now, if this old woman is not able to walk,
cut her head off," and the Indian did so—he cut her head off.'

'You saw that?'

'Yes, sir, he leave her there in the same place. We left her there
going a little ways into the forest; it was about four hours' walk after
we left the old woman, we met two women. They had no house. They
had run away. One had a child. Jiménez axed the one that had the
child: "Where is these Indians that has run away?" She tell him that
she don't know where they were. He tell her after she tell him that she
don't know that she was a liar.'

'Did he tell her this himself in her own language?'

'He tell his wife to tell her. His wife speaks Spanish too. His wife is
up there with him now at Ultimo Retiro. He tell his wife that she was a
liar. He took the child from the woman and he gave it to an Indian,

one of the Indians who had been collected to work rubber. "Cut this child's head off!" He say, and he did so.'

'How did the Indian cut the child's head off?'

'He held it by the hair and chop its head off with a machete. It was a little child walking behind its mother.'

'Was it a boy or a girl?'

'It was a boy. He left the child and the head in the same place, everything there, on the path. He went on then, he take the two women with him, but the woman was crying for her child. Well, sir, we got a little ways more inside the wood; walking we met an Indian man—a strong young fellow he was too. That is after we gets over to near the Caquetá. Jiménez say he wanted to go to the next side—the other side—of the Caquetá, but he do not know where he would get a boat, a canoe, to go over. So this time he tell the woman, his wife, to ax the Indian to tell where the boat is. Well, sir, the Indian say he do not know where it is. By that time Jiménez say the Indian lie—he was a liar, and he got a rope and he tie the Indian's hands like that behind his back. It was in the same way with the post across between two trees. He made the Indians tie a post between two trees, and he haul the Indian, like that, up to the post. His feet could not touch the ground, and he call for some dry leaves, and tell the boys to bring some dry leaves, same as the old woman. He put the leaves under his feet, and he take a box of matches out of his pocket. The man was there, shouting out, greeting. Jiménez draw a match and light the leaves, and this time, sir, the Indian start to burn, big bladders (blisters) going out from his skin. The Indian was there burning, with his head hanging like that—moaning he was. Jiménez say: "Well, you will not tell me where the canoe, where the boat is" he says "so you must bear with that." Well the Indian was not quite dead, but was there with his head hanging, and Jiménez he tell the "capitan" by name José Maria, a Boras Indian (he is chief capitan of the Abisinia "muchachos"); he says, "Give him a ball!" he says, and the Indian took his carbine and give him a ball here, shooting him in the chest. Well, sir, after I saw how the blood started I ran. It was awful to see, and he left the Indian hanging up there with the rope and everything on him.'

'Was the Indian dead?'

'Yes, sir, he was dead with the ball, and we left him there in the same place. That's all.'

Shortly after the Commission had listened to this ghastly story and while they were still numbed by its horrors, Casement was approached by Jiménez himself, who begged him to listen, as he could prove that *one* of the *Truth* charges against him was untrue.

The Casement report has all too many stories of this sort, often supported by the independent testimony of many witnesses. The slave-drivers were a repulsive collection of men, and Fonseca, Montt, Martinengui, Aquiléo Torres, Velarde, Macedo and Aguero were no less cruel and debased than Jiménez and the Rodriguez brothers, while their underlings matched their barbarities.

But probably the worst of all the Putumayo criminals was Armando Normand. Normand was as cruel as any of the others and he was better educated and more intelligent. He had been at school in England and he travelled in Europe. His letters to the Press after his capture rival Arana's in the fluency and conviction of their lies. Most of the criminals were debased animals, the scum of Loreto, itself the scrapings of Peru. All owed money to the company except Normand, who had a balance of £2,000 standing to his credit. The others had sold their souls, only to find themselves in debt as a result.

Even after reading the rest of the report the Barbadians' account of Normand's crimes is horrifying. His atrocities include 'pouring kerosene on Indians (men and women) and setting them alight, burning men at the stake, dashing out the brains of children; and again and again cutting off the arms and legs of Indians and leaving them to speedy death in this agony'. Sometimes he gave their trunks to his dogs to eat. When an Indian refused to carry a load for him he had the man's legs held apart and made Dyall beat his testicles with a club until he died. He burned children alive when their parents fled to the forest. He had a Peruvian flag soaked in kerosene and wrapped around an Indian woman, then set light to it. He flogged small children to death.

The Indians continued to run away in spite of the hideous reprisals they knew awaited them if captured, but they seldom rebelled. There was only one serious uprising in the history of the Putumayo and that was led by Katenere the Boras chief. When Katenere was in the stocks his wife was raped in front of him by Bartolomé Zumaeta, a brother-in-law of Arana. He escaped, captured some Winchesters and for a time carried out an effective guerilla war, killing many white men including Zumaeta. But Katenere's rebellion provoked a new series of atrocities.

Vasquez, quite a minor criminal by the standards of the Putumayo, was leading a punitive expedition against the rebels. They failed to find Katenere but captured some other Indians. Vasquez had one woman decapitated at once, giving no other reason than that he was in command and could do what he liked. On the way back they came across a girl about six years old said to be Katenere's daughter. She, too, had her head cut off. They then became frightened of reprisals and set off as fast as they could for the station. Several Indians who could not keep up were murdered and at the end of their journey three other Indians were shot for no reason. The survivors of this nightmare march who succeeded in reaching the post, were in their turn murdered, two of them by deliberate starvation in the stocks. When he arrived Vasquez boasted that he had 'left the road pretty'.

Katenere was eventually shot by a muchacho shortly before Casement's arrival when trying to rescue his wife. Otherwise, the Indians were so cowed by cruelty and so enervated by starvation that they had entirely lost the will to fight and indeed to survive.

The commission's task was dispiriting to the soul. They had to listen to and delve into a mountain of bestial evidence. The climate was oppressive, the mosquitoes vicious, and visiting many of the stations involved long, hot and exhausting journeys over land. Worst of all when they retired to their quarters they were often forced to share them with the criminals of whom all day they had been hearing such abominable stories. Casement was haunted by the memory and described the horror these men inspired in him in explosive sentences. 'We forced ourselves to meet and sometimes even to converse with men who richly deserved being broken on the wheel and whose presence at the table and depraved physiognomy took away appetite and often the power of speech.'

*

Back in Iquitos, Casement found in the authorities the attitude of horrified astonishment to be expected in the circumstances. The Prefect was given enough evidence to act on and 'again and again assured me that his Government was determined to deal with the criminals and protect the Indians'. In the Putumayo Tizon, the new and respectable manager, had sworn that every man tarred by Casement's brush should go. Casement told him that this was not enough and that many should be hanged. Tizon was a well-meaning man, although not a strong character, but like many Peruvians he suffered from an obsessive patriotism which over-rode all his other feelings. He wanted the criminals to flee and get lost in the wilds, thinking that this would lead to less damaging publicity than a trial.

Arana himself took the Commission in his stride. When Casement returned to London he received a letter.

'I have heard of your return and should very much like you to tell me when you will be in London, in order that I may visit you and exchange views on the reforms to be effected in the Putumayo, and if possible to have an idea of the impressions you have derived from your recent visit, as also to obtain any suggestions you may have to offer upon the better development of the Company's affairs.'

The authorities in England were horrified and those in Peru said that they were, too. The English directors were flabbergasted. The worst offenders were dismissed, but no effort was made to arrest them, although many of them were living openly in Iquitos. Others fled from the Putumayo with the same ferocity as they had inhabited it. Fonseca, Montt and Flores left with as many Huitoto slaves as they could find, hoping to sell them on the Brazilian-Bolivian borders, but were frustrated in this attempt. Although Brazil would not extradite the criminals, she detained the Indians and returned them to Peru. Aguero had burned and destroyed everything that he could, hoping to stir up the Indians, before disappearing into the wilderness with a band of muchachos and most of the Company's rifles.

There was now, of course, no doubt about the truth of the atrocities, which had indeed proved to be worse than the wildest rumours. The question was what should be done about them and the answer was simple enough. The criminals must be brought to justice and punished, and it must be made certain that the Indians of the Putumayo would never suffer such treatment again. The Peruvian Government could provide the first part of the answer by itself and the second together with the Company. But the Government seemed to share Tizon's attitude that trials would do more harm to Peru's reputation than the quiet disappearance of the criminals. They were also in an uneasy position. Arana's brother-in-law, Pablo Zumaeta, was one of their leading supporters in Loreto. All officials of any importance belonged to his political party and many of them drew a large proportion of their income from the rubber trade. Loreto was only very loosely under the control of Lima since communications were unbelievably bad. There was a mountain trail, impassable at certain times of the year, and quite unsuited at any time for a large body of men. Otherwise, the quickest route between the two points was by ship to Panama, overland across the isthmus and then by another ship to Brazil, a journey of over a month. There was a telegraph in Iquitos which had a habit of breaking down at convenient moments. Mutinies, riots and one threat of secession had been the fruits of earlier attempts to bring Loreto to heel on issues far less explosive than the Putumayo.

Thus, even if the Peruvian Government had felt the most complete revulsion at the atrocities, it was not easy for it to see that their authors were arrested, geography and political expediency being against them. In retrospect they seem to have felt only embarrassment. The ownership of the area was bitterly disputed by Colombia and any scandal would act as ammunition against Peru. The political appeal of the frontiersman carving out new provinces for the motherland cannot be exaggerated. Even Dr. Paredes, an enemy of Arana's, was obliged to introduce a report condemning his operations in terms as strong as those used by Casement with fulsome praise of his work as a pioneer.

The Government itself was not innocent. It gradually became clear that it must have known, or at the least guessed, what was happening. The atrocities had been well publicized in Peru before they had been heard of in Europe. The Peruvian army had been involved in raids on the Colombian posts, and officers and men had stayed for long periods on the Company's property. While the President of Peru was lavishing on the British Ambassador assurances of his horror at the revelations, and his determination to see justice done, the Lima newspaper *El Diario*, closely associated with the Government, was declaring in a leader, almost certainly officially authorized: 'We have no knowledge of the source of these allegations, but what we do know is that neither England nor France, or other places, has any right to treat of our affairs.' It concluded with a eulogy of Arana.

President Leguia continued to speak with two voices, one full of promises for foreign consumption, and one of sturdy defiance for use at home. The difference between Lima's promises and performance, and between Lima's orders and Loreto's actions, was the basis of a long and frustrating diplomatic wrangle, ending in the publication of the report in 1912. The bitter truth was that few people in Peru minded at all what happened to the Indians.

If the Peruvian Government was unwilling to do anything, the Company was paralysed by its past and present inefficiency. Even in 1910, the year in which rubber reached its highest price, they were sliding, in blissful ignorance, into bankruptcy. The money which should have been paid to the Indians of the Putumayo had been squandered on armies of cut-throats to persecute them, corrupt officials to ignore their plight, and newspapers to publicize their happiness. The Company's Commission, which returned to England soon after Casement, commented as strongly on the inefficiency of the rubber collectors as on their cruelty. The wretched Indians, desperate to make up the quotas and escape a flogging, would gash the trees mercilessly and mix in any other substances which might be undetected. As a result, the rubber which was already low grade, fetched an even smaller price, and the supply of rubber trees dwindled as quickly and as unnecessarily as the number of Indians to work them.

*

On June 3, 1911, Casement attended a Board Meeting of the Peruvian Amazon Company in London and saw exactly what he was up against. A typist was summoned 'and you may judge of her capacity from the fact that she describes me as "His Botanic Majesty's Consul"'. She was nevertheless too good for some of her superiors. Gubbins, the Chairman, was well named. One of his fellow Directors was completely ignorant of the Spanish language, in which most Board Meetings were conducted. Pablo Zumaeta* had mortgaged all the Company's property in South America in favour of Arana's wife for the contemptible sum of £65,000, in settlement of a debt to Arana which may never have been incurred, and yet the Directors did not even dare to withdraw his power of attorney in case 'he should sell everything and make off with the plunder'. They decided at their first meeting to send an Englishman out to take charge of the Putumayo. At their next meeting they found out that the Company could not even afford to do this. At their third meeting, on July 5, they again decided to send someone out, this time at their own expense. But decision and action were two very different things for the Company.

Casement was infuriated. 'If I had the money myself I'd buy the rogue [Arana] out and go out to the Putumayo on a well armed yacht with a party of good shots and have some of the finest big game hunting in the world. Why the devil men should go to Africa to

* The brother of the rapist shot by Katenere.

shoot 4,000 head of harmless gazelle with such fine beasts as Normand, Aguero and Fonseca to stalk I can't imagine. . . .

'I wonder if Roosevelt would take the thing up.'

The Peruvian Government's only actions by July 25, 1911, seven months after it had been informed of the atrocities, had been to send out a Commission and to issue a few indictments which it made no attempt to serve. This was in spite of threats by Great Britain to publish the report and a refusal to mediate in the Tacna-Arica dispute with Chile until the Putumayo business had been settled. There was some reaction inside the country. A Societad Pro Indigena (Society for the Protection of Indians) was formed which did some useful work, although it was too often influenced by politics and its first President was accused of being 'one of the worst slave-drivers in Peru'.

Otherwise, there was no progress. One of the officials in the British Embassy in Lima wrote privately to Casement:

'As for the Peruvian Government you probably will have read between the lines of my despatches and seen that I have never had much confidence in the sincerity of the officials. I had to pretend I have but I can tell you that I have none. The President of this Republic is one of the worst Presidents that South America has ever had and I have reason to believe that he is himself interested in the Arana undertakings.'

No one had hoped for much from the Peruvian Commission. Its leader, Dr. Paredes, was the owner of a vitriolic Iquitos newspaper named *Oriente* that had always defended Arana in the past. But, on July 25, the British Ambassador in Lima heard that Paredes had returned and had issued 215 warrants, and that four criminals had actually been arrested. This was so much more than anyone in England had hoped for that it was decided to send Casement out again to find out what was being done.

On August 29 Casement's boat stopped at Barbados and he was annoyed to be greeted affably at the quay by O'Donnell, one of the minor criminals. His irritation increased on his way up the Amazon. At the Brazilian-Peruvian frontier he found out that Fonseca and Montt were working rubber nearby on the Brazilian part of the River Javari with ten stolen Boras slaves. With great difficulty he bullied the Brazilian authorities into trying to arrest them, but the attempt was a fiasco. The Brazilians made certain that the criminals knew that they were coming, and their only official attempt to establish their presence was to ask the trader who bought their rubber whether he had seen them.

Casement arrived in Iquitos seething with fury and found little there to allay it. In May Fonseca and Montt had boarded the *Anastasia* in Peruvian waters to get a tow for their canoe and slaves. Also on board was a detachment of police whose officer asked the criminals whether they knew anything of Fonseca and Montt whom he was pursuing. The criminals at once leaped back into their canoes and cast off, brandishing their rifles. Lilley, the English owner of the boat, offered to chase them and it would have been easy enough to catch them, but the officer refused either to do this or to open fire. Later in the day the canoe again crossed their path. This time the criminals did not even bother to avoid them and made obscene gestures of contempt as they passed. This was the only 'serious' attempt made to arrest them.

Three months had passed since Paredes, as leader of the Peruvian Commission, had issued his 215 warrants, but only nine arrests had been made, and the only criminal of any importance in jail was Aurelio Rodriguez. The Prefect virtually admitted that he knew where Pablo Zumaeta was hiding. The few actions that he had taken were entirely due to pressure from Lima. A rumour was flying round Iquitos that Dr. Paredes had asked Arana for £5,000 for a favourable report.

The only pleasant note in Casement's visit was struck by Dr. Paredes himself. His paper eulogized Casement and, when they met, Paredes proved to be impressive and charming, saying that he blushed with shame to be a Peruvian. His investigations had been thorough and his report bore out Casement's in every particular, indeed adding a number of equally terrible crimes. He gave Casement a summary in confidence.

The Company's employees are described as being 'all drunkards, chewers of coca, idlers corrupted to the lowest possible degree— even to the point of idiocy, some of them illiterate ... diseased in their minds and seeing on all sides of them imaginary attacks by the Indians, conspiracies, uprisings, treasons, etc. In order to survive to save themselves they slaughtered and slaughtered without pity, entire Indian tribes, innocent beings who had no idea of escaping nor of vengeance, for the tyrannical domination of so many years holds them even to-day cowed and abject'.

The report gave the lie to the Peruvian story, circulated then and

afterwards, that the Indians were barbarous cannibals, whose
subjection would serve the cause of humanity. The Huitoto are
described as being obedient, submissive and affectionate to the
point of tenderness. 'The Indians of the Putumayo are good and
all that is needed for their government is good treatment.'

*

In spite of finding a Peruvian who saw things as he did, Casement
returned disillusioned and convinced by the lethargy and corruption
of the officials in Iquitos that it was useless to press for the conviction
of the criminals. 'We may expect the "Plenaries" or actual trial to
begin long after we are dead and the last Putumayo Indian has been
gathered, in fragments, to his fathers.' The only hope was to ensure
that such things never happened again and even here the outlook
was discouraging.

   The Company had decided to go into liquidation. Nothing had
come of the plan to send an Englishman out to the Putumayo, and
for either £65,000 or nothing* Arana had ensured that the property
which he had once valued at £1,000,000 would revert to him. In
other circumstances the collapse of the Company might have been
welcome, but with its disappearance Britain's only excuse for inter-
vening would also vanish, Arana would repossess the property and
the atrocities would continue until there were no Indians left to
murder. The only hope seemed to be to establish a mission in the
Putumayo, which might inhibit any atrocities and which would at
the least ensure the availability of reliable news. Peruvian law forbade any mission except a Roman Catholic one. But the British
public were only anxious to subscribe to a Protestant mission.

   Any hope of action from the Peruvian Government had now been
abandoned, and on July 13, 1912, Casement's Report was published
as a Government Blue Book. Feeling in England, already inflamed
by the *Truth* articles, now rose to a high pitch of indignation, and
outraged letters and petitions began to flow in to the Foreign Office.
Question followed question in Parliament. Leaders in the newspapers often showed more moral fervour than knowledge of
geography. The *Spectator*, for instance, suggested blockading the
(Pacific) coast of Peru to prevent shipments of rubber. The German

* Depending on whether the debt of £65,000, owed to him by the Company,
for which he received the mortgage of all its property in South America, was
ever incurred.

papers seemed to think that the atrocities had been committed by Englishmen. *Germania*, a Roman Catholic organ, contained this passage:

'The Biblemen who set the whole world in commotion over the alleged Congo atrocities and calumniated Catholic Belgium, have now a fruitful soil for their labours. It is worthy of note that the British took a prominent part in the Congo campaign.'

The Peruvian press responded with their usual vigour and inaccuracy. An English-language magazine, published under the auspices of the Peruvian Government, described the revelations as 'a large and disgusting amount of sensational rot'. An Anti-Gringo article appeared in *Oriente*, superb in illiterate fury:

These people [English and American] who are horrified almost to fainting at seeing a horse die in the bull ring, its intestines torn by the horns of a Miura, but who watch placidly and at times even with pleasure the agony of a human being who falls in the arena of a circus, killed by a masterful blow in boxing. They turn their thumbs down calling for the coup de grace of the modern gladiator vanquished in the sporting but brutal and savage pugilistic boxing ring.

They cannot be philanthropists, the authors of the terrible massacres of the Far West, nor those countrymen of Cromwell, who backed up Lord Kitchener when he ordered at Khartoum the shooting of 30,000 men in vengeance for the assassination of General Gordon.

'Let him that is free from sin cast the first stone' said Christ to the women of Jerusalem, who attempted to stone the erring Magdalen, a parable quite applicable to the question with which we are occupied.

The great difficulty of the Peruvian apologists was that their two versions of the story were contradictory. To protect the present Government, which took office in 1907, they had to pretend that all atrocities were committed before then; but to defend Peru's good name they had to maintain that the English company was responsible and the latter was only founded in December 1907. It was necessary for any Peruvian to pay lip service to at least one of these beliefs, if he wished to obtain a hearing.

*

In the meantime Mitchell and Fuller, the newly-appointed Consuls of Great Britain and America, had arranged to visit the Putumayo to see that the atrocities had ceased. They were accompanied by Rey del Castro, the ex-Peruvian Consul-General in Manaos, who had accepted bribes from Arana in the past, and Benito Lores, the

Government's representative who had been present at Hardenburg's capture. At the mouth of the river they were met by Arana himself and throughout their visit they were dogged by company officials. They found no evidence of cruelty. On each of the few occasions when they were able to talk to Indians undisturbed, the Indians only said that they wished the white men would go away and leave them alone.

They had few such opportunities. Mitchell writes about Rey del Castro: 'His anxiety not to lose sight of us was amusingly evident. Though totally unfitted physically for severe exercise, he followed us over fatiguing roads, through heat and storms wherever we went, while Señor Arana, a heavy man, no longer young, and suffering acutely from sciatica, also accompanied us, uncomplaining but indefatigable.'

Fat Indians were produced to dance for them and Arana was anxious that they should all call him 'Papa', a request uneasily reminiscent of the 'Ho Normand' and 'Ho Jiménez' of Gielgud's first visit. Nevertheless, as far as the present treatment of the Indians was concerned, the visit was quite encouraging, the Putumayo being now better run than many stations in the wilder parts of Amazonia. On the other hand, none of the promised measures to ensure that the Indians remained unabused had materialized. Apart from Benito Lores, there was no Government representative in the area, and its administration remained firmly in the hands of Arana. As far as the public was concerned, Mitchell was bleakly discouraging:

> The Peruvian authorities and public feeling in Iquitos are far more concerned about the sovereignty of Peru in the Putumayo than about the condition of the Indians there. The system of peonage is too firmly rooted in the country to allow any sentiment of consideration for the natives, other than their use as servants, to lead to trouble or expense, much less real sacrifice, in releasing them from a state of servitude. The only feeling in Iquitos is annoyance at the exposures. Even those who admit the truth of the allegations express no pity for the victims or a determination to prevent their ill treatment in the future. Their only preoccupation is the position of Peru in the matter.

Casement's own time on the case was nearing an end. His earlier work, particularly the Blue Book itself, had been magnificent, but for him the Putumayo had become a crusade and he could not understand that for most people it was a political weapon, awkward or convenient, depending on their position. He saw everything connected with the affair in sharply defined terms and was unable to understand the ambivalent roles of men like Benito Lores and Dr. Paredes.

'Paredes has been got at,' wrote Casement late in 1912, and again: 'Paredes has joined the enemy.' This was when *Oriente* published an article defending Rey del Castro and Arana. In fact, Paredes was an implacable political enemy of Arana's and probably felt a genuine distaste for the atrocities, but xenophobia was a more powerful cause than humanitarianism and Paredes could not allow his opponents a monopoly of it. Casement hated Peru and referred to it as 'this Iberian cess pit'.

Considering the violence with which he argued his cause, his passion and his lack of judgment, it is extraordinary how far he led the Foreign Office. Up to the end of 1912, when he retired from the case, they followed almost every suggestion made by him. The only check came from Haggard, the British Ambassador in Brazil, after Casement's change in attitude towards the 'warm-hearted Brazilians,' whom he had praised in the Blue Book. He wrote, 'I am afraid that Casement, kindly and talented fellow that he is, is but a broken reed to lean on in founding a policy.'

Casement retired from public life a popular hero, 'the Bayard of the Consular Service' as he was called by one admirer. But before his death his name was to become almost a term of execration in England, and after it millions of Irish would revere him as martyr. In 1916, when he had been arrested on a charge of High Treason, the police found a number of typewritten journals in his lodgings. These 'black diaries', as they have become known, showed Casement to be a homosexual and a compulsive writer—a fatal combination. Throughout his travels he had recorded not only every movement and every financial outlay, however minute, but also every sexual encounter. In his journey up the Amazon he left a long trail of male conquests behind him, white, black and brown from Pará to Andokes. His own account shows him having affairs with Sealey and Leavine among the Barbadians and, more discreditably, with O'Donnell, the rubber collector. He brought two Huitoto boys back to England with him but otherwise seems to have been a wistful and distant admirer of the Indians he had come to save.

But Casement should be blamed far more strongly for his selfishness than for any moral backsliding. If his perversions had been discovered on the Amazon, let alone in Iquitos or on the Putumayo, his mission would have been ruined and 10,000 Indians might have been abandoned again to the mercies of Normand, Aguero, Fonseca, Jiménez and Montt. One has only to reflect on the exquisite skill with which Arana sought to discredit Hardenburg and Whiffen to realize what he could have done with such evidence. But Casement avoided detection and his contribution to the history of the Amazon was unsullied. As we leave him, at the height of his fame, it is impossible to avoid an overwhelming feeling of compassion at the fate in store for him.

*

The inactivity of Leguia's Government had now become transparent. Martinengui had been seen in Lima and Callao and Macedo was living in Lima with no effect at concealment. The latter's name was publicly listed in the city address book and he had recently been elected to a club.

In October 1912 a new government came into power in Peru, under a leader with the reassuring name of Billinghurst. Arana's party in Loreto, the Anti-Cuevista, had been supporters of Leguia and could, therefore, look for nothing but hostility from his successor. At the same time, news elsewhere became brighter. An anonymous donation solved the Catholic Mission's financial prolems. It is a terrible commentary on the attitude of the British public that while they would write their petitions, hold their protest meetings and subscribe to Protestant missions, they refused to contribute even a modest sum towards the only measure that had a hope of success. 'Sending additional Popish monks at the expense of Protestants instead of sending the hangman' was how one idealist put it. In America the financial response was insignificant. The Franciscans set out and, turning the other cheek, their last request to the Foreign Office was that their launch in the Putumayo should be allowed to fly the Union Jack, a demand which was wisely refused.

Brazil's attempts to expel the criminals had been as despicable as the conflicting statements on the subject from her Foreign Ministry, but in November a cable arrived from the British Ambassador reporting that Colonel Rondon was to be sent to the frontier. This was the best possible news. If any man in the world could find them Rondon could, and if any South American would be merciless to the exterminators of Indians it would be the man who had devoted his life to their protection.* Unfortunately, relief on this score was to be short lived. Rondon started his expedition on February 1, but instead of being sent to the lower Javari to round up Fonseca and Montt, he was dispatched to the upper Madeira to lay down telegraph lines, over 600 miles away as the crow flies and nearly 1,500 by river.

Developments in Peru were more encouraging. In December Judge Valcarcel issued warrants for the arrest of Arana, Zumaeta, whose reputation had suffered so little that he was now acting-Mayor of Iquitos, and Vega, another of the partners in the original company. All three appealed at once and Arana and Vega were already outside the country. With the Peruvian Government in a serious mood for the first time, the extradition proceedings over O'Donnell, a minor criminal, must have been most embarrassing, the case being so ineptly prepared that the Barbadian court was forced to quash the proceedings on the grounds that he had not been properly identified.

This decision brought a last outburst from Casement about the petty-mindedness and inhumanity of lawyers, which was not the least of the grim ironies of the Putumayo affair, when one remembers that his own life could afterwards be said to hang on the presence or absence of a comma in a Norman-French Statute of Edward III.

On February 2 the High Court in Iquitos annulled the order of arrest against Arana, Zumaeta and Vega. The Government seemed genuinely annoyed, but as was pointed out afterwards, it was doubtful whether anything could have been proved against them, even in an English Court. The rest of the month went better. On February 8 the arch-villain, Armando Normand, was arrested in Bolivia and held for extradition. The Franciscan Mission arrived safely in the Putumayo and sent in quite a favourable report. Each section was now cultivating a large area; all the Indians were well-fed and there was no coercion or brutality. The Indians were friendly to the Franciscans, whom they called 'Choverames', or steel men, as all their machetes came from England. Their celibacy had caused some surprise. The missionaries had, in fact, been lucky to reach their destination so peacefully, Arana having arranged for a gang of cut-throats to greet them at Iquitos. Fortunately, their

* See Chapter 12.

boat was late enough for the Prefect to be able to ensure their safety.

The Peruvian press reacted violently to the new pressure and in particular to the indictment of Arana. *Voz del Oriente*, an extremist organ owned by his friends, was the most outspoken, but not by a wide margin. Its vicious vituperation and infantile logic, spiced with the most abject self-pity, would have been comic in a better cause. Some of its assertions at the beginning of 1913 were unbelievable. Dr. Paredes had written his report on the Putumayo because he had been bribed with the English title of Member of the Anti-Slavery Society, 'Dr. Paredes, M.A.S.S.' As so often, there was a germ of truth in its inventions. Dr. Paredes was a member, an honour which he acquired by the simple expedient of paying £2 a year. Other accusations were that the Franciscan mission were really engineers; the English Government had offered to send 10,000 soldiers free of charge to 'watch over' the district; Casement had produced his report out of spite when the company would not accept his proposal that he should become a principal shareholder.

The West Coast Leader, unwilling to be left behind, published eulogies of Normand. A series of articles appeared in a Lima paper, written by the head of the Historical Museum. A few titles are enough: 'The sovereignty of Peru and the hypocrisy of "the Dreadnoughts" ', 'International Cannibalism in the Putumayo', 'The European and Anglo-American wolves and the ewes of Spanish origin.'

Little of any importance happened in Peru for the rest of the year. In England yet another Committee produced its report, the fourth and last in the history of the scandal. This was the Parliamentary Select Committee, set up to examine the involvement of the Directors of the Peruvian Amazon Company. The English directors were severely criticized for their negligence, stupidity and greed, but were found not to have prior knowledge of the atrocities. Arana, with typical *sang froid*, came over to give evidence. Batteries of lawyers toiled through every medieval statute to find some grounds for trying him, but there were none. He told his story with ingenuity and proved almost impossible to pin down in cross-examination. But in spite of his evasions the Committee found that he must have known about the atrocities throughout.*

---

* For a fuller account of the cross-examination see *The River that God forgot* by Richard Collier. Collins, 1968.

In Iquitos the Summario, or preliminary stage of the trial, dragged on. On December 11 a letter appeared in *The West Coast Leader* from Normand complaining of the unfairness of his trial, the pampering of the Indians and the squalor of his quarters. 'The gaol here is very small and we are all forced to sleep in one room, which is very dirty and unhygienic.' On January 4, 1914, Zumaeta was elected Mayor of Iquitos, but resigned under pressure from the President. On February 23 Mr. Huckin, the British Consul, discovered that the Summario was nearly finished and that Normand and the Rodriguez brothers were severely compromised by its findings. Seventy-four warrants were to be issued.

When the Court had arrived at this decision, the Public Prosecutor or Fiscal caused consternation by demanding that the sentences be reversed, that all three judges, Herrera, Paredes and Valcarcel, should be put on trial, and that Casement should also be tried. The grounds for the objection were a technicality in one arrest, Casement's removal of the Barbadians, and a healthy contempt for justice. Peruvian law was too complicated for anyone outside the country to have anticipated a development like this. It transpired that if the Superior Court over-ruled the Fiscal's objections, he could appeal to the Supreme Court. The following month the Superior Court duly rejected his appeal and the case went to the Supreme Court in Lima.

On May 29, 1915, just before a verdict was expected, nine men including Normand, Homero and Aurelio Rodriguez, escaped from the jail in Iquitos, clearly with help from inside. Their canoe eluded the launch sent in pursuit and with them went the last chance of punishing any of those responsible for some of the most revolting crimes ever committed.

*

The First World War brought more important tragedies to the British public and the pressure on Peru stopped abruptly. Huckin, the able Consul at Iquitos, was recalled at the beginning of 1915. His last dispatch, on January 22, makes depressing reading. There were no rumours of ill-treatment, but the exodus of Huitotos continued. The Boras were retiring to the forest. Food supplies were dangerously short and disease was decreasing the numbers of those who remained. No one could work out how, in the débris of the rubber crash, it could be worth working such low-quality trees in such a remote part of the country.

After the beginning of the War two other matters brought enquiries to a complete standstill. Peru was one of the friendliest of
the South American countries, ending by severing diplomatic
relations with Germany and eventually by declaring war on her.
Casement's arrest, trial and execution for treason aroused com-
placent and enthusiastic comments from his old enemies in the
Peruvian Press. None of them seemed to feel the irony of the
situation, that of all those involved in these frightful atrocities, the
only one to be punished was the man who brought them to light
and by doing so stopped them. Casement himself may have felt this.
As he waited in the Tower for the trial that could only end one way
he received this cablegram from Arana.

On my arrival here am informed you will be tried for High Treason
on 26th June. Want of time unables me to write you asking you to be
fully just confessing before the human tribunal your guilts only known
by Divine Justice regarding your dealings in the Putumayo business.
They were all suggested by *Truth*, Anti-Slavery Colombian Government Agents Rosso Toralbo and others. Inventing deeds and influenc-
ing Barbadians to confirm unconsciously facts never happened,
invented by Saldana, thief Hardenburg, etc., etc. I hold some Barbadians' declaration denying all you obliged them to declare pressing
upon them as English Consul and frightening them in the King's
name with prison if refusing to sign your own works and statements.
You offered them good berths in Brazil to which country you brought
them deceiving Peruvian authorities making yourself their accomplice
as per your own information. You tried by all means to appear a
humaniser in order to obtain titles fortune, not caring for the con-
sequences of your calumnies and defamation against Peru and myself
doing me enormous damage. I pardon you, but it is necessary that you
should be just and declare now fully and truely all the true facts that
nobody knows better than yourself.

(signed)   Julio Arana.   14. 6. 16.*

On September 20 1916, a month and a half after Casement's
execution, a disturbing letter was sent by Father Leo Sandbrook
of the Franciscan Mission to the British Acting-Consul in Iquitos:
'Though wholesale crimes of former times have disappeared . . .

* This unpublished postscript to Casement's life can be found in the Public
Record Office, File no: FO 371 2798.

still the Indian has constantly been punished with whips, logs, chains, kicks and stocks for shortage of rubber.' A revolt was delayed only by the Indians' own lack of spirit, but when it came they killed thirteen white employees, and entrenched themselves. Several of those guilty were rounded up and it can be expected that their punishment, as well as their arrest, was more expeditious than those of their oppressors.

In August 1917, Father Ryan called at the Foreign Office. The Mission was hated by the Peruvians. During his four years there only two or three floggings had been reported, but many more were suspected. The native population was dying out, deliberately using vegetable contraceptives to avoid bringing children into a hungry and bitter world. The Franciscans wanted to leave on the grounds that they could do no more good for the natives. The last of the missionaries left the Putumayo in November 1918.

No one has ever understood why the production of rubber in the Putumayo increased throughout the War. Prices were so low that even the collectors of the finest rubber in the most accessible areas could scarcely make a profit. 'Putumayo tails' were low-grade rubber, selling at a poor price, and the estates were in a remote area. Unfortunately, the supply of figures, always unreliable, stopped altogether after 1918. In any case it is certain that production must have been abandoned at the latest in 1921, the disastrous year in which Peruvian output of rubber slumped from 4,781 tons to 133 tons, and in which the price of the material fell to an average of one third of the cost of production in the Putumayo.

Perhaps the ruin of the Putumayo estates and the miserable condition of Loreto explain the readiness with which Peru ceded the area to Colombia in 1922 in a general settlement of frontier problems. Among the few pleasant thoughts that one can take away from this foul and depressing episode is that those who had gained from the Putumayo were surely ruined by the slump, and that after all that Great Britain did to help between 1910 and 1914 it was the work of an Englishman, Wickham, on the Tapajós in 1876 which eventually led to their ruin. The cynical may also enjoy the sight of Peruvian sovereignty, in the name of which a frontier war had been fought, justice perverted and bestial atrocities condoned, abandoned so lightly when the area became unprofitable.

One might expect that, like so many other tribes of Indians, the Huitotos, the Boras, the Ocainas and the Andokes were doomed to extinction. But they have survived, although in greatly reduced numbers. Some 2,000 of them still inhabit their old land between the Cara-Paraná and Igaraparaná rivers, compared to the 50,000 found in the same area by the agents of the House of Arana.

PART FOUR

THE TWO COLONELS

Chapter Twelve

THE RIO ROOSEVELT 1913-1914

W<small>E SOON</small> found that the dogs would not by themselves follow the jaguar trail; nor would our *camaradas*, although they carried spears. Kermit was the one of our party who possessed the requisite speed, endurance and eyesight, and accordingly he led. For an hour we went through thick jungle, where the machetes were constantly at work. Then the trail struck off straight across the marshes, for jaguars swim and wade as freely as marsh deer. It was a hard walk. The sun was out. We were drenched with sweat. We were torn by the pines of innumerable clusters of small palms with thorns like needles. We were bitten by the hosts of fire-ants, and by the mosquitoes, which we scarcely noticed where the fire-ants were found, exactly as all dread of the latter vanished when we were menaced by the big red wasps, of which a dozen stings will disable a man, and if he is weak, or in bad health, will seriously menace his life. In the marsh we were continually wading, now up to our knees, now up to our hips. Twice we came to long bayous so deep that we had to swim them, holding our rifles above water in our right hands. The floating masses of marsh grass, and the slimy stems of the waterplants, doubled our work as we swam, cumbered by our clothing and boots and holding our rifles aloft . . . then on we went, hampered by the weight of our drenched clothes, while our soggy boots squelched as we walked. There was no breeze. In the undimmed sky the sun stood almost overhead. The heat beat on us in waves. By noon I could only go forward at a slow walk, and two of the party were worse off than I was. Kermit with the dogs and two *camaradas* close behind him, disappeared across the marshes at a trot. At last, when he was out of sight, and it was obviously useless to follow him, the rest of us turned back towards the boat. The two exhausted members of the party gave out, and we left them under a tree. Colonel Rondon and Lieutenant Rogaciano were not much tired;

I was somewhat tired, but was perfectly able to go for several hours more if I did not try to go too fast; and we three walked on to the river, reaching it about half-past four, after eleven hours stiff walking with nothing to eat.

This jaguar hunt was soon to be followed by a far more exhausting experience—the exploration of a totally unknown part of Southern Amazonia and one which was to result in the discovery of a river 1,500 kilometres in length, whose very existence had been pronounced impossible by reputable geographers.

One would expect the leader of such an expedition to be a young explorer, hardened in the wild country of South America, but he was, in fact, a man of fifty-five, who had never been near the Amazon in his life, and who had, until a few years before, held the position of President of the United States.

*

No one, since the defeated Disraeli began his political novel on the life of Mr. Gladstone, can have solved the problems of retirement from high office with more panache than Theodore Roosevelt. At a moment when other men would have written their memoirs, he plunged into a lengthy African Safari and wrote about that instead, displaying in his *African Game Trails* and *Life Histories of African Game Animals* an expertise which would not have shamed a professional naturalist. Roosevelt's second term of office had come to an end in 1909 and he had left immediately on his safari, which he followed by a triumphant tour of Europe.* He made an unsuccessful attempt, in 1912, to oppose his own nominee, William H. Taft, for the Republican nomination. On his defeat he organized a new Progressive Party and was again unsuccessful as its candidate for the Presidency.†

* In England his knowledge of Natural History flabbergasted Sir Edward Grey, the Foreign Secretary, himself a keen ornithologist. The two statesmen took a long walk together in the New Forest and, although Roosevelt had only been in England for one month throughout his whole life, he was able to identify every bird that they saw without error. (*Grey of Fallodon* by Lord Grey).

† Roosevelt could have won the Republican nomination (and probably the Presidency) but refused to accept the terms on which he was offered a vital fifteen votes at the Convention. In the Presidential Election he did better than Taft, the President in Office, both in popular and electoral votes, the voting being:

After these reverses Roosevelt was free to leave on a lecturing tour of South America, but not content with a programme which merely led him from one capital city to another, he decided to combine his lectures with a journey of exploration. The American Museum of Natural History of New York gave him a commission to collect specimens and appointed two eminent naturalists, Cherrie and Miller, to accompany him. The supplies of the expedition were organized by Fiala, an Arctic explorer, and it was also to include Roosevelt's son, Kermit, his secretary, Harper, his assistant, Sigg, and Father Zahm, a priest and explorer.

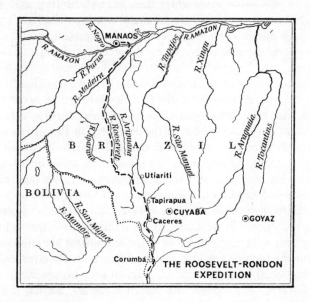

THE ROOSEVELT-RONDON
EXPEDITION

The original plan was to ascend the Paraguay River from Asuncion cross to one of the southern affluents of the Amazon, and descend it to the main river. The Museum was enthusiastic, as the head-waters of the Araguaia and Tapajós had seldom been visited by naturalists.

When Roosevelt arrived in Rio de Janeiro, the Foreign Minister of Brazil, Lauro Müller, approached him with a far more exciting proposal—that the foremost explorer in the country, Colonel

Wilson	(Democrat)	6,293,097	(435 electoral votes)
Roosevelt	(Progressive)	4,119,507	(88 „ „)
Taft	(Republican)	3,484,956	(8 „ „)

Rondon, should meet Roosevelt on the Brazilian Paraguay, and that together they should descend a river, unvisited by civilized man except in its headwaters. Its source had been discovered by Colonel Rondon himself, and, because he had no idea where it flowed, he had named it the Rio da Dúvida, the River of Doubt. Situated between the Gy Paraná and the Juruena, it might equally well augment the waters of the Tapajós, the Gy Paraná or the Madeira.

Müller's purpose in making this offer (which was accepted with alacrity) is not entirely clear. He and his colleagues in the Brazilian Government would obviously have liked some attention for the admirable pioneering work which they were sponsoring, and which Colonel Rondon was carrying out, in the Southern Highlands of the Amazon. While Roosevelt's expedition, if successful, would satisfy this purpose, the risk of his being drowned, or dying of fever or starvation was frightful. The Brazilian Government may have relied on the presence of Colonel Rondon to prevent such a tragedy, but they could certainly have diverted Roosevelt to an easier route.

As it was, his journey started in the utmost luxury. Conveyed from Asuncion to the border in the President of Paraguay's yacht, he had every opportunity to admire the endless vistas over the Chaco and to acquaint himself with the distinctive wild life of South America. He met 'an old Western friend, Tex Rickard of the Panhandle and Alaska and various places in between, who was now raising thirty-five thousand head of cattle in the Chaco'. Roosevelt becomes rapturous as he discusses the limitless herds that could be held by this wild region and he thunders against the abominable habits of the piranha fish. He potted alligators in the river with his rifle, on general principles and in order to keep his eye in.

At Cáceres, just across the Brazil-Paraguay border, he met Colonel Rondon. Together their two parties could boast a formidable volume of experience. Both Cherrie and Miller, the two American naturalists, were veterans of South American exploration, but Cherrie had enjoyed the more adventurous life; we have seen him narrowly survive a fall into a school of maddened piranha and he had had even closer escapes from death. In Venezuela, where he had become involved in revolutionary politics, he had sided against the dictator Castro, and combined the profession of ornithologist with that of gun-runner.* His revolutionary activities had earned

---

* After the revolution he paid an elegant farewell to this double rôle, by naming a new species of ant-thrush after the revolutionary general.

him two spells in prison, during one of which he had expected
daily to be taken out and shot. One night when Roosevelt's expedition were discussing the arms that should be issued to cavalry,
several of its members maintained that the lance had a unique
effect on the opposing infantry's morale. Cherrie was seen to nod
vigorously and, on being pressed, he explained that during an early
revolution against Castro, he and five Venezuelans were caught on
foot and charged by twenty lancers at a time when no quarter was
being given. They had saved themselves by accuracy and coolness
with their rifles and stopped the enemy only fifty yards away, but
the impression of twenty steel lance heads, thundering towards him
at a full gallop, would never leave his mind.

Cherrie had thought so little of the ordinary perils of the jungle
that he had taken his wife with him to the Orinoco, and there their
second child was born, 200 miles from civilization. His own comfort
had subsequently been disturbed by the frequent need to move
camp whenever their baby was disturbed by the howling of
jaguars.

Father Zahm was a theologian, a scholar and a traveller as well
as a priest. Fiala, although his explorations had been confined to
the Arctic, had served in Puerto Rico, and was so competent at
organising the expeditions' supplies that even Colonel Rondon was
unable to find fault with his arrangements. Theodore and Kermit
Roosevelt were both expert shots and used to living for long periods
in the wilds.

The Brazilian contingent included Colonel Rondon, Captain
Amilcar and three of their most experienced Lieutenants, an
army doctor, a geologist and a wretched taxidermist from Vienna
who, in Roosevelt's words 'sat on a stool, alternately drenched with
rain and sweltering with heat, and muttered to himself: "Ach,
Schweinerei!" '

But their leader was the most remarkable of the Brazilians.
Candido Mariano da Silva Rondon was of almost pure Indian blood,
a colonel in the Brazilian Army, a scholar and a Positivist. In
Roosevelt's words:

Colonel Rondon is not simply 'an officer and a gentleman' in the
sense that is honourably true of the best army officers in every good
military service. He is also a peculiarly hardy and competent explorer,
a good field naturalist and scientific man, a student and a philosopher.
With him the conversation ranged from jaguar hunting and the perils

of exploration in the 'Mato Grosso', the great wilderness, to Indian anthropology, to the dangers of a purely materialistic industrial civilization, and to Positivist morality. The Colonel's Positivism was, in very fact to him, a religion of humanity, a creed which bade him be just and kindly and useful to his fellow men, to live his life bravely and no less bravely to face death, without reference to what he believed, or did not believe, or to what the unknown hereafter might hold for him.

Rondon had been brought up on a cattle station near Cuyubá in Mato Grosso. After five years as a pupil in military school he acted for another three as professor of mathematics. Then, as a Lieutenant in the Brazilian Army, he returned home to start the work that was to make him famous.

By the time that he met Roosevelt, Rondon had been exploring the Southern Highlands of the Amazon for a staggering period of twenty-four years. During this time he had travelled 14,000 miles, mostly on foot, and by laying down over 3,000 miles of telegraph line, he had connected many isolated outposts to the rest of Brazil. The great rivers in this region run from south to north—the Xingu, the Tapajós, the Juruena and the Madeira—and most explorers had been content to follow their courses. But Rondon's travels took him against the grain of the land, from east to west. His supplies were, therefore, confined to what his animals could carry and, when they died, he would be forced to live off the country in an area where food was almost impossible to find.

On one expedition he lost every one of the 160 mules with which he had started. In his most terrible journey, in 1909, he and his companions, some of them reduced to total nakedness, others so weak that they could scarcely crawl, lived for a full four months off fruit, nuts and the occasional game that they killed.

His exploration brought even more important work to Rondon. Shortly before Roosevelt's arrival he was appointed head of the Indian Protection Service, the first organization of its type in South America. Rondon was aware of the justice of Indians' grievances and of the long and shameful history of their oppression by white men. To win back their confidence and good will he gave orders that in no circumstances, not even in self-defence, were any of his subordinates to kill an Indian. As a result of this order many brave men have lost their lives when they could have saved themselves, and many intractable Indian tribes have been pacified. When he first pronounced his policy Rondon was widely regarded as a madman,* but he survived to see it admired by much of the world. He was later promoted to the rank of General and lived on to the age of ninety-two.

*

The first part of the Roosevelt-Rondon expedition was remarkable mainly for the discoveries of the naturalists. Cherrie and Miller ranged far in front of the main party, collecting and observing, while the others hunted and watched animals and shot occasional specimens for them. The Roosevelts killed most of the local big game, jaguar, tapir, alligator, peccary and giant ant-eater, and admired colourful birds with such splendid names as hyacinth macaws, flaming orioles, tanagers, green jacmars and trogons.

In the evenings they exchanged stories of the many countries that they knew; Rondon could talk of the Mato Grosso, Fiala of the Arctic, Cherrie of Venezuela, Miller of Colombia, Zahm of the Andes and Roosevelt of the North American West, Africa and Cuba. Colonel Rondon read Thomas à Kempis on his way up the Paraguay River; Kermit read Camoens and Theodore Roosevelt anything from Sophocles to Arsène Lupin, always returning to his favourite, Gibbon.

And so, as they crossed from the headwaters of the Paraguay to those of the Amazon, part of Roosevelt's mind was in the Mediterranean, following wars, sieges and esoteric schisms, the madness of emperors and the intrigues of eunuchs, and a more virile empire rising out of the desert. The rolling sentences must have seemed to him to have been coming from another planet.

There was only one unhappy incident; Theodore and Kermit Roosevelt shared a tent, into which one morning before dawn, a pack-ox wandered, and ate their shirts and underclothes without waking either of them. But they safely followed the path previously opened up with such difficulty by Colonel Rondon and stopped at the telegraph posts which he had established a few years before. As they penetrated deep into the wilderness the expedition split up, some members returning to civilization, while one party descended Popagaio into the Juruena and then the Tapajós and another followed the Gy-Paraná down to the Madeira. Colonel Rondon,

* See the correspondence with Sir William Haggard, H.M. Ambassador at Petropolis, in the Public Records Office.

Theodore and Kermit Roosevelt, Cherrie, the doctor and one Lieutenant, with several *camaradas*,* were left to descend the River of Doubt.

During his account of this journey Theodore Roosevelt took great pains to point out the differences between the descent of a totally unknown river and that of a river already navigated by others, however wild and dangerous the latter might be. Most Amazonian rivers are interrupted by numerous rapids, some of which can be run in dug-outs. Many others, to Roosevelt's disgust, although too difficult for dug-outs, would have been child's play to a North American birchbark canoe. When the rapids were impassable it was sometimes possible to avoid a full portage by unloading the canoes, thus raising their freeboards, and manhandling them through the slowest parts of the stream. Kermit, with his experience of bridge-building, was adept at this dangerous work. The canoes would often have to be coaxed down by ropes and manpower for over a mile; a trail would then have to be found or cut through the forest, along which the expedition could carry their equipment to the bottom of the rapids. They would then reload the canoes, embark on them, and perhaps find more rapids within a half mile's distance.

Sometimes the rapids were so severe that there was no chance of lowering even empty canoes through them. Then the explorers would be forced to make a path down to the bottom of the rapids, cut about 200 straight branches for rollers and pull the canoes overland. This was a back-breaking task and only possible when the country was fairly flat. The South American dug-out canoes used by Roosevelt varied in weight from 900 to 2,500 lbs., but two or three of them would only carry the same cargo as one canvas canoe, weighing 160 lbs. Even fully loaded, the canvas canoe could survive more difficult rapids and it could be carried up or downhill without too much effort. Unfortunately, all Roosevelt's canoes were dugouts.

In the very worst conditions the rapids could be too swift to descend and the surrounding countryside too hilly for a portage. Then the explorers would have to carry their belongings down, abandon their canoes and build new ones at the bottom. Every rapid had to be surveyed to see into which category it came, and every portage had to be planned and often cut out of the jungle. All these

* Rondon's explorations were so dreaded by the *camaradas* that they had to be paid seven times their normal wages to accompany him.

delays explain why the party, with limited food supplies and anxious to press on, could cover a distance of only 110 kilometres during a full month of their journey—an average of less than two and a half miles per day.

Travellers on rivers already explored enjoy a number of advantages; they or their guides know which rapids can be shot and how to shoot them; food is more easily obtainable, the quickest paths have already been cut out round each portage; above all they know exactly what is in store for them.

After a smooth start to their passage, Roosevelt's party was soon caught up in a continuous succession of rapids, so that sometimes all its members would have to spend an entire day in the water, nursing the canoes downstream. In one such rapid, when Kermit Roosevelt's boat was upset by a whirlpool, one of his *camaradas* drowned and he himself barely escaped with his life. Once, when making a portage, Colonel Rondon's dog was shot by hostile Indians, who then disappeared into the forest without doing any more harm. The Colonel left some beads by the body to show that he was not angry and then continued downstream.

Exhaustion, the dwindling of their food supplies, constant bouts of fever and disappointment over their progress, all affected the *camaradas*. As their bruises and bites festered into ugly sores, their strength and resolution waned. One of them, a European called Julio, cracked completely under the strain, shirked his share of the work, malingered and often stole his companions' food. Paixão, a gigantic negro sergeant in charge of the *camaradas*, caught him pilfering and knocked him out. Soon afterwards Julio waited by the side of the path which Paixão was following and, when he appeared, shot him dead at point blank range.

At the time of the murder Rondon and the other Brazilian officers were well ahead and Roosevelt had to take charge. Accompanied by the doctor, he went down the trail until he found Paixão's body lying in a pool of blood. Roosevelt thought that Julio must have run amok and that he would now try to kill other members of the expedition. One man, who had been left alone and unarmed in the camp, seemed to be the obvious target, so they hurried on to it and, as they approached, the doctor said: 'My eyes are better than yours, Colonel. If he is in sight I'll point him out to you, as you have the rifle.' But Julio had disappeared and they soon found the rifle that he had used for the murder, thrown away in his panic.

H

Satisfied that he was no longer dangerous, Roosevelt saw no object in pursuing him. When, three days later, he appeared on the bank and shouted that he wished to surrender, Roosevelt felt that he would not be justified in jeopardizing the rest of the expedition by taking back a dangerous murderer, unless Colonel Rondon thought it his duty to do so.

At the next camp Roosevelt caught up with Rondon, who decided that he could not abandon the murderer, even if his presence might endanger the rest of the party. Rondon sent back two expert woodsmen to find him, but Julio had returned to the forest and was never seen again. He might conceivably have made his way to an Indian village, like many deserters before him, but it is far more likely that, unarmed and without supplies, he died a frightful and lingering death in the jungle.

*

Their journey continued in the same way, short fast dashes between long and wearing portages—their half-rations supplemented by what they could catch or shoot. At length they found cuttings in the wood by the side of the bank, left by some adventurous rubber-gatherer, and soon afterwards they found the *seringueros* themselves. Compared to what they had already endured, their journey now was luxury itself, guided as they were downstream by men who knew the river, its rapids and their portage tracks. But Roosevelt was prostrated by fever shortly before they made contact with the rubber men and he spent the time in acute discomfort.

'It is not ideal,' he wrote, 'for a sick man to spend the hottest hours of the day stretched on the boxes in the bottom of a small open dugout, under the well nigh intolerable heat of the torrid sun of the mid-tropics, varied by blinding, drenching downpours of rain; but I could not be sufficiently grateful for the chance.'

Earlier, when it became clear that the Rio da Dúvida was a major river, Colonel Rondon had produced an authority from his Government to rename it the Rio Roosevelt, a pleasant and well-earned compliment.

Guided by the *seringueros*, they descended the Rio Roosevelt until it emerged, as they now expected, into the Madeira. The Madeira is the greatest tributary of the greatest river in the world, and the Rio Roosevelt is the Madeira's greatest affluent and a considerable river in its own right, over 1,500 kilometres long.

Theodore Roosevelt returned to the United States, failed again when he tried for the Republican nomination in 1916, and campaigned for a declaration of war against Germany. When America entered the war in 1917 he applied for active service on the Western Front and offered to raise a force of volunteers, as he had for the war in Cuba.

Although a quarter of a million men responded to his appeal, President Wilson, to his intense annoyance, rejected the offer. 'This is a very exclusive war,' Roosevelt complained, 'and I have been black-balled by the Selection Committee.' He was fifty-nine at the time.

He died in 1919 and most historians agree that his life was shortened by the fever which had attacked him on the Rio Roosevelt.

Chapter Thirteen

THE FAWCETT SAGA

THE DISAPPEARANCE of Colonel Fawcett, like the identity of Jack the Ripper and the fate of the Marie Celeste, is a mystery that has seized the public's interest and held it, long after there was any real hope of its being solved. Even now, forty-two years since he was last seen, any news, however unlikely, about the Colonel will be splashed across the front pages of newspapers in England, America and Brazil. At first sight he does not seem cast for such a rôle.

Colonel Percy Harrison Fawcett was a formidable figure, 6' 1½" tall and built like a heavy-weight boxer; there was no spare flesh on his massive body but he weighed 200 pounds. He was a first-class athlete, a county cricketer and a boxer, with an obsession about physical fitness. He neither drank nor smoked and found these habits distasteful in others. His great physical strength and stamina were reinforced by an iron will, a contempt for discomfort and a virtual immunity from tropical diseases. Perhaps this last quality was the most exceptional. There were other explorers, although not many, who equalled him in dedication, courage and strength, but in his resistance to disease he was unique. Sickness was the bane of South American explorers; because of it their plans were ruined, their lives endangered and sometimes lost. Fawcett was only ill once in all his years in the Tropics and then he wrote in his diary, 'I was heartily ashamed of myself.' It was his fate instead to be held up by the illnesses of his companions and by their inability to keep up with his crippling pace.

But Fawcett, far from being an Amazonian Bulldog Drummond, was a man with many talents. His ink drawings were accepted by the Royal Academy, he built two racing yachts single-handed and patented the Ichtoid Curve. He was sensitive and broadminded in his views, tolerant for his day of social distinctions, and he hated the needless slaughter of animals. During the Putumayo scandal he was quick to point out some blemishes in his own country and her colonies and to contrast the tapir hide whip favourably with the cat o'nine tails.

He was a mystic, a spiritualist by conviction and a romantic by nature. He had a love of wild, unspoilt Indians and a pitying contempt for those corrupted by his own world. Above all he had the vocation of the true explorer; while delighted to return to his family and country, he soon became restless in civilization and he would feel as if there was something missing from his life. The call of the wilds would grow more enticing until he could resist it no more and would return, happy again, to the steamy heat, the squalor, the insects and the mysteries of the Amazon.

Fawcett was commissioned in the Royal Artillery in 1886 and spent most of his early military career in Ceylon where he married and learnt his surveying. In 1906 he volunteered for boundary delimitation work in Bolivia. The Amazon frontiers of Brazil, Peru and Bolivia had never been firmly settled, but this seemed a matter of small importance until the Rubber Boom, when it suddenly became too vital to be agreed by the interested parties. Independent survey teams were appointed. Fawcett was to work on behalf of the Royal Geographical Society, engaged by the Bolivian Government. It was his first visit to South America.

Fawcett was perfectly suited to this work both by temperament and physique. Other officers might stagger out of the wilderness, appalled by the conditions and disgusted with their masters' corrupt inefficiency, but he came back again and again, stronger, more experienced, more enthusiastic, unweakened by the cold of the Andes, the sodden descents through the watershed, the discomforts and dangers of the jungle. In 1906–7, 1908–9, 1910, 1911, and 1913 he covered almost all the vast Amazonian frontiers of Bolivia, much of them unexplored ground. He was one of the few officers who gave consistent satisfaction, but his thoughts were often far away from the problems of surveying.

Fawcett was imaginative and credulous and it would need a far duller mind than his to remain unfired by the early history and legends of South America. His intense study of the Continent's

literature was augmented by the folklore of the Indians and the
stories of other explorers. He was soon struck by the similarity of
the legends told in widely separated parts of the continent. There
were the frequent stories of white Indians and lost cities. Wherever
they occurred the undiscovered civilization seemed to lie in the same
general area, east from the Andes, north of Cuyubá and west from
Bahia.

There was documentary evidence as well. Inland from Bahia
there were known to be lost silver mines of great value, unexploited
since the early seventeenth century. Fawcett was unconcerned with
money, except as a means of enabling him to make his expeditions,
but there was a possibility of more interesting discoveries nearby.

In 1743 a bandeira had started a search for the lost mines, a
first-hand account of which is still preserved in Rio de Janeiro,
although much of the document is decayed and undecipherable. A
transcript would be too long for the purposes of this book and it
would make tiresome reading because of the many lacunae.*

When Fawcett first read this document its author's name was
unknown and, with his love of melodrama, he at once christened
him Francisco Raposo. The eminent Brazilian journalist Antonio
Collado has since revealed that the explorer's real name was João
da Silva Guimarões. His bandeira had been wandering in the wilderness for ten years,† scraping a living off a hard country. At last they
reached a vast range of mountains carpeted with some form of crystal
that gathered the rays of the sun and threw them back into the
onlooker's eye. As the mountains seemed impassable the bandeira
camped for the night and prepared to retrace its steps the next day.
But a Negro, hunting, put up a white stag and, following it, found
a pass between two mountain chains. They could not resist following
this route and after three hours they reached the top of the pass
from which they could see a long level plain. Above five miles away
from them lay a large settlement that could have been Spanish,
Portuguese or perhaps something else.

An Indian, sent forward to explore, returned terrified, but without having found any signs of habitation. A larger party confirmed
his findings. At dawn the next day the whole bandeira entered the

* The full text can be found in Lady Burton's translation in the Appendix
to Vol. II of Sir Richard Burton's *Explorations of the Highlands of Brazil.*
† Señor Collado also maintains that Guimarões started his expedition, not
as an adventurer from Bahia in 1743, but as a fugitive from Vilarica in 1730.

city clutching their weapons, frightened but resolute. They came in through three great arches, so high that none could read the inscriptions on them. They followed a broad street to a square with a monolithic column of black stone in its centre, surmounted by a statue of a man with one hand on his hip and the other pointing to the north. In each corner of the square there stood an obelisk.

The houses were inhabited only by swarms of bats that deafened the explorers and beat at their faces when disturbed. In another street they found a statue of a young figure crowned with laurels. A river ran through the valley with rice fields and swarms of duck on the far bank.

Three days' march down this river they came upon a violent cataract, to the east of which there were 'deep cuttings and frightful excavations'. All the bandeira's ropes were too short to plumb their depths. There were silver nails lying by the caverns and they panned gold dust in the river. In some ruins nearby one of the companions found a gold coin. Another party sent to explore further downstream 'after nine days good march, sighted at the mouth of a large bay formed by a river a canoe carrying two white persons with loose black hair, and dressed like Europeans . . .' Here the manuscript peters out, but it seems from the intelligible scraps that the bandeirantes fired a shot to attract these mysterious people's attention, but that they paddled away and were lost.

The expedition reached the River Paraguassu and sent a message by runner to the Viceroy in Bahia. That was the last ever heard of them and whatever happened they never reached the coast. 'Raposo's' account of his discovery mouldered in the archives in Rio until the middle of the nineteenth century, when the Brazilian Government sent an unsuccessful expedition in search of the ruins.

*

The original manuscript is in the crude Portuguese which might be expected from a semi-literate bandeirante. Fawcett argued with some force that the details given in it are entirely credible, both in the descriptions of the buildings and in the copies of the hieroglyphics on them. He maintained that it would be quite beyond the ability of an uneducated man to be so convincing about things outside his experience and that the story of Raposo's discovery must therefore be true. The part of it dealing with the mysterious white men in the canoe was supported by accounts from many explorers of the Paraguassu River and there were other stories dealing with lost cities in which Fawcett believed as implicitly.

The British Consul at Rio, Colonel O'Sullivan Beare, had told him one such story, of how he was taken to a ruined city in the jungle, similar to Raposo's but much nearer the coast. It, too, had a statue in its square mounted on a gigantic black pedestal. Unfortunately Beare's mule was drowned and lack of supplies forced him to return at once. There was also academic backing for the theory. Remains of pottery and inscriptions suggested that a high state of civilization might once have existed in Brazil.

Up to this point the evidence, although by no means overwhelming, did provide some sort of a case for the lost cities, as strong, for example, as the clues that led Hiram Bingham to Machu Picchu in 1911, and probably stronger than any indications of the existence of the last Andean lost city to be found (in 1966). Fawcett could hardly be criticized for resigning from his boundary work and devoting all his energies to their discovery.

At this point in his reasoning the credulous side in Fawcett's nature seems to have taken control of his mind. He had been presented by Rider Haggard with a black basalt statuette, which was clearly of South American origin. The British Museum declared that, if genuine, it was beyond their experience, but a psychometrist whom he consulted was less reticent. Holding the figure in one hand he wrote with the other an extraordinary account of an advanced civilization on a continent stretching from Africa to South America—advanced, that is, in power and in material wealth, but morally degenerate and given to practices of the black art. Fawcett's interpreter conveniently tuned in at the moment of their nemesis. Violent earthquakes shook the land; volcanoes erupted; the sea came in and the mighty kingdom was destroyed as thoroughly and deservedly as Sodom and Gomorrah. The time of this disaster was impossible to estimate, but it was long before the rise of Egypt.

On this slender basis Fawcett constructed an elaborate theory, of which the central belief was that the statue came from Atlantis and that it might be possible to find survivors of the Atlantean civilization at a point called 'Z' in the unexplored depths of the Mato Grosso. Even Rider Haggard must have been startled by the results of his generosity.

*

Fawcett's preparations were disturbed by the outbreak of the Great War. He left for Europe at once and served with distinction on the Western Front, winning a D.S.O. But in 1920 and 1921 he returned to the Mato Grosso to continue the search for his lost cities.

Throughout his explorations Fawcett had been hampered by his assistants, only two of whom, Costin and Manley, were of comparable physical stamina. His obsessive longing to find the lost cities made him a hard leader, intolerant of any follower who fell below his own standards of fitness and dedication. Expedition after expedition was ruined by the collapse of his assistants and after the war, when neither Costin nor Manley were available, this problem became acute. In spite of repeated disappointments Fawcett continued to accept others' valuations of themselves, and he made no serious attempt to find experienced explorers to accompany him. Perhaps this was because of his obsession with his cities; the same obsession, which made him accept any theory that fitted in with their existence as incontrovertible fact, may also have allowed him to see the next in a string of degenerate braggarts as a new Livingstone or Rondon; or he may simply have been unwilling to be anything less than the absolute leader. In any case his disillusionments were frightful.

There was the ludicrous Australian, 'Butch' Reilly, 6' 5" in height and built like Carnera, and according to his own account a V.C., a major, a bronco-buster and the owner of 20,000 acres in the outback. Fawcett had planned to spend eighteen months in the wilds. 'Butch' lasted two days, in the course of which he fell off his horse, at a walk, four times, a performance which boded ill for his next appearance in the rodeo ring. Another assistant provided the ultimate humiliation by losing his false teeth when swimming and having to be sent back because he could no longer chew any solids. Others fell sick, became frightened or cheated him.

Fawcett was already predisposed in favour of small expeditions, on the grounds that a few might live where many would starve. One cannot help feeling that he may also have reasoned that the smaller the number of his companions, the less likely they would be to include another Butch or an explorer with poorly secured dentures. He was prepared to cut down ruthlessly on equipment which others would have thought essential, guns, ammunition and food. A .22 rifle should be taken for game, although even this extra weight was unwelcome. Fawcett's arguments have some force; for a rigorous journey, lasting perhaps as long as three years and undertaken on foot, the initial supply of food was of little importance. Transport animals could not hope to survive for long. The party would soon be dependent on Indians and the fewer the mouths, the more likely they were to be fed.

For his last journey in 1925 Fawcett took only his son, Jack, and Jack's friend, Raleigh Rimmell. His plan was ambitious, perhaps foolhardy, and his goal was still the discovery of his inhabited cities. He would leave Cuyubá heading north, swing north-east across the Xingu, cross over to the Araguaia, then the Tocantins, reach the São Francisco and follow it down to the coast. He was so secretive about his route that even today its exact course is unknown, but one can say from its outlines that it was one of the most difficult and dangerous ever undertaken in the history of exploration.

In South America there is a great difference between exploring by river and by land. The Roosevelt-Rondon expedition was a good illustration of the dangers of river travel, but even if the river is unknown, interrupted by miles of boiling rapids, and hemmed in by jungle through which portages are impossible, exploration by canoe is far easier than by foot. An adequate supply of food, tools, and ammunition can be carried, fish and turtles caught in the stream and game shot on its banks. But when an explorer strikes out away from the rivers he loses all these advantages. He must now limit his supplies to what he and his animals can carry and in unexplored South America, the life of a pack animal is short. He also faces an entirely new danger—that of dying of thirst. Fawcett proposed to spend some two years on a journey which would take him across the line of three of the great southern tributaries of the Amazon, and for these two years he would have to depend for his life on what he and his companions could carry. Colonel Rondon, when making a similar expedition, would take hundreds of animals, few, if any, of which would survive. Fawcett, unable to afford such measures, took instead two young Englishmen, and a dozen mules for the first few days of his journey.

Fawcett's choice of companions for this intimidating trip was extraordinary. The young men had neither any experience of exploration nor any qualities that would necessarily fit them for it. Both, it is true, were full of enthusiasm and Jack was built like his father, with all the strength of his youth. Apart from this and his abstinence (he neither drank nor smoked and Fawcett described him as 'virgin in mind and body'), he had no obvious recommendations. Fawcett knew nothing of Rimmell and blithely assumed that he would follow Jack anywhere. On the way up to the wilds Raleigh did little to inspire confidence, calling Portuguese 'this damn jibbering language' and becoming angry when his English was not understood. Wearing in his new boots at Cuyubá produced blisters. At Bakairi, the last outpost of civilization, he rubbed a tick bite on his foot until it became ulcerous and shed great strips of skin. Jack wrote home, with careless gaiety: 'What will happen when we really meet insects I don't know!' To which Colonel Peter Fleming has replied: 'They might, one would have thought, have guessed.'

Fawcett himself had no qualms; he was now fifty-seven and he doubted his ability to keep up with his younger companions. He never seems to have doubted them or to have questioned his extraordinary choice. The little party trailed out of Bakairi, with poor Raleigh dragging his injured leg. They soon reached Dead Horse Camp, the furthest point of the 1920 expedition. Fawcett dispatched a letter back to his wife, full of confidence and ending with the words 'you need have no fear of failure'. They were to be the last words ever heard from him by the outside world.

Fawcett's estimates of the time that his expedition would take varied, but it seemed likely to last at least eighteen months. He was anxious that there should be no rescue parties, thinking, correctly, that they would only lead to unnecessary loss of life. But nearly three years after his departure an expedition was organized to investigate his disappearance, with Commander George Dyott, an experienced South American explorer, as its leader.

From the start Dyott was inundated with applications.

They came from every walk of life, lawyers, physicians, real estate dealers, engineers, steeplejacks, motion picture actors, acrobats, wrestlers, prize fighters, ex-soldiers and a host of men who apparently could not fit into any nook of civilized existence. ... One volunteer wrote eagerly that he found life particularly confusing; he was inured to hardship and had no fear of danger. 'There is only one drawback,' he explained. 'I am in jail and will not be able to get out for a little while.' Many men openly admitted that their married life was unbearable and they wanted to make a new start; a more hardened ruffian wrote 'No terror of the jungle can faze me. I have been married for 12 years'. Among the qualifications put forward by a westerner

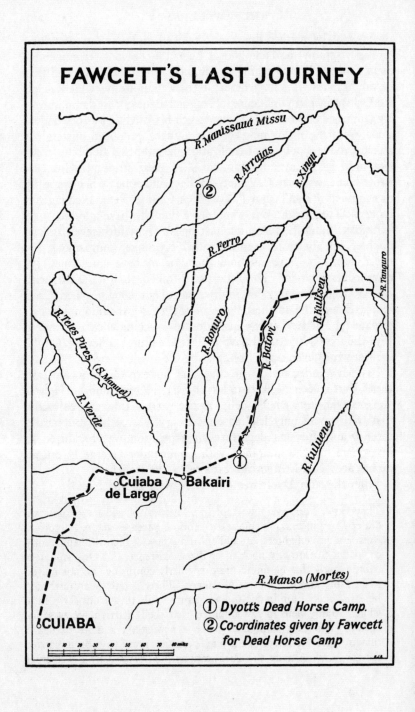

FAWCETT'S LAST JOURNEY

R. Manissauá Missu

R. Arraias

R. Xingu

②

R. Ferro

R. Tanguro

R. Teles Pires (S. Manuel)

R. Ronuro

R. Batovi

R. Kulisehu

R. Verde

R. Kuluene

①

o Cuiaba
de Larga

Bakairi

R. Manso (Mortes)

o CUIABA

① Dyott's Dead Horse Camp.
② Co-ordinates given by Fawcett
for Dead Horse Camp

0 10 20 30 40 50 60 70 80 miles

were 'I can climb anything, prefer not to shave, can dance and wear
a dress suit'. An attendant in a Turkish bath explained that he was
used to heat and would make a good companion for anyone in the
tropics.

With this wealth of talent available one would have expected
Dyott, unlike Fawcett, to choose seasoned explorers to accompany
him; but of the four young men he selected, two were experts on
photography and two on wireless. None had been on any sort of
expedition before, and one of them was to refuse throughout to eat
the flesh of any but the largest fish, on the grounds that a friend of
his had died by choking on a fish bone. The reasons for this surprising choice were that Dyott's expedition was backed by a Press
Syndicate, that if he came across any evidence he was determined to
bring back photographs, and that he wished to remain in radio
contact with his sponsors throughout.

Before leaving America, Dyott received a letter from a medium
claiming to have news of Fawcett from supernatural sources. After
their meeting, Dyott found him, somewhat severely, to be 'a
slovenly type of man, partly paralysed'. Fawcett and his party were
apparently all well, but prisoners of the Indians near the Bolivian
border, in a valley surrounded by three hills, one of which Fawcett
climbed every day to look for help. Fawcett's English dog had
returned to a farm known as Rio Novo. Dyott was advised to pay
close attention to the farmer, not to drink water near any old camp
sites, to carry rockets to frighten the Indians and if bitten by a snake,
to apply wine and bandage up the wound.

Neglecting the last piece of advice he stopped instead at the
Butantan snake farm outside São Paulo to collect serum. He then
travelled up to Cuyubá, where one of Dyott's Brazilian companions'
wife fell into a trance and proclaimed that Fawcett and his son were
prisoners of the Indians on the lower Xingu near a river called I-ti.
These messages were only the beginning of a series of contradictory
revelations that were to jam the psychic ether for the next quarter
of a century.

The inexperience of its members was the only thing in common
between Fawcett's expedition and that sent to discover his fate.
Fawcett had left with two companions and twelve mules, and three
Indians to guide him to the next village. Dyott set out with twenty-
six men, sixty-four bullocks and ten mules, radios, ciné and still
camera equipment, four canoes, a rubber raft and trunks full of

trinkets for the Indians. He must have been glad to leave Cuyubá. On his arrival in Brazil he had been greeted in the papers with the announcement that Fawcett was sitting on a mound of gold and was waiting for his accomplice Dyott to come to carry it off. No sooner had he reached the interior than he was approached by 'Captain Miranda', a revolutionary guerilla leader, who told him that Fawcett had been murdered and robbed by bandits. Theories were proliferating but facts were non-existent.

At Bakairi Dyott had the extraordinary good luck to meet an Indian called Bernadino who had left with Fawcett, 'an odd looking customer with a head as square as a brick and distorted features. Three large teeth protruded from his front jaw like the tusks of some wild animal'.

Bernadino guided Dyott's expedition out on to the same trail, through the same dry scrubland. From time to time they saw distinctive Y-shaped cuts on the trees which they thought must have been made by Fawcett. The cold at night was unbearable and the insects made the days torture. The animals suffered even more than the men. The mules' mouths were cut by the knife-edged grass and the heat was so great that the bullocks could only travel by night. It must have been with relief that they reached the Kuliseu river and were able to send back their animals. Bernadino told them that Fawcett had joined this river later on, appropriating two Anauqua canoes, and that he had accompanied Fawcett to the Anauqua village and had then returned, meeting the owners of the canoes on the way back. They had seemed understandably annoyed by their loss.

Before Dyott could set off he had to make five bark canoes, as the four he had with him and the rubber raft were not enough even for the rump of his party. They were built with great labour and difficulty from the bark of jatoba trees; Dyott continued down-river, still seeing Fawcett's signs on the banks, until they reached the Anauqua village where Bernadino had left Fawcett.

Dyott took an immediate dislike to Aloique, the Anauqua chief, and found that 'even his mouth had nothing to recommend it; it was simply a slit in his face suggestive of a treacherous disposition which his surly attitude towards us corroborated in full'. In his village they found the first concrete evidence of Fawcett's presence. Aloique's child had a trinket round its neck with inscribed on it 'W. S. Silver & Company, King William House, Eastcheap, London and in his hut there was a small metal Indian Army officer's trunk.

Unfortunately relations between the tribe and their visitors were so bad that Dyott never had a chance to look inside the trunk. They had no language in common and had to communicate entirely through signs. Some of the statements attributed to the Indians must therefore be treated with caution.

In conversation with the Anauquas Dyott suddenly heard the word I-ti, and remembering the spiritualist, he became violently excited, but the word turned out only to mean 'sun'. This was as near as any of the spiritualists' predictions came to the truth. Aloique said that he and another of his tribe had accompanied Fawcett a day's march east of the Kuluene River. Dyott sensibly split his expedition, sending the peons down the Kuliseu in boats, with instructions to wait at the junction with the Kuluene. The Americans, accompanied by Aloique and some of his tribesmen, set off towards the Kuluene, their Indian guides reluctant and afraid of the warlike Suyas to the north-east.

After three days' march they reached the country of the Kalapolo Indians, who remembered Fawcett's arrival. He had, they said, stayed one night in their village and then continued to the Kuluene. They had followed and for four days seen smoke from his camp fires, but on the fifth day there was none. In this respect the Kalapolo's evidence agreed absolutely with Aloique's, but while he suspected the Suyas and acted out a grisly pantomime which ended by his yelling 'Suyas! Bang, Bang, Bang!' at the top of his voice, Dyott and his companions suspected him of the murder. Aloique refused to guide Dyott to the place where Fawcett had been killed, on the grounds that he did not know the way.

Dyott was by now convinced that Aloique was the murderer, and decided to rendezvous with the rest of his party before trying to find Fawcett's remains. On the way down the river, he offered Aloique a rifle and a shirt if he would guide him there. In spite of his earlier denial the chief immediately accepted, thus confirming Dyott's worst suspicions. It is only fair to say that Aloique would probably have offered to guide him to New York for this reward and to repeat that no conversations between Dyott and the Indians can be taken as precisely correct.

At the junction of the Kuluene and Kuliseu Dyott realized that he had lost his chance of finding any remains. The rest of his party were camped there, miserable and surrounded by Indians all hungry for presents. Canoe-loads of importunate savages arrived daily. One of Dyott's peons deserted and on his way home took food off the Indians and told them to collect their payment from him. As the supply of presents grew lower the mood of the Indians became ugly. At last Dyott was forced to leave secretly in the middle of the night and paddle at full speed down the Xingu, pausing only, as Colonel Fleming has commented, when he was safely out of reach, to announce over his radio that he was surrounded by hostile Indians.

It is not easy to assess Dyott's contribution to the untangling of the Fawcett problem. He returned to civilization convinced that he had solved the mystery and exposed the murderer, but he had in fact done nothing of the sort. Like many explorers, Dyott never played down the dangers he faced, and a selection of some of his book's chapter headings gives an idea of its contents—'Into the Wilderness on Bucking Bullocks', 'A land of thirst and insects', 'Wrecks and River Monsters', 'Savages', 'Living with Savages', 'Surrounded' (by savages), 'Fish bones and human bones', 'A midnight escape', 'A race against time', and, finally, 'Safe at last'.

A careful reading of this book shows that Dyott was haunted throughout with the fear of being murdered by the Indians. 'Bullets have a habit of straying through the air,' he wrote. 'Knives also flash at unfortunate moments, and then another white man is reported missing or killed by Indians. That is an old game I have been long familiar with.' It was this anxiety, which may have been perfectly well founded, that prevented him from making the final effort of crossing the Kuluene to seek the scene of Fawcett's death. In spite of this failure, Dyott did achieve a great deal. He traced Fawcett's route from Bakairi to the Kalapolo village, and produced strong evidence that he had been murdered by Indians some five days' march from the banks of the Kuluene. He had not established the identity of the murderer, for Aloique, at the best, was only a slightly more probable villain than the Suyas. But, as time wore on and the likelihood of Fawcett's remains ever being found dwindled, it seemed that this was as much as anyone would discover and that the only argument left would be over the grisly details.

*

Four years later, in 1932, the whole issue exploded again. A Swiss trapper named Stefan Rattin came out of the Mato Grosso with an extraordinary story. In an Indian village in the Upper Tapajós system he had met an old white man, tall, bearded and melancholy. The Indians were annoyed by his being seen, but when they started on a drinking bout the old man approached Rattin and asked in English if he was English and a friend. He claimed to be an English Colonel and asked Rattin to tell the British Consul of his plight; he also mentioned a friend called Paget in São Paulo. When Rattin agreed, he said 'You are a gentleman,' and shook his hand.

Rattin noticed that the back of his hands were badly scratched and gave him iodine, but the Indians took it away and painted themselves with it. Rattin asked him if he was alone. He said something about his son sleeping and began to cry. Later he showed Rattin a gold locket which he wore on a chain around his neck, with a photograph inside it of a lady with a large hat and two small children.

There were several peculiarities about this story. In the first place the conversation was in English, which Rattin scarcely spoke, while both he and Fawcett were fluent in Spanish and Portuguese. The description of Fawcett's beard and eyes were wrong. The old man never identified himself, except by saying that he was an English Colonel. He gave Rattin no written message, although Rattin was actually using a pencil and some paper at the time. How had Fawcett got so far from his course, having last been seen by the Kalapolo 300 miles away going in the opposite direction? Why had he not escaped? Fawcett, even at that age, would be no pampered recusant from the pages of *A Handful of Dust*, and an Indian tribe could never have kept him captive against his will for so long.

As against this Rattin's own behaviour is perfectly credible. He identified Fawcett's photograph and claimed that it was the first time he had seen him. If he was lying he might have been expected to produce a more convincing story. If he was such an atrocious liar that he could not even do this it is odd, as Colonel Fleming has pointed out, that he should include such brilliant circumstantial detail as the story of the iodine. Furthermore Rattin made no attempt to exploit his fame, remaining instead determined to return to rescue the colonel, who, he said, would reward him in due course. He set off with two companions and was never seen again.

Attractive and mysterious as Rattin's story may be, one must admit that there is virtually no likelihood of its having been true. General Rondon, after interviewing Rattin, declared to the Press that he was unconvinced and still believed Fawcett to have been killed by the Indians. He also took the opportunity of referring to Dyott's expedition as 'a complete fiasco since it contributed nothing to geographical knowledge and left the Indians excited'.*

Rattin was followed by many less convincing witnesses. Rumours of Fawcett's presence and stories of his death came pouring in from every corner of Amazonia, varying in conviction from the unlikely to the ridiculous. They reached perhaps their nadir in 1934, when a book by a Tex Harding appeared, entitled *The Devil's Drummers*. Mr. Harding, described in the introduction as 'a world hobo' and 'thorough-going roughneck', claimed to have rescued the beautiful Indian maiden Tana as she was about to be sacrificed to the sacred anaconda. In her very proper gratitude she told him that the three men had been captured and killed by the Indians in a feast to the Sun God, which was accompanied by the foulest cannibalistic rites.

*

In 1950 a far more serious theory was advanced and one which may well provide the true answer to the mystery. Since Fawcett's disappearance things had altered in the Mato Grosso. Science has wrought two dramatic changes in the Amazon system, the first through the invention of the steam ship, the second through that of the aeroplane. If the steamer made the main river accessible for thousands of miles, the aeroplane has done the same for the most remote parts of the Amazon Valley. Fawcett and Dyott had spent months reaching the Kuluene. They had first to take a steamship up the Paraguay to Cuyubá, then to face the exhausting trek overland to the Kuliseu, then to build or borrow their canoes and fight their way down or round the rapids in that river, finally they had to strike out overland for the Kuluene. It was almost impossible to ascend a turbulent river like the Xingu. But, after the invention of the aeroplane, a small advance party could clear a landing strip, establish a post, and then be reinforced and supplied without any difficulty.

The area in which the Kalapolo, the Suya and the Anauqua live was pacified by these methods, and the tribes who inhabited it

---

* Many an explorer has found this attitude infuriating. Nothing could be more wounding to a man's self esteem than to be told that his death at the hands of Indians would be lamentable because it might jar the delicate sensibilities of his murderers.

taken under the wing of the Central Brazil Foundation—an admirable if xenophobic body. Their administrators, Orlando and Claudio Villas Boas, are heirs to many of Rondon's ideals. These two brothers live a strange and isolated life, dedicated to the preservation of the Xingu Indians. As a result of their devotion they are trusted by the Indians in a completely different manner to other white men. Even twenty-five years after Fawcett's disappearance, any theory on his death from such a source must be taken seriously, especially when it is circumstantial.

Orlando Villas Boas lived for a year with the Kalapolo tribe. During this time he became convinced that they had killed Fawcett, and by the end of the year he had persuaded the chief Izerari to show him the grave. But before he had a chance of doing so, Izerari died and the next chief, Yacuma, was too frightened to help. His successor, Comatzi, after the most solemn promises that there would be no reprisals, showed Villas Boas the grave. Villas Boas dug and found some bones and a machete.

The Kalapolo story was that three men, one old and two young, had come from the west with the chief of a neighbouring tribe, the Nahukuas, clearly the Anauquas, since different writers give their own phonetic renderings of Indian names. A Kalapolo, Cavuquira, took them out hunting the next day. Fawcett shot a duck, and, when Cavuquira ran to retrieve it, something about his behaviour made Fawcett think that he intended to keep it for himself. Fawcett grabbed hold of the Indian and slapped his face. That evening in the Kalapolo village Cavuquira made much of this insult and begged the chief, Caiabi, to allow him to kill the white men. It was also evident that, while Fawcett had beads and others gifts in his pack, he had no intention of distributing them to the Kalapolo.*

* I am taking Colonel Eggeling's version of the Kalapolo's story. Colonel Eggeling was a member of the first expedition to go out to the Xingu to investigate this version of Fawcett's death and he has made a deeper study of the subject than any other writer. The conclusions of this chapter are, I think, broadly in agreement with his views, but the last word on Colonel Fawcett cannot be written until his book *Murder in Mato Grosso* is published.

Adrian Cowell stayed for some months with the Villas Boas brothers and wrote an interesting account of his experiences in *The Heart of the Forest* . . . He quotes Orlando as saying that, after the duck episode, Fawcett slapped the face of an Indian child who was pestering him, and that this was the final straw that persuaded the Kalapolo to kill him. It seems likely that one face slapping, probably that of Cavuquira, may, over the years, have grown into two. Indians are grossly unreliable witnesses.

These considerations were powerful enough to decide the Indians on his death. In the morning, three young warriors, Cavuquira, Bororo and Cuiuhi, ferried the doomed party across a narrow lagoon. A small boy called Krahi sat in the canoe and witnessed the tragedy. At the top of the far bank the three Kalapolo suddenly turned on the Englishmen, caught them entirely by surprise and clubbed them to death. They threw their bodies into the lagoon and returned to their village, the wound to their honour assuaged.

Three days after this massacre the chief became worried about its discovery and ordered Cavuquira to find Fawcett's body, take it out of the lagoon and bury it. The bones which Villas Boas found twenty-one years later were missing a leg and an arm—evidence that was consistent with the skeleton's having spent three days in a lagoon infested with piranha and alligators.

At first sight the story was wholly convincing. There is no serious argument that Fawcett and his companions in fact went to the Kalapolo village. There was the concrete evidence of the bones, found exactly in the right place. There was no motive for the Kalapolo to admit to a murder of which they were innocent, and indeed they were reluctant in their confession. Their story tallied remarkably well with the few known facts, and Orlando Villas Boas was not the sort of man who would fabricate evidence. Most of the inconsistencies with Dyott's account could safely be put down to inaccuracy in remembering details after so long and to his own imperfect understanding of what he was being told. Fawcett's irritable behaviour, while out of character, could well have been the result of frustration at Raleigh Rimmell's unfitness.

The bones were reverently returned to England, handed over to his family in the unfunereal setting of Claridges Hotel and taken off for examination by the Royal Anthropological Institute. Their finding was devastating. Fawcett was well over six feet, but the bones belonged to a man of about 5′ 7″ and probably to one who was either Indian or part-Indian. If any further evidence was needed the teeth bore no resemblance to Fawcett's. Jack was taller than his father and Raleigh Rimmell was much taller than the skeleton. It was certain that the bones belonged to no member of Fawcett's expedition.

If the Kalapolo had failed to produce Fawcett's body, their confession alone would have been plausible, but once they had disinterred bones which could not possibly have been his, their whole story seemed less than convincing. The supporters of the bones theory suggested that the Kalapolo, frightened by enquiries about Fawcett, might, at some time, have changed his bones for others, or alternatively, that their nerve might have failed them at the last moment and that they had then deliberately shown Villas Boas the wrong grave. But neither of these explanations can be described as more than uninspired guesswork.

A party of Brazilian journalists, accompanied by Colonel Eggeling and Fawcett's surviving son, Brian, set out to inspect the grave, interview the Kalapolo and discover the truth. Unfortunately most of the journalists had already written on the subject and they were more anxious to justify the flights of their own imaginations than to find out what had happened to Fawcett. Brian Fawcett, on the other hand, was convinced that his father had never been near the territory of the Kalapolo tribe* and that the entire bones theory was, therefore, untrue. With most of the visitors holding strong and contradictory views, any consensus of opinion was out of the question. Cavuquira himself was dead, but Bororo and

* Brian Fawcett maintains to this day that the expedition never went near the Kuliseu or Kuluene rivers, and that Dead Horse Camp, from which his father sent back his last message, was not where Dyott and Bernadino had described it—at 14° S in the headwaters of the Batovi—but some hundred and forty miles away between the Araias and the Manitsaua-Missu at 11° 43′ S, 54° 35″ W. He bases his theory on his father's letter from Dead Horse Camp which gave these co-ordinates and claims that any report of the expedition in the Kuliseu–Kuluene area is necessarily mistaken. Brian Fawcett thus sets himself against a mass of evidence. Separate eyewitness accounts confirm almost all of Fawcett's journey to the Kuluene. Bernadino accompanied him for the first part of the expedition. Aloique and the Anauqua received him in their village on the Kuliseu and escorted him to the Kuluene; the Kalapolo remember his arrival at their village and confess to his murder. Dyott's discovery of the Y cuts, the stolen canoe, the trinket and trunk in Aloique's hut all confirm the Kuliseu–Kuluene route.

Even without this evidence, it would be impossible to believe that Fawcett could have reached this Dead Horse Camp in time to write his dispatch. It is over a hundred and fifty miles from Bakairi to the co-ordinates given by Fawcett and the country in between is dense tropical jungle. An expert on the area estimated that it could take three fit men several months to complete this journey. To have been on the Manitsaua-Missu when he wrote, Fawcett, impeded by pack animals and a lame man, must have taken only nine days which not even he could have done. As it is also impossible that an adept surveyor could have mistaken his position by one hundred and forty miles after so short a journey, we are left with the certainty that Fawcett deliberately falsified his co-ordinates to prevent others from following him to his lost cities. Such an action is entirely consistent with his passion for secrecy.

Cuiuhi repeated their confessions and Krahi his testimony. Their account of Fawcett's death was endorsed by the rest of the tribe. It is easy to imagine Villas Boas's relief when his guests departed. He does not encourage visitors at any time, on the grounds that they may unsettle the Indians. As the argument grew louder and the flash bulbs exploded one can see this extraordinary man—short, bearded, stout and formidable—glowering at such an unparalleled intrusion.

*

The bones theory is the last serious attempt to solve the riddle of Fawcett's disappearance and whether it is accepted or rejected, there remain a number of irritating inconsistencies which are worth examining in detail.

Taking the case in favour of the bones theory, the report of Fawcett's arrival is circumstantially correct. He came from the right direction with the chief of the right tribe. Raleigh Rimmell had got a bad leg and the description of the party was exact. The machete found with the bones was traced back to a German firm trading extensively in England at the time. The Kalapolo had no conceivable motive to confess to the murder if they had not committed it, and the environment in which dozens of false confessions may be received for the same crime is one of the many social amenities missing in the Matto Grosso.

The Kalapolo's fear of reprisals gives their story a ring of truth, strengthened by the belief in it of Orlando Villas Boas who knew these Indians better than anyone. If the Kalapolo had not murdered Fawcett it is most unlikely that they would have remembered his short visit so vividly for more than twenty years. Above all, if one rejects the bones theory, the confession of the Kalapolo must be explained, and it should be repeated that the testimony of the two surviving murderers was supported by an eye-witness and corroborated by the entire tribe. The very length of time which elapsed between Fawcett's disappearance and the Kalapolo confession adds to its plausibility.

On the other side there are firstly the bones themselves, to start with the strongest evidence in favour of the theory and then damning against it. The switching of bones by the Kalapolos is unconvincing. One can understand their removing Fawcett's bones through fright, but not their replacing them with others which, as far as their own knowledge went, would be just as incriminating; how on earth would they know about pathology? The accuracy of their account of Fawcett's visit is not in dispute, only that of his death, and even allowing for distortions over the years there are some discrepancies. At the same time the accuracy of the Kalapolos' version of Fawcett's arrival does dispose of any outside chance that they might have murdered an entirely different party.

We have seen that Dyott's account suffers from his linguistic limitations, but that of the Kalapolo is open to different objections. The passage of twenty years and many repetitions must have changed their original version to an extent that we can never know. And it is not, therefore, unfair to contrast some of their statements with those of Dyott. When Dyott questioned Aloique and the Kalapolo, they both told him, with vivid gestures,* that the smoke from Fawcett's fires could be seen for four or five days after he had crossed the Kuluene. Aloique actually said that he had accompanied Fawcett for a full day of his last journey, and a day's march would have taken him well beyond the place where the Kalapolo afterwards claimed to have commited the murder.

We must also describe as valueless Aloique and the Kalapolos' claim to have seen smoke from Fawcett's camp fires for four or five days after his departure. There are no natural eminences on the banks of the Kuluene, from which one can look out over the roof of the forest, and it would therefore be impossible to see smoke anything like as far as four days' march away. Any smoke that was seen could not be identified as coming from Fawcett's camp rather than from the fires of Indian hunters. It is an interesting question why Aloique and the Kalapolo told the same lie while blaming the murder on different culprits, but the answer would shed more light on Indian psychology than on Fawcett's fate.

In their story to Villas Boas, the Kalapolo maintained that they were afraid of the Nahukua learning the truth. When questioned by

---

* Aloique first imitated a white man walking and commented, 'caraiba (white man) puc puc puc.' Then he pointed to the east, exclaiming 'Iti'—a word which Dyott knew to mean the sun. He moved his arm slowly over his head from east to west, still saying 'Iti', and, when the 'sun' had set, he lay down and snored. He repeated this performance four times to indicate the passage of four days. On the fifth day his arm stopped after threequarters of its course to show that the murder took place at about 3 p.m. He then gave his dramatic mime of the Suyas springing from ambush. Aloique would have been brilliant at parlour games.

Dyott they accused Aloique and his Nahukua of the murder, while Aloique blamed it on the Suya. Both of the Kalapolo statements argue against any collaboration between the two tribes, and yet the rest of Aloique's testimony supports what they told Dyott, and, if they were both speaking the truth on that occasion, the Kalapolo could not have done what they claimed later, since Fawcett would have been alive four days after crossing the Kuluene.

But this is a tenuous argument. While the Indian sign-languages seem to have been clear enough, Aloique, even by the elastic standards of his race, was a wretched witness. He contradicted himself frequently and Dyott believed that the purpose behind his story was to lure him into a convenient place, murder him there and steal his rifle, which he greatly coveted.

In fairness to Colonel Fawcett one must point out that during many of his expeditions, his life had depended on the friendship of Indians, who were sometimes members of tribes far more dangerous than the Kalapolo. He was no stranger to pain, discomfort and frustration and he would be most unlikely to behave so rashly under what, for him, would still be slight pressure. Fawcett's success with Indians had always been based on gentleness and the avoidance of any form of aggressive action. Slapping Cavuquira, let alone the child, would have been alien both to his nature and his training.

Writers, who on Fawcett's marches would have done little better than the unspeakable Butch, have accepted the Kalapolo story without reservation, and described him as having brought about his own death by his 'petulance'. In dismissing such childish arrogance we must remember that the Kalapolo had over twenty years in which to develop their own story of the murder, and that the version that finally emerged was unlikely to do them discredit. A cold-blooded murder committed for the sake of a few beads, may, by partisan repetitions, have been transformed into a manly defence of tribal honour. It is surely significant that, as late as 1952, the beads in Fawcett's pack were admitted to be part of the Kalapolos' motive.

Any attempt to assess the bones theory must founder on the contradiction between the bones themselves and the mass confession of the Kalapolo. We can dismiss any of the fringe theories in which Fawcett never went near the Kuluene. The evidence gathered by Dyott proves beyond any reasonable doubt that he did and that he reached the Kalapolo village by the confluence of that river and the

Tanguro. To come to any firm conclusion as to what happened afterwards one must offer a convincing explanation, either to the problem how the wrong bones were in Fawcett's grave, or to that of how an entire tribe described a murder which they did not commit. No answer based on the existing evidence can be more than a wild hypothesis and we are unlikely ever to learn more. The Kalapolo could for example, have let the party cross the lagoon and, over the years, have built up a fantasy of having killed them, in which they eventually came to believe. They could have killed Fawcett elsewhere, perhaps well on the far side of the Kuluene, and have confused the place with the grave of some Indian victim.

It may be significant that the skeleton which was disinterred should be without an arm and a leg. No Indian could hope to survive the loss of a single limb, let alone two, and it is almost certain that the limbs were removed after death. This in its turn suggests that the body was in the lagoon where alligators could reach it. According to the bones theory Fawcett's body was also in the lagoon for three days, after which one would expect it to be dismembered and unidentifiable. A possible explanation is, then, that an Indian's body, which for some unknown reason was in the lagoon at the time, was retrieved in mistake for that of Fawcett and buried in his place.

A false confession by an entire tribe to a murder in which two of its members claimed to be guilty parties seems far less likely than a mistake of this sort about the body or confusion after so many years as to the site of the grave. There are several theories to account for the wrong bones having found themselves in the grave, none of which are convincing but all more likely than any explanation of the Kalapolo confession. We can therefore say somewhat tentatively that Colonel Fawcett and his companions were murdered by three Kalapolo Indians on the bank of a lagoon near the confluence of the Kuluene and Tanguro rivers in the state of Mato Grosso.

EPILOGUE

EPILOGUE

IT SEEMS conventional to finish any book about the Amazon Valley with a panegyric on its future. Over one hundred years ago Lieutenant Herndon wrote '... I have no hesitation in saying, that I believe in fifty years Rio Janeiro without losing a tittle of her wealth and greatness, will be but a village to Pará, and Pará will be what New Orleans would long ago have been but for the activity of New York and her own fatal climate, the greatest city of the New World; Santarem will be St. Louis, and Barra, Cincinnati.' Edwards, writing even earlier, considered that, 'were Pará a free and independent state, its vast wilds would in a few years be peopled by millions and its products would flood the world'. We have already seen Colonel Church's references to 'a land as fair as the Garden of Eden'; Spruce, as enthusiastic as anyone, wished that his country owned the Amazon Valley instead of India; and Casement was thinking in the same terms when he wrote: 'Germany in South America, the Teuton on the Amazon would work more amazing things than the British in India.'

It is possible to continue such quotations indefinitely. Before, during and after the Rubber Boom foreign visitors were unanimous in predicting a golden future for the Amazon and it seemed that there were grounds for their optimism. Its rivers sweep through a vast, fertile country unsurveyed and almost untouched. There is no telling what oil, minerals or precious stones lie under its soil and even without them, an uncultivated area the size of Western Europe must be of vast importance to a hungry world. The very idea of a sub-continent lying fallow seems absurd. Once malaria, yellow fever and smallpox had been conquered, the Amazon seemed free to take its place as the storehouse of the world.

But the quotations we have seen were all made before the collapse
of the Rubber Boom. Since that time of unparalleled poverty, the
Amazon Valley has seen some progress, but it has been pitifully
short of all predictions. The advance has indeed been more a matter
of recovery than of growth, and the Amazon's importance, both to
Brazil and to the world, is far less now than in the golden years of
the Rubber Boom.

If Fawcett could be reincarnated to set out once again on that
terrible journey from the Kuluene River to the coast, he would find
his path as desolate and very nearly as dangerous as in 1928. If
Bates could return to Ega or Spruce to Tarapoto, they would find
them little altered after a century's absence. Wallace, on the Rio
Negro, might find his canoe swamped and himself deafened by a
passing hovercraft, but he might also meet Indians as primitive as
those he had found a hundred years before on the Uaupés. The Rio
Roosevelt is as wild as at the time of its discovery, and as yet none
of the light industries and vast ranches, dreamed of by the President,
grace its banks. Nor has the Putumayo been hauled into the twentieth century by colonies of industrious and wonder-working
Teutons. If La Condamine, Father Fritz or even Orellana once more
descended the river, they would find much of it familiar.

Nevertheless the Amazon Valley has changed in small but
important respects. Two towns on the river, Belém by its mouth and
Pucallpa 2,500 miles away on the Ucayali, are connected with the
outside world by road. It is an awe-inspiring sight when great yellow
Caterpillar machines scoop out the jungle in huge bites, push down
the highest trees and leave behind an avenue covered only with
bare earth. How easily the Madeira-Mamoré railway could have
been built with such tools!

The importance of these roads can be judged from the amount
of traffic using them, which, considering their quality, is enormous.
The road from Lima to Pucallpa starts impressively enough with a
paved surface running across the coastal desert. It climbs up into
the Andes, reaching a height of nearly 16,000 feet, plunges into
valleys and soars again over the next range of mountains. After
two thirds of its distance the hard surface is replaced by gravel and
mud* which is churned into a foot-deep slush by the torrential
rainfall of the Eastern Andes. The road is closed after each rain and
it is so narrow that traffic flows in one direction only, according to

* The road will soon have a hard surface throughout its length.

the day of the week. It is blocked by landslides with sickening regularity. But in spite of all its shortcomings, the road to Lima has had far more effect on Pucallpa than the link with Brasilia or Belém. In 1935 Pucallpa had a population of some 500. The road was completed in 1943 and now it is a sprawling, insanitary town with more than 30,000 inhabitants. Through Pucallpa the products of Loreto can take the only overland route to the main markets of their own country.

The obsession with rubber at the time of the Boom blinded the people of the Amazon to the value of any other material. But now there is a fair-sized oil-field in the Bolivian Amazon, several smaller fields in Peru and a refinery outside Manaos. Every kind of forest product is gathered, although often on a small scale. The woods yield not only timber of excellent quality—teak, mahogany, cedar and many others—but also more precious by-products, fibrous textiles, guarana, nuts, vegetable oils, sarsparilla, resins, tannin, cacao, jute, many kinds of nuts and fruits, and spices and oils essential to the making of such diverse products as chewing gum, scent and insecticides.

The animals of the Amazon contribute their toll to its recovered prosperity. Skin-factories in Manaos, Iquitos and Belém each export tens of thousand of hides annually. The great fish, pirarucu, filota and piraiba, are speared, cut into strips, dried and sent off for sale. Smaller fish, tropical birds and monkeys are captured alive and sold to collectors or scientific institutions.

But these developments have fallen so far short of what was universally expected of the Amazon, that it may be worth turning to the river's one model industry to see whether, by contrasting it with them, we can discover why so little progress has been made.

Rich and extensive deposits of manganese ore were discovered in Amapá Territory to the north of the Amazon's mouth. I.C.O.M.I. a Brazilian company, sold a forty-nine per cent interest to Bethlehem Steel and work began in the late 1940's.* The project has been a success from every point of view; annual production should soon exceed one million tons and a loan of $67,500,000, made by Bethlehem Steel when mining began, has already been repaid. But more important is the effect on the lives of the people of Amapá territory. In 1948 they were typical *caboclos*, ignorant, fever-

* A full description of I.C.O.M.I.'s operations can be found in an article by Douglas Botting in *The Geographical Magazine*, July 1966.

ridden and under-nourished, living in riverside slums with an infant mortality rate of fifty per cent. Now the mineworkers live in a model township, in comfortable and hygienic conditions; they can relax in a lavishly equipped club room and eat in the best restaurant in Amazonia. Men whose previous skills were limited to the control of a dugout canoe now work with sophisticated mining machinery and are paid accordingly. The infant mortality rate in the township is lower than in the United States.

American skill and capital have been crucial in achieving this transformation, but once they had been provided, the *caboclos* learned at great speed and now less than one fifth of I.C.O.M.I.'s employees are of American or European origin. Twenty per cent of the company's profits are paid in royalties to the Government and reinvested in the territory of Amapá. This constant flow of money will create new industries and the increased prosperity of the region has already attracted private investment. The Government is planning a hydro-electric dam, a Dutch firm is building a plywood factory and plans for other industries are well advanced. This process would seem to be self-perpetuating, so that in time the prosperity of Amapá will no longer depend on the manganese that created it.

The distinguishing feature about Amapá is that it offered a concentrated and large source of wealth, on which an American company would be prepared to lend the considerable sum needed for its development. Amapá has shown how the Amazon should be developed; but it is useless as a prototype, since the rest of the river's attractions are more nebulous. We may wince at the sight of this vast area still covered by unreclaimed jungle, at a million square miles of unfelled timber, at a fifth of the world's running water pouring out, its energy untapped, into the ocean. We may wonder what is hidden under its unsurveyed soil. But there is no compelling reason to do anything about it.

The countries owning the Amazon—Brazil, Bolivia, Peru, Ecuador, Colombia and Venezuela, take much the same attitude. With the exception of Venezuela they are poor and they are, without exception, lightly populated and backward. Their possessions in the Amazon Valley show these characteristics at their most extreme.

The most natural use of the Amazon would be for agriculture and forestry. But the alluvial land, although rich and accessible, cannot be exploited without flood control. Much of the soil inland is lateritic—incapable of containing nutrients except when protected by the jungle. Once exposed to the elements the rich lateritic soil soon loses its fertility, until, after three or four crops, cultivation becomes impossible. Few of the countries concerned farm more than five per cent of their land and they all have undeveloped lands which, compared to the Amazon Valley, are accessible and easy to clear.

While the countries owning the Amazon are reluctant and unable to provide the capital for its progress, they often discourage foreign investment. The British-owned utility companies in Belém and Manaos were expropriated at the end of the Second World War and compensation in some cases has still to be paid. The attitude towards foreigners, particularly in Brazil, is one of deep suspicion. At the lowest level this can be comical, as when we found two devoted American missionaries whose vocations had been sadly misinterpreted. Their less reputable neighbours, dazzled by the riches of their speedboat, their houseboat and the seaplane which they shared with other missions, concluded that such powerful men could only be interested in smuggling gold—an uncanny repetition of the attitude of the citizens of Quito towards La Condamine's expedition 200 years before.

The same xenophobia can be dangerous when held in official circles. Artur Reis, who was until recently the Governor of the State of Amazonas, is acknowledged to have been among the finest governors in Brazil. His administration was entirely beneficial to the state and he managed miracles with the pitiful allowance given to him by the Federal Government. I quote Señor Reis only to show that this state of mind is universal on the Brazilian Amazon, even among its most enlightened and intelligent citizens.

Señor Reis's book, *The Amazon and International Greed*, lists every outrage perpetrated in Amazonia since the first Dutch colonists established their forts on the Xingu River. The scientists of the nineteenth century are greeted with a combination of pride and alarm—pride that they should have been attracted from the other side of the world by the natural wealth of the Amazon, and alarm at the secret designs they might have on the river.

Herndon's and Gibbon's well publicized journey caused suspicion in Brazil; Schomburgk, 'did not have the appearance of a man of science', and made the further mistake of describing Brazilians as ignorant Indian-killers. The many boasts by English, German and

American travellers of how much better their countries would administer the Amazon are given sinister undertones. But poor Spruce comes in for the heaviest abuse. He posed as a lover of the Amazon, while in fact carrying out a diabolical mission to export rubber seeds for the British Secret Service. It seems unlikely that Señor Reis has read Spruce's own book, for he quotes the passage about India and the Amazon from Von Hagen's essay on him in *South America Called Them* (he also confuses Spruce's removal of cinchona seeds from Peru with Wickham's coup in Brazil.) And this imaginary exchange of colonies, rather than the 8,000 botanical species collected by him, 'makes it clear what Spruce was really doing on the Amazon'.

This deep distrust still limits foreign participation in the development of the Amazon, but it is only fair to the Brazilians to admit that their suspicions were sometimes justified. Herndon was on a secret mission for the Confederacy to see if the Amazon could be an alternative home. During the Rubber Boom foreign businessmen plotted to bring in coolie labour; and whatever the precise circumstances of his departure from Pará, the Brazilians had no reason to feel indebted to Wickham.

With the exception of Roosevelt and Bates, few of the foreign writers on the region had anything good to say about its inhabitants and their arrogance must have exasperated the Brazilians, particularly since most foreign achievements on the Amazon have been anything but impressive and a few have been ludicrous. The most spectacular of these fiascos concerned the greatest industrialist ever to have invested in the Amazon, the fairy godfather of rubber, Henry Ford.

During the slump in rubber in the early 1920's the British Government started a system of Rubber Regulation to support prices. But the scheme worked too well and was abandoned in 1928 after protests from America. In the meantime both Ford and Firestone, infuriated by the soaring price of this vital material, started plantations of their own, Firestone in Liberia and Ford in Brazil. In 1934 Ford exchanged 700,000 acres of his original concession of 2,500,000 for an equivalent area nearer the mouth of the Tapajós by Belterra. By 1940 12,000 acres were growing rubber.

Ford took care to ensure that Belterra should be as efficient, as modern and as well run as any plantation in the East. The finest strains of rubber were encouraged through every refinement of selective breeding and bud-grafting. The same formula that had worked so brilliantly in Detroit was applied to his *seringueros*, who were paid wages which, by local standards, were beyond the dreams of avarice. Their physical health was protected by regular medical inspections and serious sicknesses could be treated in the company hospital. They had excellent housing, clubs, canteens, sports grounds and even an ice machine. It was a glorious departure from the waterlogged sties in which the earlier rubber workers had languished during the rainy season.

But the *seringueros* were not advanced enough to appreciate such treatment. If they could earn enough in a day to support themselves for a week, they saw no reason to return to work until they needed more money. Their stomachs rebelled at the rich food they were given; they resented the medical inspections and shunned the sports ground. Ford's generosity, far from raising productivity, actually lowered it and shortage of labour, always one of the Amazon's problems, aggravated the position.

The undoubted charm of the *seringueros*' attitude can lead one into exaggerating its importance, for these were only teething troubles. There can be little doubt that, if the rubber had grown satisfactorily, Ford's methods would have succeeded on the Tapajós as they had in Detroit—and as a similar approach would soon succeed in Amapá. But rubber would not grow in Belterra. The young trees were attacked by a virulent form of leaf disease that spread through the plantation like smallpox through an early Reduction. The only cure for the epidemic was a process known as double grafting which was uneconomic.

Ford loyally kept his plantation running throughout the Second World War, and, during this period of acute shortage of rubber, the Amazonian industry was given its last chance of recovery. The United States Government planted thousands of acres and sent 20,000 *caboclos*, trained in the latest tapping techniques, out into the jungle. But the buyers of rubber were as greedy and dishonest as their predecessors; medical supplies intended for the *seringueros* were diverted instead to the Black Market. Thousands of workers died without producing enough rubber to make a significant contribution to the war effort. Despite the limitless capital and expertise behind it, the Amazon Industry had failed its final test. The synthetic rubber factories which filled the gap can be regarded as the last nails in its coffin.

After the war Ford sold Belterra to the Brazilian government for $250,000. He is estimated to have spent $30,000,000 on it. The Brazilians were no more successful in planting rubber there and it is now an experimental agricultural station.

The general lesson to be learnt from these examples seems to be that, in the absence of any discoveries of oil or minerals in abundance, the progress of the Amazon will continue at a leisurely rate; and because surveying is difficult and foreigners are not encouraged to take part, one cannot expect many important finds in the near future.

*

The Hudson Institute has, however, made a plan which would certainly accelerate progress on the Amazon* and might lead to dramatic development. What the Hudson Institute proposes is an artificial Great Lakes system which would link up the Paraguay with the Guaporé, and the Rio Negro with the Orinoco. Rapids would be eliminated or by-passed and a direct inland route developed from Buenos Aires to the mouth of the Orinoco. Smaller lakes would improve communications on the Caquetá, the Ucayali and other rivers. The Amazon itself could be dammed by Monte Alegre and a vast freshwater sea recreated, stretching as far upstream as Tefé.

This project could initially be achieved at a low cost and expenditure increased as the benefits of the lakes began to be realized. Communications vessels could be stationed in the lakes, to replace the cumbrous radios that carry messages around the Amazon at present. The land around the fringes of the lakes would be free of the hazards of inundation; every sort of industry—mining, petroleum, fishing, agriculture and forestry, would become possible where they are now impracticable. The vast deposits of iron ore near the river's Northern and Southern headwaters might be opened up economically. The electricity generated would be almost embarrassing, since the damming of the Amazon alone would bring in one quarter of the installed electrical capacity of the United States. Bolivia would at last realize her ambition of a port with access to the sea. This kind of activity could produce, on a far

* *New Focus on the Amazon.* Herman Kahn, Robert Parnero, Hudson Institute 1965, and *A South American Great Lakes System.* Robert Parnero, Hudson Institute 1967.

greater scale, the same self-generating prosperity as is developing in Amapá.

*

Whatever the future of the Amazon there are two aspects of its life which cannot be left without the most profound sense of depression. The threat to its animal life grows each year. If one sails up the river every floating hut has long rows of skins and hides lying outside it to dry in the sun. In Manaos and Iquitos the factories work steadily to process tens of thousands of skins every year. Iquitos alone exports 50,000 live monkeys annually. Greed has already pushed the otter and the cock of the rock to the verge of extinction, and made the turtle and the heron lamentably rare; it is now eroding almost every form of wild life. This tragic and thoughtless destruction is a repetition of events in Africa and North America and an example of man's inability to learn from his mistakes.

The future of the Indian population of the Amazon is equally threatened. They put up little effective resistance to the occupation of their country. The most ferocious tribes were satisfied with raids on villages and ambushes on small expeditions. They have never put a formidable disciplined force into the field, and any independence they may have retained is due to the impenetrable country in which they live. There are no Isandhlwanas, no Little Big Horns in the history of the Amazon. A long process of slavery, slaughter and infection has reduced the numbers of tribal Indians in Brazil alone from over one million at the time of the conquest to some 75,000 today.

A report from the Brazilian Government has recently revealed that this persecution continues undiminished. They have been terrorized, enslaved, tortured and murdered to make their land available for colonization. New settlers have pushed the few surviving tribes of wild Indians into the interior, where they are forced to live in a country which can only support the smallest of villages. Officials of the Indian Protection Service, who should have reported these outrages, have instead, abetted them, and two former directors of the I.P.S. have been accused of committing numerous crimes against the Indians. Entire tribes have been exterminated by deliberate infection with smallpox and by gifts of sugar laced with arsenic; they have been mown down by machine-guns and blasted with home-made bombs from the air—all to make their land available for new settlement.

One cannot doubt the good faith of the Brazilian Government
in this matter. Since the days of Rondon their attitude towards
Indians has been impeccable. But the Governments of some States
involved are less progressive and some of their underlings—and
those of the I.P.S.—would qualify for employment by the Peruvian
Amazon Company. Unless the right kind of men are speedily sent
out into the troubled areas with the power to deal with the criminals,
the Indian tribes will continue to be annihilated and perhaps an
entire race put in danger of extinction. Rondon and Vieyra must be
turning in their graves.

BIBLIOGRAPHY

Unpublished

Public Records Office. Diplomatic and Consular dispatches from Peru, 1908–14. Series FO 371, 507–3709; FO 177, 395–404.
Rhodes House. Archives of the Anti-Slavery Society. *The Historical and Geographical Description of the Great River of the Amazons ... and of the several Nations inhabiting that ffamous country, or rather Mightie Realm, or Empire of above 3,000 leagues in Compass, part of which I have seen myself* (Major John Scott, *circa* 1670, Rawlinson MSS, Bodleian Library, A 175, No. 356).

Historical

McClymont, J. R.: *Gabriel Añes Pinçon*. Quaritch 1916.
Medina, José Toribio: *Descrubimiento del Rio de las Amazonas*. Seville 1894. Translated and annotated by Bertram T. Lee for the American Geographical Society. New York 1934.
Millar, George: *Orellana*. Windmill Press 1954.
Prescott, W. H.: *The Conquest of Peru*. London 1854.
Inca da Vega, Garcilasso: *Historia general de Perú*. Cordoba 1617.
Oviedo y Valdes: *Historia general y natural de las Indias*. Madrid 1851–5.
Raleigh, Sir Walter: *The Discoverie of the large and bewtiful Empire of Guiana*. Preface by V. T. Harlow, London 1928.
Southey, R.: *History of Brazil*. London 1810–19.
—— *The Expedition of Ursua and the crimes of Lope de Aguirre.*
Simon, Father: *The Expedition of Pedro de Orsua and Lope de Aguirre in search of El Dorado and Omagua*. Translated by W. Bollaert, Hakluyt Society 1861.
Williamson, James A.: *English Colonies in Guiana and on the Amazon. 1604–68*. Clarendon Press 1923.
Edmundson, The Rev. Dr. George: *The Dutch on the Amazon and Rio Negro in the seventeenth century.*
—— *Portuguese Dominion on the Rio Negro 1638–1732.*

—— *Dutch trade in Penoenÿ 1678–1706*. English Historical Review 1901–04.

Boxer, C. R.: *The Golden Age of Brazil 1695–1750*. University of California Press 1964.

Cunninghame Grahame, R. B.: *A Vanished Arcadia*. Heinemann 1901.

O'Neil, Father George, S. J.: *Golden years on the Paraguay*. Burns, Oates and Washbourne. 1934.

Fritz, Father Samuel: *The Journals of Father Fritz*. Translated by the Rev. Dr. George Edmundson. Hakluyt Society 1922.

Lacombe, Robert: *Sur terre comme au ciel*. A review of Hochwaelder's play. Science Ecclésiastique. October, 1955.

McFadyean, Sir Andrew: *The History of Rubber Regulation*. George Allen and Unwin 1944.

McColl, René: *Roger Casement*. Hamish Hamilton 1956.

Bruhns, Carl: *Alexander von Humboldt*.

Bingham, Hiram: *The Lost City of the Incas*. Atheneum. New York 1963.

Madriaga, Salvador de: *The Rise of the Spanish American Empire*.

—— *The Fall of the Spanish American Empire*.

Reis, Artur: *A Amazonia y la Cobica internacionale*. Rio de Janeiro 1965.

Freyre, Gilberto: *Mansion House and Shanties*.

—— *The Masters and the Slaves*.

—— *Brazil, an interpretation*.

St. Clair, David: *The Mighty Mighty Amazon*. Souvenir Press 1968.

Maw, H. L.: *Journal of a passage from the Pacific to the Atlantic*. J. Murray, 1829.

Acuña, Christoval de: *Nuevo Descubrimiento del Gran Rio de las Amazonas*. 1641.

Natural History and Scientific Exploration

La Condamine, Charles Marie de: *Relation abrégée d'un voyage fait dans l'intérieur de l'Amérique Méridionale*. Maestricht 1778.

Humboldt, Alexander von: *Personal narrative of a voyage to the equinoctial regions of America*. London 1814–29.

Vues des Cordillères. Paris 1816.

Edwards: *A voyage up the River Amazon*. New York 1847.

Waterton, Charles: *Wanderings in South America*.

Bates, Henry Walter: *A Naturalist on the river Amazons*. J. Murray 1863.

Wallace, Alfred R.: *A Narrative of travels on the Amazon and Rio Negro*. Reeve and Co. 1853.

Spruce, Richard: *Notes of a botanist on the Amazon and Andes*. Edited by Wallace. Macmillan 1908.

Agassiz, Professor and Mrs. Louis: *A Journey to Brazil*. London 1868.

Cherrie, George K.: *Dark Trails*.

Gardner, George: *Travels in the interior of Brazil 1836–41*. London 1846.

Burton, Sir Richard: *Explorations of the Highlands of Brazil.* Tinsley Bros. 1869.

Castelnau, Le Comte de: *Expédition dans les parties centrales de l'Amérique du Sud.* Paris 1850–59.

Santa-Anna Néry, Baron de: *Le pays des Amazones.* Paris 1899.

von Spix, J. P. and von Martius, C. F. P.: *Atlas zur Reise in Brasilien.* Munich 1823–31.

Roosevelt, Theodore: *Through the Brazilian Wilderness.* Scribner 1914.

Whiffen, Captain T.: *The North West Amazons.* Constable 1915.

Brown, John: *Two against the Amazon.* Travel Book Club.

Guenther, Konrad: *A Naturalist in Brazil.* Allen and Unwin 1931.

Dorst, Jean: *South America, a Natural History.* Hamish Hamilton 1967.

Bates, Marston: *South America.* Life Nature Library 1964.

Cutright, Paul Russel: *The Great Naturalists explore South America.* Macmillan 1940.

von Hagen, Victor: *South America called them.* Robert Hale 1944.

—— *South America, the green world of the Naturalists.* Eyre and Spottiswoode 1951.

Gates, R. R.: *A Botanist in the Amazon Valley.* H. F. and G. W. Therby. London 1927.

Herndon, Lieut. W. L., U.S.N. and Gibbon, Lieut. L., U.S.N.: *Exploration of the Valley of the Amazon.* Washington 1854.

Maw, Lieut. R.N.: *Journal of a passage from the Pacific to the Atlantic.* London 1829.

Schomburgk, Richard: *Travels in Guiana 1840–41.*

Smyth, Lieut. W., R.N. and Lowe, Mr. F., R.N.: *Narrative of a journey from Lima to Pará.* J. Murray 1836.

Ulloa, Antonio de and Juan, Jorge: *Voyage historique de l'Amérique méridionale.* Amsterdam and Leipzig 1752.

Dessalines d'Orbigny, Alicide: *Voyage dans l'Amérique méridionale.* Paris 1835–47.

Miller, Leo: *In the wilds of South America.* Scribner 1918.

Marcoy: *Voyage à travers l'Amérique du sud.* Paris 1869.

The Rubber Boom

Wickham, H. A.: *The Cultivation and Curing of Pará Rubber.*

—— *From Trinidad to Pará.* W. H. J. Carter 1872.

Woodroffe, Joseph: *The Rubber Industry of the Amazon.*

—— *The Upper Reaches of the Amazon.* Methuen 1914.

Akers, C. E.: *The Rubber Industry in Brasil and the Orient.*

Macedo Soares, José Carlos de: *Rubber, an Economic and statistical survey.*

Hardenburg, W. E.: *The Devil's Paradise.*

Collier, Richard: *The River that God forgot.* Collins 1968.

Baum, Vicki: *The Weeping Wood.*

General

Barrington Browne, C., and Lidstone, William: *15,000 miles on the Amazon and its tributaries.* London 1878.
Craig, Neville B.: *Recollections of an ill fated expedition.* Philadelphia 1907.
Fawcett, P. H.: *Exploration Fawcett.* Edited by Brian Fawcett. Hutchinson 1953.
Fawcett, Brian: *Ruins in the sky.* Hutchinson 1958.
Fleming, Peter: *Brazilian Adventure.* Cape 1933.
Dyott, G. M.: *Man hunting in the jungle.* Bobbs Merill 1930.
Price, Willard: *The Amazing Amazon.* Windmill Press 1952.
Church, G. E.: *The aborigines of South America.*
Smith, Herbert H.: *Brazil, the Amazons and the Coast.* New York 1879.
Wagley, C.: *Amazon Town.* New York 1953.
Huxley, M. and Cornell Capa: *Farewell to Eden.* Chatto and Windus 1965.
Whitney, Caspar: *The Flowing Road.* New York 1912.
Bryce, Lord: *South America. Observations and impressions.* Macmillan 1912.
McGovern, W. M.: *Jungle paths and Inca ruins.* Hutchinson 1927.
Haskins, Caryl P.: *The Amazon. The life history of a Mighty River.* Doubleday Doran 1943.
Up De Graff: *The Headhunters of the Amazon.* Hebert Jenkins.
Tomlinson, H. M.: *The Sea and the Jungle.* Duckworth 1912.
Singleton Gates, P. and Girodias, M.: *The Black Diaries of Roger Casement.* Olympia Press 1959.
Kahn, Herman and Parnero, Robert: *New Focus on the Amazon.* Hudson Institute 1965.
Parnero, Robert: *A South American Great Lakes System.* Hudson Institute 1967.
Maxwell, Nicole: *Witchdoctor's apprentice.*
Waugh, Evelyn: *Ninety two days.* Duckworth 1934.
Cowell, Adrian: *The Heart of the forest.* Gollancz, 1960.
Matthieson, Peter: *The Cloud Forest.* André Deutsch 1962.
Maybury Lewis, David: *The Savage and the Innocent.* Evans Bros. 1965.
Guppy, Nicholas: *Wai Wai.* Penguin 1961.
MacCreagh, Gordon: *White Waters and Black.* Doubleday 1961.
Zahm, Father: *Following the Conquistadores.* New York 1910.
Keller-Leuzinger, Franz: *The Amazon and Madeira Rivers.* Chapman and Hall, London 1874.
Schultz, Harald: *Hombu.* Rio de Janeiro 1961.
Phelps, Gilbert: *The Last Horizon.* Bodley Head 1964.
Collado, Antonio: *Esqueleto na Lagoa Verde.*
Huxley, Francis: *Affable Savages.* Rupert Hart-Davis 1956.

INDEX

INDEX

Kitchener, Lord, 191
Klüver, Dr. Heinrich, 137
Krahi, 230, 232
Kuliseu River, 224, 225, 228, 231
Kuluene River, ix, xi, 225, 226, 228, 231, 233, 234, 235, 240

La Chorrera, 176
La Condamine, Charles Marie de, 14, 33, 67, 73, 74, 75, 85–90, 97, 99, 100, 101, 117, 119, 124, 147, 240, 243
Lago Hyanuary, 127
Laguna, 90, 95, 96
Land and Wildlife of South America (Bates, M.), 135, 137
Lange, Algot, 133
Lauricocha, Lake, 9
Leavine, 193
Leguia, President, 186, 194
Lidstone, William, 10, 141
Life Histories of African Game Animals (Roosevelt, T.), 204
Lilley, 189
Lima, x, 67, 70, 85, 99, 108, 121, 172, 185, 186, 188, 189, 194, 196, 197, 240, 241
Llamoso, 46–7
Lores, Benito, 191, 192–3
Loreto, 90, 91, 183, 185, 186, 194, 199, 241
Lupin, Arsène, 209

Macdonald, Juan Alvarez, 41, 124
Maceda, Father, 61
Macedo, 171, 183, 194
Machiparo, 27, 28–9
Machu Picchu, xi, 218
Macintosh, Charles, 147
Madeira River, 4, 5, 29, 30, 51, 72, 130–1, 160, 161, 165, 166, 195, 206, 208, 209, 212
Magdalena River, 39, 99, 106
Malay Archipelago, The (Wallace, A. R.), 120
Mamoré River, 70, 72, 143, 160
Manaos, ix, xi, 51, 113, 119, 121, 127, 150, 152–4, 155, 157, 159, 160, 169, 176, 191, 241, 243, 247
Manley, 219
Maracaibo, Lake, 40
Marajó Island, 5, 64–5
Maranhão, Bishop of, 66
Marañon River, 36
Margarita Island, 44, 45, 46, 47
Maria, José, 182
Mariocay fort, 51
Markham, Sir Clements, 44, 47, 154, 155, 156
Martinengui, 183, 194
Martius, C. F. P. von, 111, 112

Mato Grosso, xii, 60, 71, 72, 110, 129, 156, 208, 209, 218–19, 226, 228, 232, 235
Matteson, Matthias, 53
Matthieson, Peter (At Play in the Fields of the Lord), xii
Maximilian (Mexican Emperor), 161
Medina, José Toribio (Discovery of the Amazon, The), 23
Metternich, 109
Mexia, Diego, 26
Mexiana Island, 136
Miller, Leo, 123, 129, 205, 206, 209
Miranda, Captain, 224
Mississippi River, 4, 131
Mitchell, 191, 192
Montgomery, Colonel, xiii
Montoya, Father, 61, 77
Montt, 183, 185, 188, 189, 194, 195
Montufar, Carlos, 108
Morgan, Captain Henry, 42
Moxo Indians, 66, 67, 70, 72, 74, 76
Müller, Lauro, 205, 206
Murder in Mato Grosso (Eggeling, Colonel), 229
Mutis, Dr., 106

Nahukuas, see Anauqua Indians
Napo River, 9, 18, 24, 30, 68, 169
Napoleon, 98, 109
Nassau, fort, 49, 51
Naturalist on the River Amazon, The (Bates, H. W.), 118, 139–40
New Focus on the Amazon (Kahn, H. and Parnero, R.), 246
Newton, Sir Isaac, 84, 86
Nheengaiba Indians, 65, 66
Nicholls, Patrick, xiii
Nile River, 5, 131
Nobrega, 54–5, 77
Normand, Armando, 174, 176, 177, 179, 183, 188, 192, 194, 195, 197

Obidos, 7
Ocainas Indians, 168, 178, 199
O'Donnell, 188, 193, 195
Oiapoque River, 49
Omagua, chief, 27
Omagua Indians, 40, 41, 44, 66, 67, 68–70, 89, 147
Omaguas (Peru), 95
O'Neill, Father, 61
Orange, fort, 49, 51
Ordaz, Diego de, 48
Orellana, Francisco, xi, 12, 13–14, 16–17, 20–5, 28, 29, 30–9, 42, 44, 46, 48, 53, 88, 124, 141, 147, 240
Orinoco River, 10, 15, 29, 32, 44, 45, 88, 99, 100, 102, 104–6, 119, 121, 122, 127, 207, 246

256